THE FRENCH ECONOMY

J.R. Hough

HOLMES & MEIER
PUBLISHERS, INC.
New York

First published in the United States of America 1982 by
Holmes and Meier Publishers, Inc.
30 Irving Place, New York, N.Y. 10003

Library of Congress Cataloging in Publication Data

Hough, J.R.
　The French economy.

　Includes index.
　1. France – Economic conditions – 1945 –
2. France – Economic policy – 1945 –　　. I. Title.
HC276.2.H677　1982　　330.944'083　　82-11943
ISBN 0-8419-0821-4

Printed and bound in Great Britain

CONTENTS

TABLES AND FIGURES

Tables

Figures

PREFACE

My grateful thanks are due to a number of individuals and organisations who have assisted me in various ways in the writing of this book.

The British Academy generously awarded me a research grant of £319 to finance a visit to Paris in December 1981. Whilst I was there various officials at the Commissariat Général du Plan, Ministère du Commerce Extérieur, Ministère des Finances and Ministère de l'Industrie provided useful comments and suggestions relating to draft chapters which they had read. Monsieur J.P. Milleron of INSEE (the French government's institute for statistical and economic studies) read much of the draft manuscript and was particularly helpful on many points. Monsieur Claude Tibi of IIEP and Monsieur Bernard de Canecaude assisted in facilitating arrangements for my visit and in making introductions. Staff at the libraries at INSEE, La Documentation Française and SciencesPo were all helpful in providing facilities and assisting in a variety of ways.

At Loughborough University the staff of the university library, and particularly Mrs C.M. Lincoln, went to a great deal of trouble on my behalf to seek up-to-date sources and to check references. I am grateful to Professor Dennis Swann for originally suggesting to me, some ten years ago, that in view of my background I should develop and maintain a teaching and research interest in the French economy, and to Professor Leonard Cantor, my Head of Department, for his constant support and encouragement in all my work.

I have to thank Monsieur Robert Julet and Monsieur Bernard de Canecaude, with both of whom I worked in Paris some 25 years ago, for their generous assistance to me over a long period of years, and for inculcating in me persistent Francophile tendencies. I trust that the latter have not imparted any undue bias to the writing of this book. Mrs G. Brentnall, Miss T. Geary, Mrs A. McNamee, Ms J. Oselton and Mrs M. Salsbury all shared the work of typing at various stages and Mrs McNamee typed most of the final manuscript with her usual cheerful efficiency. Finally, my thanks are due to my wife and family for more than I could ever express on paper.

Final responsibility for the text and for any errors and/or omissions does, of course, lie with myself alone.

As with my previous book, arrangements have been made for all author's royalties to be remitted by the publishers direct to Christian Aid.

J.R. Hough,
Loughborough University

1 INTRODUCTION

France and its Economy

Interest in France

Few Anglo-Saxon economists have taken any serious interest in France and its economy, in contrast, for example, to such fields as politics, geography or history in each of which there are in the UK numerous well known students of French affairs. That enigmatic fellow, 'the ordinary man in the street', if asked about the post-war economic experiences of West Germany and France, would in all probability be conversant in general terms with the successful record of the former but know nothing at all of the latter. If he were then told that for a long period of years during the 1960s and 1970s France's economic performance consistently exceeded that of West Germany year by year, his reaction might verge on the incredulous. These, at least, have been the writer's experiences with the final-year undergraduate students (of economics and European Studies) at Loughborough University to whom he has given a course of lectures on the French economy for the past ten years or so.

Space does not permit us to explore here the reasons for this lacuna, but they would have to include (a) the language barrier — few Englishmen, still, seem prepared to make a serious effort to learn the French language (the same problem does not seem to occur, or at least not to the same extent, in the case of West Germany, since so many German people speak English and since much information of an economic nature relating to Germany is published in English, which is certainly not the case with France) — and (b) the remarkable love-hate relationship which often seems to exist between the British and French nations.

Political Links

On 11 September 1981, which was seen at the time as one of the more remarkable turning points in Anglo-French relations, there was talk of a new phase of goodwill and friendship 'on a scale missing since before the era of General de Gaulle':[1] at the press conference held at the close of President Mitterrand's talks with Mrs Thatcher, so pro-British and friendly were the President's remarks that they met with 'silence and incredulity' on the part of the assembled media representatives. The reopening of the Channel Tunnel project as what the French experts

called 'une liaison permanente' between the two countries was inevitably
seized on by the media as the symbol of the new era; even, however, if
that project should fail, as it well might, the new spirit of understanding
between Britain and France seemed likely to continue whilst Mitterrand
remains President, unless of course political change in Britain meant that
one day a serious attempt is made to withdraw Britain from the EEC. It
seemed, indeed, one of the most remarkable paradoxes of recent political history that, whereas relations between President Giscard d'Estaing
and Mrs Thatcher (both right-wing politicians ideologically committed
to monetarism, the strengthening of the private sector and the reduction
in scope of the welfare state) were always described by such adjectives as
'fraught' and 'frankly difficult', Mrs Thatcher's relations with President
Mitterrand (ideologically her complete opposite to the extent that it was
suspected that they would not agree on any single policy issue) were
apparently warm and friendly from their first meeting. Mitterrand's
Anglophile sentiments do, of course, date back to the two years he
spent in London as an 'exile' in 1942-4.[2] As one French correspondent
put it, 'You now have in Paris, for the first time in three decades, a
French President who is not seeking to erect obstructions when he goes
into talks with the British.'[3]

Perhaps inevitably, by late 1981 the supposed Franco-British *rapprochement* appeared to have worn rather thin in the face of what the
French saw as continuing British obduracy within the EEC over compensation for Britain's budget contribution and limitation of expenditure
on agriculture, and foreign policy disagreements over the Middle East,
in addition to which French Ministers were taking an increasingly
serious view of Britain's economic difficulties. 'End to rapprochement
that never was' was how the headline in *The Times* summarised the
situation.[4]

Economic Success

A major theme in this book will be the quite remarkable success of the
French economy in the post-war (post-1945) period. From almost immediately after the Liberation, France experienced high rates of economic growth continuously year after year until the mid-1970s. From
an economy in ruins and with much of its physical capital and social
infrastructure destroyed or damaged, thirty years later France had one
of the most successful economies in the world. Whereas 1945 saw the
average Englishman with a standard of living some one and a half times
that of his French counterpart, by the mid-1970s their relative positions
were almost exactly reversed.

Only with the onset of the successive oil crises did France's long period of increasing prosperity seem to come, temporarily at least, to a halt: in the latter half of the 1970s and into the 1980s the country experienced mounting unemployment (although, as we shall see later, the available statistics are not easy to interpret), recurrent balance of payments deficits, rates of inflation continuing in double figures, and rates of economic growth much lower than those to which she had become accustomed. Whilst all other developed economies have been experiencing broadly similar difficulties in recent years, these have often given the impression of being more acute and/or longer lasting in France than in most other countries: by the early 1980s, for example, the French rate of inflation was the highest on the mainland of Europe. Only the economy of the UK has seemed to be faring consistently worse than that of France in respect of each of the problem areas indicated above and in this sense the situation has to be seen in perspective: the low rates of economic growth that caused anxiety in France (2-3 per cent against the previous 5-6 per cent) were generally above those that the UK economy could achieve in its best years; France's worries about a level of unemployment exceeding 2.1m early in 1982 have to be compared with the UK's figure of some 3m.

Subsequent chapters of this book will be devoted to examining various aspects of the country's remarkably successful economic record since 1945, and trends in the more difficult period after about 1975. The remainder of this chapter will consider briefly various aspects of the historical, political and social context into which that record has to be set.

Historical Development

'In the eighteenth century France was the strongest and richest power in the world.'[5] This statement is perhaps truer of the earlier years of the eighteenth century than of the years after 1763, and inevitably begs such questions as whose the riches were and where they came from; nevertheless it does indicate the extent of development and unification France had achieved a century or more before Germany as a country even came into existence. After the traumas of the French Revolution and the, in retrospect, brief Napoleonic heyday, France was to spend most of the nineteenth century apparently dwelling on past glories and ignoring the processes of modernisation taking place in both Britain and Germany. Whilst both the latter countries rapidly industrialised, sought new markets for their products overseas, and saw social and legal changes in line with their economic development, France, broadly speaking, did none of these and continued to stagnate. The loss of Alsace and Lorraine to Germany in 1870 is usually referred to for its implications in terms of politics and national morale, but its economic effects were no less pronounced and certainly helped to delay the advent of industrialisation in any meaningful sense.

Some industrialisation and economic modernisation came at last in the later years of the nineteenth century and the period before 1914, but too late and too slowly to prevent France falling even further behind her potential competitors: from 1870 to 1913 France's annual rate of economic growth averaged only 1.6 per cent, compared with the UK's 2.2 per cent, Germany's 2.9 per cent and the USA's 4.3 per cent.[6] From 1880 extensive tariff barriers protected French industry from exposure to foreign competition and removed much of the incentive to hasten the pace of change. France had spent huge sums (which she could ill afford) on her newly acquired colonial empire, but had done little to promote development at home. The coming of the First World War found France totally unprepared for a long period of intensive warfare, from all points of view, including the economic, and by 1918 much of northern and eastern France had been flattened by the successive waves of warfare, to say nothing of the tragic loss of manpower (some one and a half million Frenchmen died).

The French economy recovered well after 1918 and for the ensuing eleven years was as buoyant and prosperous as it had ever been. Right-of-centre governments, known colloquially as the 'Bloc National', under a succession of prime ministers and then under Poincaré from 1922, sought modernisation without undue change and stood for no nonsense from the left. The gradually increasing prosperity, heavily dependent on the emergence of a number of new industries such as chemicals and mechanical engineering, came to a sudden end in 1930 with the world economic crisis, which hit France particularly badly; from then on until 1939 the country never really recovered. The Popular Front government of Leon Blum (1936-7) pioneered social reforms but had rather little economic impact, except perhaps to make new investment less likely. The franc was devalued in 1936, 1937 and 1938 (twice) as successive governments sought financial stability,[7] tariff protection for French agriculture was increased, but little or nothing was done to aid industrial development or stimulate aggregate demand.

It is hardly necessary to add that the Second World War was a catastrophe for France, not least from the economic point of view. With many of her industries out of action, buildings destroyed, communications severed and manpower lost, by 1944 total industrial production was less than half of the level achieved in 1913. Yet so great was the devastation that perhaps it brought new possibilities for reconstruction and a fresh start.[8] Perhaps also it changed attitudes and brought to the surface new leaders, all rather non-ecomonic explanations[9] for the dramatic change from stagnation and decay to growth, modernisation and prosperity, a change which seems to have taken place quite suddenly around 1944-5. Whatever the reasons (and doubtless economists and historians will continue to argue about them for many years yet), the French economy went through a remarkable re-birth at the end of the Second World War, from which it has never looked back.

Political System

A recent summary of the French political system referred to 'the strong presence of central government with its traditions going back to the *ancien régime* and to the more centralised forms of Napoleonic France'.[10] After its election to power in May-June 1981 the socialist government under President Mitterrand made serious efforts to reverse this centuries-old tradition of centralisation and to decentralise or 'return the power to the people': by early 1982 a series of radical reform measures had been promulgated and more were promised.

The present, Fifth, French Republic has to date adhered to broadly the same principles as its predecessors save that its Constitution, enacted in 1958, vests considerable authority in the President of the Republic, previously a titular figure with no real powers. The President can now take the leading role in forming and dissolving the government, appointing the Prime Minister, and is sometimes seen as reigning supreme in connection with all major policy decisions. There can certainly be little doubt that President Mitterrand has, since election, proceeded with the implementation of a series of policy measures to which he was personally committed.

In fact, however, the President of the French Republic is subject to the approval of the National Assembly (legislature) for all legislative and financial measures and is thus in a position quite similar to that of the President of the USA: if he has a clear majority of his own political party in the legislature (as has President Mitterrand), he should presumably have little difficulty in carrying through his measures, but where the majority of the legislature are opposed to him, this is much less likely to be the case. It is worth remembering that General de Gaulle, the supposed personification of a strong presidency, resigned when he was unable to carry through his plans for regional reforms, the majority of the votes cast in a referendum going against him. It can even be said that the French President has markedly less power than the President of the USA since the latter is in immediate control of the executive,[11] but this is an interpretation that is open to some dispute. It is significant that in the event of a political deadlock he may dissolve the National Assembly, a power which has no parallel in the USA. Elected for seven years by a two-stage universal suffrage, his major decisions must be counter-signed by the Prime Minister, who is appointed by the President but who cannot be dismissed by him.

The French Prime Minister clearly has less power or status than his counterpart in other comparable countries. All major decisions are taken by the Council of Ministers, which is chaired by the President of the Republic, not the Prime Minister. Major international initiatives usually involve the President — thus the re-opening of cordial relations between the UK and France in 1981 came as a consequence of negotiations between the French President and the British Prime Minister. Clearly, however, the personality of the individual Prime Minister is of considerable importance here: no one could doubt, for example, that Raymond Barre as Prime Minister under President Giscard d'Estaing exerted a very powerful personal influence on the whole sphere of government policy, but particularly on all financial and economic matters.

Since its inception in 1958 the Fifth Republic has been marked by stability of governments with rather few Ministerial upheavals; even the cataclysmic events of May 1968 brought, directly at least, little in the way of political change (in contrast to the frequent changes of Prime Minister during the Fourth Republic). Government Ministers must resign their seat in parliament upon appointment and subsequently may speak but not vote in the Chamber; thus is continued the two-hundred-year-old tradition of the separation of the executive from the legislature. Each Minister chooses a cabinet of advisers, whose importance has tended to grow in recent years: there are even accusations that many decisions are now taken by consultation between cabinets rather than in the Council of Ministers or in parliament. Parliaments have tended to feel that their powers have been declining during the lifetime of the Fifth Republic.

Within parliament the National Assembly, elected by direct universal suffrage, has far more status and authority than the Senate or upper chamber,[12] elected by indirect voting by local authorities. Within the National Assembly the splinter parties which characterised the Fourth Republic have since 1958 formed into four main political party groups, with the further nominal agreement of a 'Common Programme' between the socialists and the Communists from 1972 to 1978. The Gaullists remained the largest party until the socialists' triumph at the elections of 1981.

At the local level, France remains divided into 96 départements, each headed by a prefect appointed by and responsible to the central government. He has to work with an elected *conseil général*, but also with the hundreds of small representative bodies in each urban or rural locality. The prefect is a career civil servant who does not come from the area and who will be moved on elsewhere if he develops local sympathies which from the centre appear too strong. This is a centralist tradition which President Mitterrand on election undertook to change without delay. Each President since de Gaulle has toyed with various attempts at devolution to more significant local levels but little in the way of effective change took place before the elections of May-June 1981.

The Mitterrand Government

The elections of May-June 1981 brought to power, for the first time in the history of post-war France, not only a socialist President, François Mitterrand, but also a socialist majority in the National Assembly, exactly 45 years after the introduction of paid holidays by the socialist regime of Leon Blum. Within days of coming to power the new President had increased the basic minimum wage by 10 per cent to the equivalent of £254 per month for a 40-hour working week, increased family allowances by 25 per cent (from July), old age pensions by 20 per cent to £154 per month, and had increased housing subsidies by 25 per cent from July and a further 25 per cent from December. Sharp increases in government expenditure were announced, adding £500m to welfare expenditure, creating 54,000 new jobs in the civil service at a cost of £200m in 1981, with additional expenditure of £235m on low-cost housing and £272m on industrial aid. These measures would be financed partly by 'soak-the-rich' taxes (surtaxes on high incomes, windfall profits tax on banks and insurance companies and, eventually, a wealth tax) and by tolerating larger budget deficits.[13] Further nationalisations in such areas as banking and the aerospace industry were announced by the new President even before the two-stage June elections were completed.

By the close of his first 100 days in office President Mitterrand was 'comfortable in the knowledge that he has already done enough to reshape the face of France to guarantee himself a niche in history'.[14] His 'quiet French revolution', which was proving extremely popular with the French electorate, included a variety of economic and social measures but had come to focus more and more on the decentralisation of political power. Mitterrand was determined to reverse the centuries-old centralist tradition of increasing political power being concentrated in Paris, by demolishing the powers of the Paris-appointed prefects at the head of France's 96 départements and handing these over to locally elected general councils, and by devolving effective power, in a variety of ways, to local authorities and communes.

By September 1981 an opinion poll found that only 12 per cent of French people considered that the Mitterrand dose of socialism was 'too much'.[15] In addition to the measures mentioned above, the negotiation of a 39-hour week plus a fifth week of paid holiday, talks on legal retirement at age 60 and the immediate recruitment of 100,000 extra postmen and teachers had been announced. The nationalisations comprised eleven dominant industrial groups, including such famous names as Cie. Générale d'Electricité, Saint-Gobin, Pechiney Ugine Kuhlmann, Rhone-Poulenc and Thomson-Brandt,[16] plus the remainder of the steel industry and 36 French-owned banks; these were in future to be managed with workers' participation, whilst smaller firms were to be helped by cheaper credit and tax rebates.

On the social front the new government abolished the notorious guillotine, the special security court, a kind of latter-day star chamber, the army's special courts and the repressive criminal procedure introduced by the previous government. One prisoner in seven was set free and the police force 'famed for bullying and pseudo-fascist methods'[17] was earmarked for radical reform. In the case of immigrants, including those in France illegally, a number of reforms were introduced to alleviate the previous harsh regime. Plans were announced to decentralise the school system, to curb the rather autocratic powers of university rectors and to pump extra funds into scientific research, into the Ministry of Culture and into France's ailing film industry.

Some 23 years ago Mitterrand opposed the new Constitution of the Fifth Republic for giving too much power to the President. Now that same concentration of power had enabled him to introduce a long series of reforms with surprising speed, the major single thrust of reform being, paradoxically enough, the decentralisation of power.

That President Mitterrand will have left a definite mark, and possibly an indelible one, on France at the close of his period of seven years in office can scarcely be doubted. One well respected observer of the French scene described him after a few months in office as 'a combination of idealist and pragmatist' and 'a quiet revolutionary'.[18] Eschewing undue personal publicity and some of the trappings of high office – he has appeared only infrequently on television and declined to fly in Concorde for his visit to Canada on the grounds that it was too expensive — he has adopted broad continuity with the past in such areas as foreign affairs, defence and nuclear energy, to the surprise of those who expected a more radical approach.

Social Questions

The population of France at the turn of the twentieth century was some 40,700,000; by the close of the Second World War it reached barely 40,500,000: thus, starkly, can be seen the terrible losses of French men and women during the two world wars. By January 1981 the population had reached 53,800,000: the considerable increase in population in the years since 1945 in fact took place largely in the late 1940s and early 1950s when birth rates were very high. All but 1 million of the increase had been achieved by 1973, so that thereafter the population was rising by only some 140,000 per year.[19] In the mid-1970s birth rates in France, in common with those in all other developed countries, fell to very low levels before recovering somewhat, at least temporarily, in the later 1970s/early 1980s. With net immigration effectively nil after 1976, any net increase in population can only come from natural causes; and if French women of childbearing age continue to have on average only 1.87 children each during their fertile years, not enough to replace the previous generation, any net increase in population can only result from the tendency to live longer. By early 1982 some regions of France had static or even declining populations and in some quarters it was being seriously argued that the government must introduce further measures to encourage families to have more children. This perhaps brought back memories of the 1950s when any woman managing to have nine children would be presented with a medal by the local Prefect.

France's total population of nearly 54m may be compared with the UK's 56m or West Germany's 62m; since, however, France has a far greater land mass, her figure for population per square kilometre of the country (95) is far smaller than that of either the UK (220) or West Germany (250). French people have tended to move, and are still tending to move, from rural areas to those loosely termed urban, i.e. including the peripheral areas around towns. As Table 1.1 shows, for most major French cities, whilst the central area has been losing population (except in the south), the city as normally defined has been gaining population at a far more rapid rate than the rate of growth of national

Table 1.1: Population Growth in Urban Areas, 1968-75

	The City[a]		Town Centre Alone		Wider Area including Periphery	
	Population (thousand)	Pop. Growth 1968-75 (per cent)	Population (thousand)	Pop. Growth 1968-75 (per cent)	Population (thousand)	Pop. Growth 1968-75 (per cent)
Paris	8,550	+ 3.6	2,300	− 11.2	9,943	+ 7.0
Lyons	1,171	+ 7.5	457	− 13.5	1,450	+ 9.9
Marseilles	1,071	+ 5.9	909	+ 2.2	1,134	+ 7.1
Lille (French Sector)	936	+ 5.1	172	− 9.6	1,099	+ 5.4
Bordeaux	612	+ 7.5	223	− 16.3	755	+ 7.9
Toulouse	510	+ 14.1	374	+ 0.8	592	+ 17.2
Nantes	453	+ 11.8	257	− 1.4	499	+ 12.4
Nice	438	+ 11.4	344	+ 6.8	794	+ 13.7
Grenoble	389	+ 16.9	166	+ 2.7	471	+ 14.8
Rouen	389	+ 5.1	115	− 4.6	523	+ 7.1

Note: a. Conventional definition.
Source: G. Vincent.

population, and the more extensive area including the periphery has in almost every case been growing even more rapidly. Table 1.1 also shows that the rates of population growth, as expressed in percentage terms, now tend to be slower in the largest cities, including the capital, than in the somewhat smaller towns. It is, of course, also important not to lose sight of the number of people involved: 7.0 per cent of Greater Paris with its population of 9.9m,[20] i.e. 693,000, represents far more people than any of the other percentage increases shown in the right-hand column of the table.

Nearly 7.7 per cent of France's population still (1981) work on the land: even though this figure has fallen steadily in the years since 1945 it remains significantly higher than that for the UK (1.8 per cent) and marginally higher than that for West Germany (7.2 per cent). Of the total working population of some 21,500,000, some 37 per cent were female at the time of the 1975 census, a percentage that had been rising slowly but steadily as female labour participation rates rose, but which may now have stayed constant or even fallen due to the large-scale unemployment of recent years. Some 1.6m 'foreigners' work permanently in France, mostly from the poorer countries of southern Europe or North Africa.

Gross inequalities of income, wealth and standard of living continue to exist in France and are most noticeable in the case of those rural communities which, despite all the developments of the last thirty years, still frequently lag far behind their urban counterparts for many of the basic amenities of life: 'The French peasant has become more aware of his lower income for harder work and longer hours than town people and of the lack of cultural facilities and modern conveniences.'[21] Far from being adequately protected by the welfare state, isolated rural communities have been largely excluded from its protection: they have, for example, shorter life expectancy, higher infant mortality and larger families than their compatriots in the towns, and tend to make much less use of the medical or educational facilities provided by the state.

Some mention must be made of the 'events' of May 1968 which seemed at the time cataclysmic, even possibly portending another French revolution, although in retrospect they seem to have had rather little long-term effect. After repeated riots and attempts at brutal repression by the police, by May 1968 the Latin quarter in Paris was the scene of repeated battles between students and police, with paving-stones torn up to provide barricades and missiles. When large-scale strikes broke out all over France and the country became paralysed, the government of de Gaulle seemed out of touch and out of control. The phase of unity between the habitually warring rival trade union confederations did not last long, but the flight from the franc and the dwindling of the country's foreign exchange reserves continued until the end of 1968 and beyond. De Gaulle refused to revalue the franc, suffered acute loss of prestige, and the scene was set for his defeat the following year.[22]

Education System

France has traditionally had a very centralised system of education, with all ultimate control vested in the Ministry of Education in Paris. Only in the 1970s did this centralist tradition begin to break down so that it ceased to be true that the Minister knew, at any hour of the day, what each schoolchild at each age right across France was doing at that particular moment.

Education in France has mushroomed during the years since 1945, partly as a result of the sustained 'baby boom' of the late 1940s and partly as a result of gradually increasing participation in secondary education and, later, in higher education.

The French tradition has been that of a strict separation between primary and secondary schools with largely only the children of the bourgeoisie, and especially civil servants, going on to the prestigious lycées (or grammar schools) which could offer entrée to higher education and professional careers. The Fifth Republic has seen some, albeit rather limited, dilution of this tradition via the establishment of some middle schools (bridging the primary/secondary divide) and, more importantly, collèges d'enseignement secondaire (CES). The latter were to offer, as theoretical comprehensive schools, the advantages of secondary education to pupils from a wider range of social backgrounds, but their impact was disappointing: although selected pupils could continue through to take the baccalauréat, or school leaving certificate, at age 17, many chose to drop out at an earlier age and of those who persevered as many as 40 per cent failed the examination.[23]

Possession of the baccalauréat confers automatic right of entry to a university course; hence first-year university courses are often intolerably crowded and after a stiff examination to thin out numbers at the end of the first year (as many as 40 per cent may fail), what is sometimes known as the 'course proper' begins in the second year. Many of the most able students will, however, seek to bypass the universities and enter the grandes écoles, prestigious institutions of higher education for which no equivalent exists in the UK. Entry to them may require a further two or three years of study after leaving school to prepare for a stiff competitive examination which will include mathematics to a very rigorous level. The grandes écoles, which are all in or around Paris, will embrace the future leaders of the civil service, industry and the country's political life, and the close contacts forged between these are often alleged to have an important bearing on the country's economic and administrative success. Whilst this is difficult to prove, it takes on an added perspective when it is realised that the typical career of a high-level civil servant will normally include periods spent in some state-owned industrial or commercial concern and/or in some political office.

In the fifteen years to 1967 the number of university students trebled and continued to grow, albeit at a less frenetic rate, thereafter. With only 22 universities (the UK had 46), each institution tended to be very large and to create a feeling of alienation on the part of the students: it is often overlooked that the 'events' of May 1968 really commenced when the students at Nanterre University (which by then had some 25,000 students, far more than any university in the UK except for the federal University of London) threw the Minister of Education into the swimming pool he had just opened. Decentralisation of the University of Paris into smaller and more manageable units took some years to achieve. The social class bias inherent in both secondary and higher education appeared to have remained largely intact during the era of rapid expansion (as in other countries, including the UK).

After 1968 the new Minister of Education, Edgar Faure, committed to reforming the out-of-date administrative structures and teaching methods and ossified syllabuses of French universities, instituted the 'Loi d'orientation de l'enseignement supérieur', of which the twin key principles were autonomy and participation. The old-style centralist direction was to disappear forever, but at the practical level reform was slow to happen and discontent of one kind or another was to rumble on in French universities for much of the 1970s.

The Capital

Paris and its hinterland dominate the industrial, commercial and cultural life of the country to a far greater extent than any other capital on the mainland of Europe. Not only is Paris so much larger than any other French city, as was shown in Table 1.1, but most historical develop-ments over the last two or three hundred years have favoured the French capital at the expense of other locations. A glance at the railway network shows that all major routes lead to Paris and a similar remark could be made, with only marginally less accuracy, of the country's much newer (and very impressive) motorway system.

Paris is at once the major centre of employment and by far the largest market for practically all products. It was therefore only to be expected that the newer industries established during the first half of the twentieth century (and especially between the two world wars) should be attracted to locate there and that they in turn should attract population movement from other parts of France. When eventually serious attempts were being made to develop regional economic policy during the 1950s and 1960s, perhaps the main objective was to stem this human flow which both denuded the provinces and rendered much more acute congestion and shortages (especially of housing) in Paris. Only in the 1970s was the in-flow eventually converted into a net out-flow.

Administratively the division of Paris and its environs into the départements of Seine, Seine-et-Oise and Seine-et-Marne lasted from 1790 to 1965; by the latter date the problems of administering nearly 10m inhabitants had become so great that eight new départements were formed in place of the previous three, with Paris-ville becoming a département on its own.

Parisians have a longer expectation of life, lower rates of infant mortality and better provision of such welfare facilities as medical care and education than their compatriots elsewhere. They also have to cope with worse problems of congestion, including on the roads, though this is confidently stated to have been declining steadily in recent years.[24] A visitor to Paris could be forgiven for having his doubts, especially if he is rash enough to try to park his car anywhere near the centre.

Of the approximately 4,800,000 persons in the Paris region in employment, at the time of the 1975 census, over 60 per cent worked in the tertiary sector, i.e. in 'white-collar' jobs in offices, such as in banks, insurance companies or the civil service, a proportion that was continuing to rise (for Paris itself the figure was 70 per cent). Tertiary-sector jobs have proved very resistant to the attractions of regional ecomonic policy and have tended to stay in or around the capital; this is true also of most French Ministries or other governmental offices. On average, Parisians earn between one-quarter and one-third as much again as French men or women elsewhere, but they do face much higher costs, especially for housing. Of all workers in Paris itself, over 45 per cent are female, a far higher proportion than for any other location in France.

Most large French industrial and commercial companies have their head office in or around Paris, even if their principal factory locations are elsewhere; there are in France some 95,000 industrial jobs in companies whose head offices are located in or near the Champs-Elysées.[25] Only in recent years, with the stricter controls on new industrial buildings in the Paris region, have numbers of jobs been growing more slowly there than elsewhere in France, thus reversing the trend of the previous two hundred years.

Economic Links

The remainder of this book will concentrate on various aspects of the French economy, but wherever possible links will be drawn with some of the historical, political and social questions mentioned above. Some of the points touched on above will be referred to again in the concluding chapter.

Notes

1. *Guardian*, 12 Sept. 1981.
2. Just as, at a more modest level, the author's Francophile sentiments date back to the time when he lived in Paris as a student. Every effort has been made to prevent such sentiments from influencing the writing of this book, but doubtless they show through from time to time.
3. Quoted in the *Guardian*, 12 Sept. 1981.
4. C. Hargrove, *The Times*, 4 Dec. 1981.
5. John Ardagh, *The New France*, 3rd edn (Pelican, 1977).
6. J-M. Albertini, *L'Economie Française* (Editions Du Seuil, 1978).
7. L. Lagnace, *La Croissance Economique* (PUF, 1980).
8. Ardagh, *The New France*.
9. C.P. Kindleberger, *France: Change and Tradition* (Gollancz, 1964).
10. R.B. Jones, *The Making of Contemporary Europe* (Hodder and Stoughton, 1980).
11. Jones, *The Making of Contemporary Europe*.
12. Although a French colleague commented, 'But it does twice as much as the House of Lords.'
13. Brian Moynihan, 'Liberté, egalité, but not much realité', *Sunday Times*, 14 Jun. 1981.
14. J. Swain, 'The 100-day gallop', *Sunday Times*, 19 Aug. 1981.
15. W. Schwarz, 'Can Mr Mitterrand keep his state of grace?', *Guardian*, 7 Sept. 1981.
16. K. Page, 'France to nationalize private banks', *The Times*, 10 Sept. 1981.
17. Schwarz, 'Can Mr Mitterrand keep his state of grace?'
18. C. Hargrove, *The Times*, 10 Sept. 1981.
19. G. Vincent, *Les Français 1976-79* (Masson, 1980).
20. J. Beaujeu-Garnier, *Atlas et Géographie de Paris et de l'Ile-de-France*, vol. 1 (Flammarion, 1977).
21. A. Hoyles, 'Social Structures' in J.E. Flower (ed.), *France Today* (Methuen, 1971).
22. H. Tint, *France since 1918*, 2nd edn (Batsford, 1980).
23. M.S. Archer, 'Education' in J.E. Flower (ed.), *France Today* (Methuen, 1971).
24. Beaujeu-Garnier, *Atlas et Géographie de Paris et de l'Ile-de-France*, vol. 1.
25. Beaujeu-Garnier, *Atlas et Géographie de Paris et de l'Ile-de-France*, vol. 2.

2 INDUSTRY

Introduction

The remarkable resurgence of the French economy in the post-war years could not have taken place without a long period of sustained renewal and expansion in the industrial sector. After a review of the latest national statistics relating to composition of Gross Domestic Product by the principal industrial sectors, this chapter will consider the developments in each of a number of the major industries in turn before going on to discuss more general questions.

The latest available statistics for the composition, by industrial sectors, of Gross Domestic Product at market prices, with trends over the decade 1970-80, are given in Table 2.1.

The table shows that much the largest sector of industry, in terms of final output for 1980, was building and civil engineering with 182,935m frs., followed by the energy sector with 114,103m frs. and transport with 106,583m frs. Then followed a relatively close grouping of automobiles and inland transport equipment, 68,769m frs., mechanical engineering, 67,528m frs., iron and steel, 65,173m frs., electrical engineering, 65,036m frs. and chemicals, 63,531m frs. The right-hand column of Table 2.1, which has been calculated from columns 2 and 3, shows that over the decade 1970-80 major changes have occurred in the relative positions of the major sectors, as evidenced by their record of growth in volume. Thus building and civil engineering, the largest sector, had one of the lowest rates of growth (second only to textiles, clothing and leather), and if present trends continue, looks certain to lose its position of pre-eminence at some future date. At the other extreme, each of naval and aeronautical equipment and electrical engineering more than doubled output over the decade and had much more rapid rates of growth than any other industry. The only other industries to exceed 50 per cent growth were chemicals and automobiles and inland transport equipment, although the growth for transport was only just below that level.

No other industrial sector grew sufficiently to maintain its share in Gross Domestic Product at market prices, which grew in volume by 43.1 per cent. The latter includes, in addition to industry, the large and increasingly important services sector which grew by 58.4 per cent,

26

commerce, 39.3 per cent, and agriculture and food products, 24.3 per cent. Indirect taxes grew more rapidly than GDP, especially in the staggering increase of 159.6 per cent in customs duties.

Table 2.1: Composition of Gross Domestic Product at Market Prices, 1970-80

	1980[a] (current prices) (million frs.)	1970 (current prices) (million frs.)	1980[a] (at constant 1970 prices) (million frs.)	Increase 1970-80 (at constant prices) (per cent)
Agriculture and food products	227,219	82,307	102,325	24.3
Energy	114,103	35,569	50,812	42.8
Ferrous and non-ferrous metals	38,419	15,568	21,518	38.2
Construction materials and glass	36,637	10,585	14,539	37.3
Chemicals	63,531	18,355	27,979	52.4
Iron and steel	65,173	20,834	23,490	12.7
Mechanical engineering	67,528	21,625	27,229	25.9
Electrical engineering	65,036	20,519	41,815	103.8
Automobiles and inland transport equipment	68,769	15,455	23,237	50.3
Naval and aeronautical equipment	29,330	6,000	13,969	132.8
Textiles, clothing and leather	51,741	21,291	21,793	2.4
Building and civil engineering	182,935	58,315	58,605	4.9
Transport	106,583	32,605	48,313	48.2
Other industries	85,146	41,520	58,267	40.3
Commerce	253,244	79,632	110,963	39.3
Services	998,330	229,049	362,905	58.4
Total gross value added	2,503,724	709,229	1,007,759	42.1
Value added tax	244,856	70,865	105,625	49.1
Customs duties, etc.	6,301	2,466	6,401	159.6
Gross Domestic Product at market prices	2,754,890	782,560	1,119,785	43.1

Note: a. Provisional.
Source: *Rapport sur les Comptes de la Nation 1980*, vol. 4 (INSEE, 1981).

Readers conversant with the method of presentation of industrial and economic statistics elsewhere, including the UK, are frequently puzzled by the practice in France of presenting statistics in terms of 'value added'. Table 2.1 shows, however, that the total value added is simply the sum of all the sectoral outputs to which indirect taxes (VAT and customs duties) are added to arrive at Gross Domestic Product at market prices. Therefore total value added is, quite simply, what is known in the UK as 'Gross Domestic Product at factor cost'. Total value added is labelled 'Gross' even though it is net of intermediate consumption, the 'Gross' referring to the fact that no deduction has been made for capital depreciation.

The statistics given in Table 2.1 have been compiled from much larger tables published by INSEE, which give further detailed breakdowns in respect of a number of the sectors. Thus within 'Agriculture and food products' agricultural output as such has developed much less rapidly than the food-producing industry which utilises an increasing share of agriculture's products. Similarly, within energy, the production of electricity and gas doubled in volume over the decade, a much more rapid increase than that for the remainder of the energy sector. Non-ferrous metals more than doubled in volume, whereas ferrous metals rose by less than 17 per cent. Within electrical engineering, however, the two component sectors, industrial electrical equipment and household electrical equipment, recorded almost identical rates of growth.

Table 2.2 presents details, on a similar basis, for the major sectoral groupings over the years since 1975, their relative position in the overall industrial structure and their respective annual rates of growth. Table 2.2 shows that the share of GDP at current prices attributed to all industry continued to decline, from 36.5 per cent in 1975 to 35.6 per cent in 1980, as also did the share of agriculture and fishing. Within the industry total the only sector to increase its share in GDP was energy, in response to the primary importance attached to increased domestic production of energy in the wake of the oil crisis. The 'industry' subheading in the table corresponds to the narrower of the two definitions conventionally used in France and therefore excludes the category of building and civil engineering, which is shown separately; the latter had a larger fall in its share of GDP than any of the other industrial categories shown and larger than that for 'industry' (narrowly defined) overall. The share of consumption goods also decreased significantly, from 6.4 per cent to 5.4 per cent. The increase in GDP share for other services from 29.1 per cent to 33.5 per cent shows the continuing trend for the relative expansion of France's tertiary sector.

When the same statistics are presented, on the right-hand side of Table 2.2, as annual growth rates in volume, only building and civil engineering consistently declined over the years shown, although a number of other categories recorded falls in 1980. Most industrial groupings saw their volume growth rates decline steadily and none of them withstood the pronounced effects of the recession in 1980. Other services, however, continued to prosper throughout.

Table 2.2: Structural Change by Major Sectoral Groupings, 1975-80

	Structure (per cent of total) (at current prices)		Annual Change in Volume (per cent)				
	1975	1980	1976	1977	1978	1979	1980
Agriculture, fishing	6.1	5.1	–5.3	4.8	7.9	8.1	0.4
Industry of which:	36.5	35.6	6.7	4.9	2.0	3.0	0.2
Food-processing	5.1	5.0	3.0	2.6	2.8	–0.5	2.0
Energy	4.7	5.1	4.3	9.7	1.5	7.5	–0.2
Intermediate goods	9.9	9.9	12.3	3.4	2.3	4.6	1.0
Capital goods	10.4	10.2	7.1	6.0	3.3	1.6	–0.8
Consumption goods	6.4	5.4	2.0	3.6	–0.8	1.9	–0.8
Building and civil engineering	9.2	8.1	–3.4	–0.2	–3.8	–1.0	–0.1
Commerce	12.9	11.2	4.5	–1.6	1.4	0.5	–1.1
Transport and telecommunications	6.2	6.5	6.6	5.2	6.1	4.8	2.6
Other services	29.1	33.5	4.9	5.4	5.3	4.0	4.6
All	100.0	100.0	4.2	3.4	3.0	3.1	1.1

Source: *Rapport sur les Comptes de la Nation 1980*, vol. 2 (INSEE, 1981).

Finally under this heading, Table 2.3 gives a comparison of growth of industrial production between France and her principal competitor countries for the years 1975 to 1980. It is immediately apparent that the consistently high rates of growth which France enjoyed for the period of thirty years after the Second World War did not continue into the latter half of the 1970s. All the countries listed clearly felt the effects of the world economic recession and the successive oil crises, but to varying degrees. Table 2.3 shows that France, which had become used to annual volume increases of around 5-6 per cent, fared relatively worse than most other comparable countries from 1975 onwards, as the country was particularly hard hit by the escalating cost of energy: France's average growth rate for industrial production for those years, 1.2 per cent, is lower than those for many other countries and lower than the averages cited. Each of 1975 and 1980 were particularly bad years, with industrial production in volume actually falling. Of the intervening period only 1976 (with a 9.0 per cent increase) and, to a lesser extent, 1979 (4.4 per cent) were successful years.

Table 2.3: Industrial Production: Comparative Annual Growth Rates, 1975-80 (per cent)

	Average 1975-80	1975	1976	1977	1978	1979	1980
Belgium	1.1	−9.9	9.0	0.0	1.8	4.5	2.0
Denmark	1.6	−1.0	2.4	0.8	2.3	4.3	0.8
France	1.2	−8.9	9.0	0.9	2.7	4.4	−0.3
West Germany	2.1	−5.7	7.3	2.9	2.2	5.3	1.1
Ireland	4.5	−6.1	9.0	8.3	9.3	6.2	1.5
Italy	2.6	−8.8	11.6	0.0	2.0	6.8	5.5
Netherlands	1.1	−4.8	8.0	0.0	0.9	2.8	0.0
UK	0.3	−4.8	3.0	4.9	2.8	3.6	−7.0
Total EEC	1.8	−6.1	8.0	1.9	2.7	4.4	0.5
USA	2.2	−8.9	10.8	5.9	5.7	4.4	−3.5
Japan	4.1	−10.5	11.1	4.1	6.2	8.3	7.1
Total OECD	2.3	−6.1	9.0	3.7	4.4	4.2	−0.5

Source: OECD (quoted in *Les Comptes de la Nation 1980*, vol. 2).

Some Major Industries

Building and Civil Engineering

The building and civil engineering industry, with a total value added of 182,935m frs. in 1980, is the largest industrial sector in France (total *gross* production in 1979 reached 304,000m frs.). The industry employs a labour force which, at some 1.9m, is larger than that for any other industry and represents around one-quarter of the total French industrial labour force. Some indication of the difficulties in collecting adequate statistics for this industry is given by the fact that, alone of the major industries, these figures cannot conveniently be subdivided into sectoral components.

The building industry has a large number of very small firms scattered throughout France, although with an obvious concentration in the main urban areas. Of the total labour force some 1,200,000, or 61 per cent, work in firms with fewer than 50 employees, and some 528,000 (27 per cent) in firms with five or fewer employees: these figures embrace some 266,000 firms, out of the industry's total of 270,000; there are just 28 firms which have over 2,000 employees each, concentrated much more heavily at the civil engineering end of the industry and involved in the construction of, *inter alia*, roads, power stations, sports complexes and drainage systems. Overall the industry's most important sphere of work was the construction of housing and commercial units, whether multiple-flat blocks, office blocks or, increasingly in recent years, single private houses. The industry's overall growth rate exceeded the national average for all industries each year until 1967, since when the position has been reversed.[1] From a growth rate averaging 10.2 per cent per year for 1960-5 the industry declined to an average growth rate of only 3.3 per cent for 1970-5, with only 'Maintenance' work remaining relatively buoyant.

The building industry has many low-paid jobs and an average wage per employee which is less than that for almost any other industrial sector. As a consequence it has become an increasingly unattractive form of employment for French people and has resorted more and more to the use of immigrant workers. Perhaps 30 per cent of all the industry's labour are immigrants, but the figure reaches 90 per cent on some large sites in Paris.[2] Many of these workers are newly arrived from foreign countries, especially those in southern Europe, and speak little or no French, which tends to mitigate against productive speed and efficiency.

Total employment in the industry continued to rise, although at declining rates, until 1970, since when it has fallen. Between 1975 and 1979 some 165,000 jobs were lost. The shake-out of labour has been most marked in the provinces and from the smaller firms, so that the gradual tendency is for the industry to become somewhat more concentrated in larger units and in the Paris region.

This industry more than any other is greatly affected by the booms and slumps of the economic cycle, since not only is building work the first to be cut back in any economic crisis, but also there have been very high rates of inflation for both land and construction materials. Further, since some 80 per cent of the industry's total work stems directly from the state (including local government authorities and nationalised industries), and since the latter tends to reduce or delay building works during any recession, this effect is accentuated. Professor Baleste cites as an example the public expenditure cuts which accompanied the recession of 1977 which directly led to the bankruptcies of 2,900 firms and the loss of 70,000 jobs (between March 1977 and March 1978).

It took perhaps twenty years to make good the massive destruction suffered during the Second World War and the severe housing shortage, accentuated by the rapid growth of population and the trend towards younger marriages, continued until well into the 1970s. An official report in 1977 estimated that 13.4 million people, or more than one household in every five, still lived in conditions classified by INSEE as overcrowded.[3] The aim has been around 500,000 housing starts per year but by 1977, with a figure of only 475,000, this was not being achieved and by 1979 the figure had fallen to 430,000. Nevertheless the proportion of the Gross Domestic Product invested in housing, 6.7 per cent, was higher in France than in other comparable countries.[4] Within this total a considerable boost to the construction industry came with the development of a 'secteur social', or subsidised housing sector, to provide 'Habitations à Loyer Modéré' (HLM) or moderate rental housing, to enable more young and lowly paid workers to have the chance of securing adequate housing. This sector is quite distinct from the blocks of high-quality offices and apartments commissioned, for profit, by independent promoter companies, especially in and around Paris and along the Mediterranean coastline. The leading French banks are often prominent shareholders in such companies.

To a casual observer it might appear that production processes in the construction industry have not changed for many years, but in fact there has been a considerable trend towards industrial prefabrication in factories of parts, and sometimes whole sections, of buildings subsequently assembled on site. Further specialist subsidiary firms have been set up to supply standardised windows, doors, roofings and other parts, without delay, rather analogous to the specialist suppliers to car manufacturers. The previous trend towards larger and larger buildings, as evidenced by a casual glance at the new Paris skyline, has, however, now been reversed, partly due to the ban on new tower blocks imposed in 1973.

In face of the relatively declining domestic market the industry has made a noted endeavour to export its expertise in the field of major civil engineering projects and by 1979 30 per cent of total income for civil engineering emanated from overseas.

Transport Equipment

The transport equipment industry comprises both automobiles and inland transport equipment (total value added 68,769m frs. in 1980) and shipbuilding and aeronautical production (29,330m frs.). In 1979 the former had *gross* production of 143,000m frs. and employed some 500,000; since 1970 it had seen its share of GDP rise from 8.7 to 12.7 per cent, with a further 50,000 jobs created. Shipbuilding and aeronautical production employed a further 159,000 people.

Interest in this sector of industry tends to centre on France's world-famed car industry. It is certainly true that the inland transport equipment sector is dominated by the production of motor cars, with over 90 per cent of each of value added, exports and labour force. In 1979 France produced 3,220,000 private cars plus 390,000 commercial vehicles, around 10 per cent of the world's total, rather less than West Germany but some 50 per cent more than the UK. The industry's two 'giants', Peugeot-Citroen-Talbot and Renault, produced 1.8m and 1.4m cars respectively, i.e. very nearly the whole of the sector's total: the addition of Talbot (ex Chrysler-France and Simca) to Peugeot-Citroen made this group the second-largest in Europe after Volkswagen (*c.* 1.9m vehicles per annum) and the fifth-largest in the world. Talbot had previously left the Fiat group only to become largely (80 per cent) American-owned. Citroen, formerly controlled by Michelin, had been linked with Peugeot since 1974. Under an agreement concluded in 1978 links were established between Renault and the American General Motors which were intended to lead to the development of exports of Renault vehicles to the USA as well as to joint production processes.

The whole of the inland transport equipment sector produced an external trade surplus of over 30,000m frs. in 1979, a truly remarkable achievement.

What Professor Baleste and Mr Roux-Gaillard both describe as this brilliant industry is responsible for the livelihood of some 2 million people, or one-tenth of the active population. Despite being, in view of the nature of its products, particularly sensitive to economic booms and slumps, the industry has enjoyed unparalleled growth and success over the last twenty years; not only have its exports established significant positions in the vehicle supply market in many other countries (in 1979, 53 per cent of all vehicles produced were exported), but it has also managed to resist foreign penetration of the French domestic market.

The traditional location of the industry has been in the Paris region, close to both markets and sources of supply, but the 1960s and 1970s saw a significant trend towards decentralisation, particularly towards the west. Thus Renault now has manufacturing sites at Le Mans, Cleon (near Elbeuf), and Le Havre-Sandouville, Citroen has plants at Rennes, Caen and Metz and Simca (now Talbot) factories are to be found at La Rochelle and Valenciennes. Amongst European countries only West Germany (just) has more vehicles on the roads than France, which had nearly 20 million by the early 1980s. By then, however, the industry was expressing real fears that the market was close to saturation point (a view which will be shared by anyone who has tried crossing Paris by car during the rush hour) and that it could not hope to maintain such buoyant growth rates in the future. At about the same time foreign cars, especially from West Germany, Italy and Spain, were starting to sell well in France and had captured around 20 per cent of new car sales; it was also becoming increasingly clear that vehicles of nominally French manufacture included to a significant and increasing extent parts emanating from foreign subsidiaries or suppliers: by 1975 French motor manufacturers had established a total of 78 factories in 38 foreign countries,[5] although few were opened subsequently in the face of the fall in demand.

The automobile industry has relatively few technically qualified or female employees. Since around 1960 it has had high levels of investment and a marked trend towards mechanisation and capital/labour substitution. The industry's labour force continued to grow steadily until 1973, since when it has probably fallen somewhat.[6] If the French automobile industry is to maintain its position in the extremely competitive world markets, high levels of investment in automated systems plus further industrial restructuring will be required.[7]

An independent report[8] published in late 1981 predicted that the new car market in France would continue to stagnate until at least 1986. The major possibilities for further expansion may well lie, therefore, with the hitherto less publicised sectors of the industry, including commercial vehicles.

Aeronautical and related production has had a very successful record, the French aircraft and aerospace industries being the most important in the EEC with full commitments to such products as Airbus and Ariane. Productivity is high and exports account for more than half of total sales. The state is directly involved and owns or controls the major firms, for reasons of both security and prestige.[9]

Mechanical Engineering

The mechanical engineering industry had a total value added of 67,528m frs. in 1980 from some 550,000 employees, some two-thirds of each relating to heavy and medium engineering, the next largest sector being precision engineering with some 14 per cent of each; the remainder covers a variety of machine tools, agricultural machinery and related operations. The range of products is very wide from, at the heavy end, boilers and industrial plant, to, at the precision end, watches, clocks and optical instruments. The industry is characterised by medium-sized firms, nearly one-half of the labour force being in firms with between 50 and 499 employees. Some 85 per cent of employees are male. Locations are spread more evenly throughout France than is the case with most other industries, but the Paris region and Rhone-Alps (Lyons) have traditionally been, and remain, important centres.

The industry's total production grew at around 8.5 per cent in volume per annum over the period 1959-74, i.e. considerably in excess of the national industrial growth rate, but with this average falling somewhat in the latter part of that period.[10] Thereafter the industry was particularly badly hit by the gathering recession and total production effectively did not expand at all over the years 1974 to 1979. Of the industry's products some 50 per cent are used for investment purposes, 25 per cent as intermediate consumption by firms and 25 per cent is exported. The industry is particularly subject to the ups and downs of economic cycles, in view of the typically cyclical nature of investment decisions.

Both exports and imports have been very large since around 1960 and in the years prior to 1975 national demand for mechanical engineering products grew even more rapidly than the industry's output with the consequence of increased imports, especially from West Germany and the United States: throughout the 1960s and early 1970s there were net balance of trade deficits before an eventual recovery. As Table 2.4 indicates, the subsequent years have seen healthy trade surpluses as, in the light of low demand and spare capacity at home, the industry has turned its attention to export markets.

Table 2.4: Mechanical Engineering: External Trade Balance, 1970-9 (thousand million francs, current)

1970	−0.9
1972	−1.4
1973	−0.9
1976	+6.8
1977	+8.4
1978	+9.5
1979	+7.5

Source: P. Roux-Vaillard, 'L'Industrie' in J.P. Pagé (ed.), *Profil Economique de la France au Seuil des Années 80* (La Documentation Française, 1981).

Significant trade deficits continue, however, in the case of certain types of product where the industry is unable to satisfy domestic demand, notably ball bearings and, rather surprisingly, agricultural machinery, and this trend showed no signs of slackening into the early 1980s.

Structurally, the industry consists of firms which are on average much smaller than their competitors in West Germany or the UK and this was seen as one of its major weaknesses.[11]

Energy

If the whole of the energy sector is grouped together it forms a massive 'industry' with a total value added in 1980 of 114,103m frs, comprising petroleum products and natural gas 47,805m frs., manufactured gas, electricity and water 58,203m frs. and solid combustible fuels 8,095m frs. The whole sector employed some 290,000 people, and had a 4.8 per cent share in GDP and 8.3 per cent of gross national investment.

Presenting the results as 'value added', i.e. as contribution to GDP, in some respects masks the efforts made by the coal industry since a large part of its output is subsequently used for the production of electricity and manufactured gas; nevertheless it remains true that France's coal output, at some 22m tons, compared very unfavourably with the output of some twenty years previously (1962 = 55m tons). The coal industry's labour force fell steadily from some 250,000 in 1958 to some 70,000 by the end of the 1970s. In the latter 1970s strenuous efforts were made to arrest the downward trend of the coal industry in view of the country's massive energy crisis, but had to contend with the twin problems that a number of usable coal seams, including those in the Nord-Pas-de-Calais region, were close to exhaustion and were earmarked for closure in 1985, and that productivity was extremely low (2.7 tons per miner in France against 12 tons in the USA). By 1980 only two major clients remained for coal, namely the steel industry and coal-fired power stations; the industry's employment was concentrated in the Paris, Nord-Pas-de-Calais and Lorraine regions, with only Lorraine still having large reserves of high-quality coal.

The solid fuels sector is far more labour-intensive and less efficient than the remainder of the energy sector. The crucial importance of the energy problem to France's current economic situation is referred to throughout this book, with energy giving rise to a far larger balance of payments deficit than any other sector. Apart from the much-publicised oil crisis, France is also a heavy importer of coal and has imported more in volume than the total of domestic production each year since the mid-1970s, the principal suppliers being West Germany, Poland and the USA.

Coal-mining has undergone a radical reformation during the post-war years with extraction being concentrated on the larger and more cost-effective pits, aided by the installation of automated extractive machinery. With the increased competition from other energy sources, output steadily declined until about 1976, since when it has approximately stabilised in the wake of the oil crisis and following the stimulus of the

Bettencourt Plan. Most mines were nationalised in 1946, when Charbonnages de France took over from the independent companies. With the
setting up of the European Coal and Steel Community in 1951, inter-
European co-operation in this field pre-dated the formation of the EEC
by some years. Following the oil crisis, Electricité de France dramatic-
ally increased its purchases of coal from around 5.2m tons in each of
1973 and 1974 to around 17m tons by 1978, but three-quarters of this
total had to be imported. The annual deficits of Charbonnages de France
have risen steadily, to reach 3,500m frs. by 1978.[12]

Electricity and gas production are nationalised. Electricité de France,
with 106,000 employees, is the largest single firm in the energy sector;
electricity production has had an extremely successful record of growth
(around 7 per cent per annum) and diversification for many years, with
an acceleration of the nuclear power programme from 1974 onwards.
Nuclear energy was providing 7 per cent of the nation's energy requirements by 1980 and was planned to supply 30 per cent by 1990. Of
electricity production, 23 per cent came from nuclear power stations
in 1980 and by 1990 the figure should be around 73, and could reach
80, per cent.[13] Electricity also comes from lignite and gas, as well as
coal, and from the hydro-electric schemes that have been developed
successfully in all the main mountainous regions, and along major rivers
such as the Rhine and the Rhone. Coal-burning power stations remain
important and have become much more efficient: one kilowatt of electricity is now produced from 400 grams of high-quality coal, whereas in
1952 670 were required.[14] Natural gas has been found in large quantities
in the south-west of France, especially at Lacq, and is also piped across
the Mediterranean from Algeria.

France has some small petrol fields, the most important of which is
the Parentis field in the Landes region near Bordeaux; the smaller field
at Lacq, in Aquitaine, has virtually been exhausted. Total production
from all fields amounted to around 1.2m tons in 1979, i.e. just under
1 per cent of the nation's needs, and significantly less than the figures
for 1960 (1.9m tons) or 1970 (2.3m tons). There are high hopes of
finding petrol in the coastal waters to the north and west, but as yet
the searches have been disappointing. French refineries dealt with 126m
tons of crude oil in 1979, mostly from the Middle East and Venezuela;
much the largest supplier was Saudi Arabia with 44m tons. Imports of
already refined products have been kept down to 9m tons. To achieve
these imports, France has the sixth-largest fleet of super-tankers in the
world, including three giant vessels of over 500,000 tons each. French
refineries could handle over 170m tons annually and have a global

problem of excess capacity, leading to the closure of the refinery at Ambès. The refineries are mostly located along the Seine between Paris and the sea, in the south near Marseilles and on the west coast near Bordeaux. In the wake of the oil crisis, storage capacity for refined products is being increased and oil pipelines now criss-cross France from south to north and from west to east.

France is, perhaps rather surprisingly, not a heavy user of energy, her total consumption being only some two-thirds of that of either the UK or West Germany, but French consumption has tended to rise more rapidly in recent years. Dependence on imported energy products has risen remorselessly from only 41 per cent in 1960 to well over 70 per cent by the late 1970s.

Chemicals

Chemicals and allied industries had a total value added of 63.531m frs.: of this total some 38 per cent stemmed from basic chemicals, some 17 per cent from auxiliary chemical products and some 13 per cent from rubber goods, with the remainder divided fairly equally between plastics processing, glass and pharmaceuticals. Total manpower in the industry amounted to 335,000 in 1979, but with the spread of labour across the various component sections of the industry being only poorly correlated with the above figures for value added: basic chemicals, for example, employs only some 24 per cent of the industry's total labour force, and the rubber goods sector employs more labour than does auxiliary chemical products. The chemical industry made a positive contribution to the French trade balance of some 11,000m frs., of which some 66 per cent emanated from the basic chemicals sector. Of the total industry's profits of 15,486m frs., basic chemicals were responsible for some 57 per cent.

Traditionally the industry has centred around the production of inorganic chemicals (acids, alkalis and fertilisers), which has been facilitated by the availability in France of raw materials such as sodium chloride, potash and sulphur.[15] The basic chemicals sector produces the full range of inorganic and organic chemicals, including very large quantities of compound fertilisers, phosphate slag, acids, alkaloids and compressed gases; auxiliary chemical products include explosives, paints, soap, glues, films and photographic software and inks; much the most significant output of the rubber goods sector relates to vehicle tyres, the principal plastics products are polyethylene, polyvinyl chloride, polystyrene and a variety of plastic sheetings, whilst 75 per cent of the products of the glass sector comprise glass bottles of various kinds. This very heterogeneous industry, which has over 20,000 different products,[16] ranks sixth, by volume of output, among the chemical industries of the world, coming just behind that of West Germany but ahead of the UK, and is responsible for some 21 per cent of the EEC's production of chemicals. The location of the industry is concentrated in the Paris region and in Rhone-Alps, which together are responsible for some 40 per cent of the industry's total employment, with the regions of Nord (around Lille) and Auvergne also being important centres. Many of the industry's largest companies are foreign subsidiaries or branches of multinationals, such as Société Colgate Palmolive France, Société Kodak-Pathé-SAF, Dunlop, Firestone France and Goodyear; among the most significant French-owned companies are Michelin, Rhone-Poulenc and Kleber-Colombes, each of whom employs well over 2,000 people. There are also three large public sector groups including C de F Chimie which has taken over all the former chemical subsidiary operations of Charbonnages de France.

The economic characteristics of the French chemical industry resemble those in other comparable countries in that it is concentrated in large units to reap the benefits of the massive economies of scale and is highly capital-intensive, employs a highly qualified manpower (a survey in 1967 showed that 47 per cent of all employees had a technical qualification of some kind) and has a high proportion of female workers (around 25 per cent).[17] It is one of the most dynamic of French industries with a vigorous record of growth and diversification. From 1960 to 1973 total value added in the industry increased by an average of 10 per cent per year, a quite remarkable performance, this being accompanied by a continued trend towards greater capital-intensiveness and improved productivity: over the same period the annual increase in the industry's labour force averaged only 2.1 per cent. On the other hand, the effects of international competition were felt much more sharply during the 1960s and the industry's foreign trade balance relative to its total output has tended to decline (and, for the first time for many years, the balance even became negative during 1971-3, before subsequently recovering). During the same fifteen-year period the industry's self-financing ratio did not improve, remaining fairly constant at approximately 15 per cent, but nevertheless gross capital per employee increased by some two-and-a-half times in real terms.[18] The same years saw the average working week in the industry reduced from 45 to 42 hours. From 1974 onwards much slower rates of growth were recorded and the total labour force fell by some 12,000 between 1974 and 1979, assisted by significant improvements in productivity. In the face of severe international competition, including from newly industrialised countries, there emerged a serious problem of excess capacity, which remains to this day.[19]

Professor Baleste points out that the French chemical industry is characterised by smaller units of production than those in the main competitor countries, a relatively weak export performance (the Swiss chemical industry exports 45 per cent of its production, the German 25 per cent, but the French less than 20 per cent) and a considerable problem of excess capacity. It therefore seems almost paradoxical that whereas the chemical industry has been one of the most successful in France during the post-war period and has emerged as one of the country's most important industrial sectors, its future is now viewed with concern by some independent observers.

Within the chemicals and allied industries, the pharmaceuticals sector, with perhaps one-third of the industry's total value added, is one of the most successful in the world.[20]

Electrical and Electronic Engineering

Electrical and electronic engineering contributed total value added of 65,036m frs. in 1980 and had 457,000 employees. The industry is sub-divided into electronic household and trade equipment (41.6 per cent of value added, 44.9 per cent of employees), electrical equipment (32.8 per cent of value added, 36.8 per cent of employees), office machines and data-processing equipment (16.9 per cent of value added, 7.8 per cent of employees) and domestic equipment (8.6 per cent of value added, 10.2 per cent of employees).

This industry has one of the highest degrees of concentration and includes the two giants Compagnie générale d'électricité (some 170,000 employees) and Thomson Houston-Hotchkiss Brandt (115,000) (1978).[21] Over 60 per cent of the labour force are in firms with 2,000 or more employees and 78 per cent are in firms with 500 or more employees. This tendency to large-scale organisation is not surprising in view of the high level of capital-intensiveness and very large economies of scale in this industry. This French industry is considerably smaller than its UK counterpart and is only half as large as that in West Germany. The most significant categories of products are (in descending order of value of sales) insulators and insulating components, data-processing equipment, telephone and telegraphic equipment, a variety of domestic electrical appliances, electronic and radio-electric trade equipment, and insulated wires and cables.

The industry has had a rapid growth rate, averaging over 10 per cent per annum in volume over 1969-74,[22] but declining to the still high rate of around 6 per cent per annum for the later 1970s, and remains one of the most dynamic and successful of French industries from the point of view of growth. External trade performance was disappointing until around 1970, since when exports have multiplied by around 3.3 times (to 1979), mushrooming from some 23 per cent of the domestic market to over 40 per cent. Imports also grew rapidly but less so than exports, so that by the years 1976 to 1979 healthy annual surpluses were being achieved, that for 1979 being 4,700m frs. The principal geographical orientation of this trade was to the other EEC countries.

The industry's growth over the last twenty years has taken place in the provincial regions, away from its traditional centre in and around Paris: the regions to have benefited have been especially those southwards and westwards from the capital. Some 60 per cent of all the industry's employees now work outside the Paris region. Total employment in the industry increased steadily until 1974, since when it has stayed fairly constant overall, although employment of qualified engineers, scientists and technicians continued to increase. By 1979 the total volume of business of the industry, including the informatics sector, was 107,423m frs. at factor cost.[23]

In view of the nature of its products, highly technical, science-based and constantly being updated, the industry employs a highly skilled and well qualified labour force which tends to receive high wages. Its most successful products can compete with the best in the world, including its contribution to France's very successful aerospace industry, automatic control mechanisms in industry and massive power-plant installations for electricity supply. On the other hand, the level of capital per worker is less than in other French engineering industries, in recent years there has been intensive competition on the French market from foreign suppliers, and the industry is even reported as having cash-flow problems.[24] Azouvi concludes that modernisation of outdated equipment and techniques has proceeded too slowly and that the industry's recent problems are by no means over.

Within the new field of 'informatics' the French government inspired and helped to organise the creation of a joint French-American company, CII-Honeywell-Bull, to assure increased participation in the rapidly growing world market. The new company was assured of both subsidies and privileged access to public-sector markets. The large Saint-Gobain-Pont-à-Mousson took over control of CII-Honeywell-Bull in 1980, a merger which opened up new possibilities of expansion.[25]

Metals (including Steel)

The original INSEE statistics from which Table 2.1 was compiled show three separate categories relating to the mining and production of metals: ferrous minerals and metals (value added 26,773m frs.); non-ferrous minerals and metals (value added 11,646m frs.); and iron and steel (value added 65,173m frs.). Whether this group should in fact be called an industry is a moot point, since it comprises the three quite distinct sectors. French steel production totalled 23.4m tons in 1979, significantly below the 1974 figure of 27m tons. Iron ore production amounted to 31.7m tons, significantly below levels in earlier years (pre-war production reached around 50m tons).

Interest tends to centre on the French steel industry, which is concentrated into large units, with the two largest companies, Usinor and Sacilor, each producing around 12m tons of steel annually and employing nearly 7,000 people. It has traditionally been located close to the sources of supply, especially the Lorraine and Nord regions, followed by Rhone-Alps and the Paris regions. During the 1970s, however, very large-scale sites have been developed around Fos, on the Languedoc coast, to the west of Marseilles, and near Dunkirk, using high-quality imported steel. Products go to serve the needs of all other industrial sectors. There is consistently an overall balance of trade deficit, even though both the iron and steel and primary steel processing sectors usually record significant surpluses. Productivity is low, output per employee being significantly below those in all major competitor countries: the figures for 1977 were 149 tons per person for France, 190 in West Germany, 249 in the USA and 327 in Japan.

The excess capacity problems of the world's steel industries are well known and France is no exception: her share of total world production has been declining steadily for the last thirty years, largely due to the inexorable rise of the Japanese steel industry.[26] As the 1970s progressed, the problems showed no signs of lessening until at last both 1978 and 1979 saw small increases in production.[27] The industry has seen very high levels of capital investment and a steady process of technical innovation and change, both directly aided by the intervention of the French government, which has always taken a close interest in the affairs of the steel industry in view of its vital role in the industrial life of the country. July 1966 saw a significant step forward in this relationship with the conclusion of a state-industry agreement detailing a programme of rationalisation and investment and the level of aid from public funds over the next five years. As part of this agreement a number of smaller firms have been merged into larger units and public funds have been ear-marked for the development of the sites at Fos and Dunkirk, intended to have eventual capacities of around 7m and 8m tons respectively.

The mining of iron ore has declined steadily as older seams have been nearing exhaustion and as cheap foreign imports have become more readily available: domestic extraction fell from 68,900 tons in 1960 to some 30,000 tons by the late 1970s and the employed labour force fell even more rapidly as significant efforts were made to mechanise and improve productivity. Only in Lorraine do abundant good-quality supplies remain, and these now furnish 96 per cent of national output. French production of cast iron rose by 60 per cent over 1960-77, based largely on imports from Sweden, Brazil, Liberia and Canada to the new plants at Dunkirk and Fos,[28] but thereafter output stayed relatively constant.

In view of the gravity of the crises facing all their steel industries, the EEC member countries agreed to the 'Davignon Plan' under which they would voluntarily limit their production and maintain minimum price levels fixed for various categories of products.[29]

Industry Overall

Public Ownership

As the writer has noted elsewhere,[30] the French government has through-out the post-war period intervened in the national economy and in the affairs of industry in a more complex and detailed manner than has been the case in most comparable countries. Prominent among the methods of intervention used has been direct participation in the ownership of industrial and commercial companies, this participation ranging from full-scale nationalisation to quite small holdings in a very large number of companies. Probably in no other Western industrial economy has direct state ownership or co-ownership of private enterprise been so extensive. Some nationalisations, of munitions factories and aircraft manufacturers, took place (primarily for strategic reasons) in the late 1930s, but it was the post-war chaos that led to a major wave: over 1944 to 1947 the electricity, gas and coal industries, the Banque de France, four deposit banks, 32 insurance companies and the Renault car firm were all nationalised.

Further, in subsequent years 'public holdings',[31] i.e. majority or min-ority shareholdings, have been acquired in many companies, primarily where a company either covered an important sector of the economy or was important in the financial sector: thus the state effectively can control or influence the petroleum industry via ERAP (Enterprise for Research and Control of the Petroleum Industry), the chemical industry via EMC (Mining and Chemical Enterprise) and construction via SCET (Construction and Planning Company). As an indication of the extent of state ownership, ERAP has some 150 subsidiary companies. SNCF (French railways − rather surprisingly not a nationalised industry but a private-sector company in which the state is the major shareholder), Air France, ORTF (radio and TV) and PTT (posts and telephones) are other major concerns that are all effectively under state control. The extent of the relative importance of 'public enterprises' (which the state either owns or effectively controls) in various industries is summarised in Table 2.5.

Table 2.5: Share of Public Enterprise Production in Total Production

Share	Position	Industries concerned
More than 80 per cent	Monopoly	Manufactured tobacco, matches, coal lignite and compressed coal dust, distributed gas, electricity, natural gas, telecommunication services.
Between 40 and 80 per cent	Very important	Coked products, electrical and mechanical auto equipment, products of aeronautic industry, armament and ammunitions, various minerals, transports by land, air and sea.
Between 20 and 40 per cent	Important	Crude oil, automobiles, inorganic chemistry, health services.
Between 5 and 20 per cent	Secondary	Household appliances, organic chemistry, public works and buildings, transportation auxiliaries, housing service, services rendered to enterprises.

Source: R. Drago, 'France' in W. Friedmann (ed.), *Public and Private Enterprise in Mixed Economies* (Stevens, 1974).

The public sector in France is relatively larger than that in any other major industrialised country, being exceeded only by Austria. It has been estimated[32] that the state is the majority shareholder, either directly or via holding companies, in some 500 industrial and commercial companies; it is also a minority shareholder in over 600 others, many of which have received loans from one or other of the various official funds (discussed below) which frequently require, as a condition of the loan, a minority participation in the share capital and representation on the board of directors.

The extent to which the French government in fact 'intervenes' in the operation of the various companies indicated above is not entirely clear: on the one hand many of their top managers and other executives have been transferred from senior positions in the civil service and often take with them specific instructions or strategies to be followed, and the concerns undoubtedly have to adhere to the general framework of government policies. For example, the purchasing policy and power of Electricité de France have been used to enforce the reorganisation of the heavy electrical equipment industry. On the other hand, in their day-to-day operations the firms are left fairly free to run themselves much like any company in the private sector: Renault, for example, appears to have almost complete freedom to innovate, expand and modernise, with none of the bureaucracy or red tape sometimes associated with state-owned organisations. Indeed, many state-controlled firms seem to have been well able to resist pressure from the relevant government departments to move out of the Paris area and relocate their activities in the poorer regions of France. On the other hand, the success of the recent 'contractual' approach to certain economic policies, considered in Chapter 6, has undoubtedly been aided by its ready 'acceptance' by state-controlled firms.

It is in the financial sector (outside the scope of this chapter) that the state's intervention has been more extensive than in any other part of the economy, and this has been of crucial importance for the state's control over economic developments.

If everything written above was true before the election of the Mitterrand government in 1981, many of the points mentioned become even more true in respect of the subsequent period. A detailed programme of further nationalisations and outlined interventions in industry in a variety of ways were announced by the new government during the course of 1981 and are detailed elsewhere in this book (see Chapters 1 and 9). It may confidently be predicted that more such measures will follow during the next few years.

Post-war Growth

1945 to mid-1970s

After some twenty years of stagnation and failure to innovate during the inter-war years, and from being largely devastated by 1945, French industry has throughout the post-war years recorded exceptionally high rates of expansion, investment and modernisation.[33] For most years from 1945 to 1976, including the whole of the period from 1959 to 1974, the rate of growth of industrial production equalled or exceeded 6.5 per cent per year. For 1959-74[34] the rate of increase was highest for the production of investment (capital) goods (8.6 per cent per year) and lowest for consumer goods (4.6 per cent per year). The overall annual rate of increase did not fall below 3.5 per cent (1974) or exceed 8.6 per cent (1964 and 1968), although some individual sectors of industry recorded rates of growth reaching 9 per cent or even 10 per cent on a number of occasions.

This pattern of continuous rapid growth was accompanied by a notable, if uneven, expansion in France's exports of industrial products, but also by a steady worsening of the rate of coverage of foreign trade in volume (defined as (exports-imports)/total internal production), which fell from over 3 per cent in 1959 to –0.1 per cent by 1974, the deterioration being particularly pronounced in the case of consumer goods industries.

The total labour force in the whole of French industry rose by only 1 per cent per year over the same fifteen-year period, value added per head rising on average by 5.4 per cent per year (8.4 per cent for the energy sector). It was, paradoxically, in the capital goods sector that the least capital-intensive (or the most labour-intensive) expansion took place. The sustained increase in productivity per employee for industry overall is all the more remarkable since it coincided with a steady reduction in weekly hours of work for each employee. The total stock of gross fixed capital continued to grow, at over 5 per cent per year, as also did the self-financing ratio and the trend towards capital/labour substitution.

Labour costs tended to rise more rapidly than other costs and distributed profits showed a steady increase, but company tax payments fell significantly: the former, including associated social security charges, comprised 45.6 per cent of industrial costs in 1959 and 50.3 per cent in 1973, whereas the latter fell from 24.3 per cent to 17.8 per cent over the same years. The trend towards relatively more female workers in industry had been expected to help to hold down labour costs, but this did not happen to any great extent.

From mid-1970s

As already seen above with the studies of individual industries, a quite new set of circumstances applied from the mid-1970s onwards in view of the successive oil crises and the gathering world economic recession. Even some of France's apparently most successful industries found themselves confronted with severe competition in international markets and, in some instances, increasing penetration of the domestic market by foreign competitors. The index of production for all industry, narrowly defined (i.e. excluding building and civil engineering), set at 1970 = 100, reached 126 in 1974, 126 again in 1977 and 134 in 1979.[35] Other statistics told the same story: in each of the years 1975 to 1980 the level of investment (in volume, i.e. with price fluctuations removed) remained below that for 1970,[36] whilst labour productivity, which had risen by an average of 5.5 per cent per annum over 1959-73, could rise by only 2.5 per cent per annum over 1973 to 1978.[37]

Even though, broadly speaking, all other comparable countries were undergoing similar difficulties and even though total production in France in fact fared better than that for the average of all developed countries, there were clear signs that France had, in certain respects, been particularly badly hit and nowhere was this more true than in the case of her external balance, as considered in detail in Chapter 8. The significant decline in the number of industrial jobs is considered in Chapter 4.

Structural Change

Considerable structural change has occurred in French industry in the post-war period, both in the sense of the amalgamation of firms into larger units and in the sense of relative inter-sectoral gains and losses. With regard to the former, a constantly repeated theme in industrial studies has been that the average size of French firms has been, and still is, too small, and that amalgamations, whether at the level of firms or establishments or both, are to be encouraged. Only by so doing could French industry reap the benefits of economies of scale and hope adequately to challenge its competitors in other countries.[38] There can be no doubt that such mergers have been pursued with considerable success: the number of take-overs of smaller firms by larger ones increased each year throughout the 1950s and 1960s; the average number of employees per firm rose from 109 in 1962 to 130 in 1970 and to 150 in 1974, the latest year for which such figures have been published, whilst over the same period the average number of employees in those firms with over 1,000 employees rose slightly from 4,166 (1962) to 4,224 (1974). Of all industrial concerns, employment in those firms with more than 1,000 employees comprised 43.1 per cent of the total in 1962, 46.2 per cent in 1970 and 48.1 per cent in 1974.[39]

Some indication of how confusing the relevant statistics can be may be gained from the fact that the number of firms with over 1,000 employees actually fell over the same period, from 466 to 445.[40] Other indicators made it clear that the same trends continued until at least 1979.[41] Overall the average size of both firms and establishments in France remains smaller than those in West Germany or the UK, however this is measured. A count in 1979 of firms with a volume of business of over US$ 2,000m showed that West Germany had 32, the UK 36 and France only 21. One older study found that the percentage of Gross National Product emanating from the twenty largest firms (for 1969) was: West Germany 19.44 per cent, UK 27.51 per cent, France 15.57 per cent.

With regard to structural change in the inter-sectoral sense, significant relative fluctuations have occurred, whether measured by total number of employees in each industry or by value added: the number of workers employed in each of the textiles, clothing and leather goods sectors has declined, those in the raw materials industries have risen only slowly, whilst those in such areas as vehicle production and electrical machinery have risen rapidly; cars, motor cycles and cycles recorded an increase in the number employed by 62,000, or 18.7 per cent, over the period 1969 to 1973 and electrical machinery and equipment saw an increase of 66,000 workers, or 17.2 per cent, over the same period. The relative changes considered previously in respect of Table 2.1 are also relevant here. The regional effects arising from such relative inter-sectoral changes are obvious and will be discussed in Chapter 7. There appears to be some interaction between the rates of increase of the industries' labour force and the rate of reduction of the average working week, since the trend has been for the latter to fall more significantly in the capital goods industries than in the consumer goods industries, but this interaction effect is probably rather small.[42]

International Competition

One of the greatest causes for concern in recent years has related to the competitiveness of French industry in the face of increasingly severe international competition not only from her traditional competitors but also from the emerging industries of Asia, South America and Southern Europe.[43] All countries, faced with the prolonged effects of the oil crisis since 1974, have made renewed efforts to promote their industrial exports and French domestic markets for a wide variety of products have seen serious inroads by imports of low price and good quality. France's production in the fields of motor cars, military aircraft, rail stock, glass, tyres and electronics are still among the finest in the world, but these have to be offset against particular weaknesses in other sectors. Capital goods production is generally weak and there is heavy reliance on specialised imports: despite having a large and well protected agriculture, the food products sector is poorly developed and manages to export only some 14 per cent of its production; much agricultural machinery is imported and even Renault tractors have German engines; domestic paper production is inadequate, the largest deficit item in the balance of trade after petrol being for imports of paper; neither furniture nor domestic electrical machinery have been produced in sufficient quantity and quality to satisfy the large and buoyant home markets; for machine tools the deficit on the balance of payments is 'chronic' and the industry 'resembles that of a developing country';[44] the steel, textile and shipbuilding industries have been particularly susceptible to competition from countries with cheap labour costs; whilst in the fields of informatics and micro-chips French production is now expanding well, but from a very small base.

Government Intervention

In a speech to parliament in 1978 the Minister for Industry specified five conditions for successful industrial development: healthy financing, access to innovation and new technologies, encouragement for exports, more favourable conditions for smaller firms and facilitation of the setting up of new companies. In particular, the traditional routing of preferential cheap credit towards housing and agriculture must cease, in favour of industry.[45] In some fields at least joint production projects with suppliers in other European countries will be essential for survival.

In the current situation even right-wing economists see the need for active government intervention to aid the restructuring of industries, ensure the provision of adequate finance, research and retraining facilities, and assist in the achievement of an adequate balance of payments equilibrium.[46] An official report from the Ministry of Foreign Trade suggested that much more active steps would have to be taken to curtail production in those sectors where world demand is declining and reorientate towards products for which demand is increasing or for which France has special advantages, and urged positive action to achieve this. France was seen as being not well placed in those industrial sectors for whose products world demand is rising strongly and this gave cause for concern, especially when linked to the apparently increasing propensity to import. The report particularly urged that research and investment should not continue to be channelled into sectors the prognosis for which was bleak.[47] During the 1970s France has seemed even more vulnerable than before to import penetration and economists have urged that industrial policy must give at least as much attention to import substitution as to exports.[48]

Financial Crises

In view of the mix of factors outlined above, it is not surprising that many French industrial companies have run into financial difficulties in recent years.

The French banking sector has largely been unwilling or unable to provide aid and the companies in question have had to turn to CIASI, an inter-Ministerial committee set up by the government to provide emergency assistance. These appeals have come mainly from small and medium-sized firms, but have also included some large groups such as Boussac (11,000 employees) and Manufrance (3,500). The sectors worst hit have been mechanical engineering, textiles, building and public works and leather goods, but no section of industry has remained unaffected. Many workers have had to be laid off, thus adding to the country's growing total of unemployed. Since the turndown in demand has, for many products, been more acute on the domestic market than in other countries, the tendency has been for those companies without substantial export interests to be the worst hit.[49]

Fears that product price increases would cause yet further decline in sales have led companies to make strenuous efforts to absorb cost increases. Inevitable consequences have been that, as profit margins have fallen, investment programmes have been postponed or cancelled, thus in turn causing a downturn in demand for other sectors. It has, indeed, been extremely difficult to persuade firms of the need to re-invest in a situation in which the Ministry for Industry estimated that not more than 80 per cent of existing productive capacity was being utilised. Drastic reductions in the labour force in such industries as steel, textiles and furniture production have been the inevitable consequence.

Concern

It is clear that some elements of the current situation facing French industry have given rise to widespread concern. It is hardly surprising that it should feel the effects of the world economic recession as, as has been seen above, in certain respects its position was more vulnerable than those of its competitor industries in other countries. Overall, however, such a view should not be exaggerated: the remarkable success of the French economy in the post-war years has been built largely on the very successful record of most of France's major industries. When the upturn in world demand eventually comes, it is to be hoped that the country's industries will have largely put their domestic problems, some at least of which are essentially short-term, behind them and will be ready to face what seems certain to be a new era of acute competition from industries in other countries, for both domestic and export markets.

Government Industrial Policy

As noted above, throughout the post-war period there has been concern that the average size of French industrial and commercial firms was too small in comparison with those in neighbouring countries, and the government has pursued an active policy of encouraging mergers and industrial concentration since the early 1960s. Substantial tax concessions were available to companies merging or acquiring subsidiaries, an aim of the policy also being that unprofitable or badly managed firms should be taken over.[50] Major restructuring of whole sectors of industry has been achieved in only a few sectors, notably chemicals and metals, but there have been significant regroupings in the chemical, aviation, shipbuilding and motor industries, and also in banking and insurance. Significant mergers achieved have been those of Saint-Gobin with Pont-à-Mousson, Péchiney with Ugine Kuhlmann and Evian and Kronenbourg with BSN (Boussois-Souchon-Neuvesel), and the setting up of the Creusot-Loire group. Perhaps the most famous recent case was that of the Peugeot-Citroen, and now Talbot, link.

Such developments were aided by the setting up in 1970 of the Institut de Développement Industriel (Industrial Development Institute), modelled on the United Kingdom's IRC (Industrial Reorganisation Corporation), a rare example of France following the economic example of Britain. The IDI operates as an autonomous body with a governing board comprising largely industrialists from the private sector, its capital being derived 49 per cent from the state, 51 per cent from banks and financial institutions. It seeks to aid primarily rapidly growing medium-sized firms by (i) providing additional capital either by taking a shareholding or by granting a loan normally for a maximum of five years, and (ii) giving advice after in-depth sectoral studies. With regard to this latter, the IDI takes the initiative, not waiting for industrialists to approach it but going ahead with studies especially of those sectors given priority under the current Plan. Regarding the provision of capital, funds have been made available to many smaller and medium-sized firms, often via the IDI taking a minority shareholding which is sold to the other shareholders at the termination of the loan. Such participation has never exceeded the 24 per cent stake it took in Compagnie Internationale pour l'Informatique, the IDI's policy being not to take control of the companies it is aiding. The work of the IDI has been hampered by shortage of funds and it has not achieved the status that the IRC has enjoyed in Britain: the IDI has capital of only 500m frs., nearly half of which has been used for a major restructuring of the paper industry and to aid Compagnie Internationale pour l'Informatique in the computer field. Prior to 1981 further expansion of the IDI seemed unlikely in view of the fact that it has been seen as competing with the banks which are its shareholders, and in view of the government's stated policy of encouraging credit to be provided via the normal private-sector market mechanism rather than by the intervention of the state.

The work of both the Institut de Développement Industriel and the Commission Technique de la Concurrence, considered in more detail below, must be seen as an integral part of the French government's active industrial policy, which has been set out in detail in successive plans. The focus of this policy has been to increase industrial competitiveness in order to achieve the sustained high rate of economic growth to which France became accustomed, to increase significantly France's industrial exports, which have tended to lag behind those of her competitor countries, and, more recently, to create more jobs with a view to reducing unemployment. To this end productive investment has been encouraged by both tax incentives and preferential credit terms. The government also took steps to remove legal or other hindrances to expansion, such as the law which required a 'comité d'enterprise', with employees' elected representatives, to be set up in any company which had fifty or more employees. One company with which the writer is familiar remained with a staff of 49 for some years before eventually dividing itself into two fictitious legal entities enabling it to expand to a staff of 98, to escape the provisions of such laws. Professor Chardonnet's view is that industrial concentration is still discouraged, for example by the fact that on the occasion of a merger the taxes to be paid, notably stamp duties, cost more in France than in any other EEC country.

Unfortunately, there can be little doubt that the achievement of a coherent and unified industrial policy has been impeded by the differing viewpoints of the plethora of Ministries and other governmental or semi-official bodies which the author has described in detail elsewhere.[51]

Competition Policy

There do not exist in France any direct equivalents of the UK's NEDC, Monopolies Commission or Restrictive Practices Court. The functions of the former, and many more, are carried out by the Commissariat Général du Plan which is, of course, of far greater importance and which will be considered below. Policy against monopolies and restrictive practices has not been so extensive in France as in the UK, even though there has been a general trend towards greater competition over the post-war period. Competition policy has been directed by the Commission Technique des Ententes et Positions Dominantes (recently renamed the Commission Technique de la Concurrence), operating under the aegis of the Ministry of Economy and Finance, which is now governed by an Ordinance of September 1967, replacing earlier provisions of 1953. Inter-firm agreements are prohibited if they 'prevent, restrict, or falsify the effect of competition', but may be permitted if they are deemed to favour economic progress. Abuse of a 'dominant position' may also be declared illegal: the existence of a market monopoly is not in itself considered wrong, merely its abuse, and this is defined as:

> Activity of a firm or a group of firms occupying a dominant position in the domestic market, characterised by a monopoly situation or by an evident concentration of economic power, when these activities have as their object, or may have the effect of, interfering with the normal functioning of the market.[52]

Both definitions are, therefore, delightfully vague and the Commission has had considerable freedom to place its own interpretation on them. Apart from its educative role, it has in fact taken an extremely liberal attitude: in pursuit of the former it has issued a series of reports and has emphasised that its long-term aim is control via having a better-informed public rather than by any coercive measures. In investigating individual cases, the Commission has been anxious that its work should not impede the government's policy of industrial concentration (considered essential for sustained economic growth and for the success of the Plan) and it has taken the view that since oligopolies were becoming more numerous it should seek means of justifying them.[53] In order for there to be a 'dominant position', the Commission stated that there must be 'stable, important and direct' financial links between the firms in question and that something more than merely defending a dominant position was needed to constitute abuse. Thus in 1969 high selling prices for cement were accepted on account of the industry's special need for self-financing of investment.

The most common infractions have been minimum prices, rigid quotas, cartels, compensations and penalties of various kinds, but after the effective commencement of the policy on anti-competition practices in 1955, the first legal prosecution did not take place until 1966 and the second not until 1969. In all, Le Pors concludes that the Commission appears to have achieved rather little: from 1966 to 1974 it investigated a total of only 101 cases, mostly of minor economic importance.[54] One must bear in mind that 84 of these cases were not permitted to continue in their previous form (19 of these being permitted after modification or restriction) and it seems likely that, as in the United Kingdom, the threat of legal action was sufficient to ensure co-operation. Overall, however, relatively little seems to have been achieved and inter-firm agreements are still widespread. The report of the Committee on Competition for the 6th Plan concluded that the nature of competition must vary from one sector to another, so the emergence of a unified or more coherent national policy seems unlikely. Professor Chardonnet concludes that 'save in certain highly concentrated sections, pricing agreements are rare in France . . . and as for restrictive practices they are forbidden by law.'[55] On balance, this seems to be less supported by the evidence than the conclusion of Dyas and Thanheiser that 'discussions and negotiations between competitors are a fact of life.'[56]

Monopolisation has never been so extensive in France as in many other developed countries and this is given as the reason why no organisation exists for the control of monopolies on the lines of those in the USA, Canada, UK, Japan or West Germany.[57] Proposals for control at the European level are, however, now well advanced after being discussed at the European summit conference of October 1972.

The educative role has recently been taken up by a new body, the Institut National de la Consommation, as the vogue of consumer protection has affected France much as in other countries;[58] forms of non-price competition, labelling and advertising will all receive closer attention in the future.

Externally, there is still considerable protection for French producers from such institutions as the European Coal and Steel Community, the European tin-plate Convention, and the administered price and quota systems for agricultural products and the food-processing industry, but extensive liberalisation of trade within the EEC has taken place since the signing of the Treaty of Rome. French tariff barriers, formerly the highest in Europe with an average rate of over 18 per cent, plus a whole series of additional regulations, quotas and customs controls, have disappeared for intra-European trade and, as discussed in Chapter 8, there was a massive expansion of imported manufactured and semi-manufactured goods (which perhaps quadrupled in the ten years from 1959 to 1969). There can be little doubt that the marked increase in foreign competition provided a sharp incentive towards increased productivity and effectiveness on the part of French firms.

Prior to the latest developments, the overall attitude of the French government to industrial problems may be summarised in the words of Green:

> According to the Minister of Industry the adjustment problem has brought home to the French government that it is no longer possible or even desirable to attempt to support or maintain a presence in every industry. If choices have to be made the most logical decision is to maximise France's natural advantages, especially in the industries of the future. At the policy level the government has attempted to free entrepreneurial initiative (the abolition of price controls and measures to assist company liquidity) to enable French companies to adapt to international competition. It should, and will, reinforce this action by facilitating the spread of the new technologies and by encouraging innovation in all forms.[59]

The Mitterrand Government

Since the election to power in May-June 1981 of the socialist government under President Mitterrand there has been a major shift in government industrial policy, quite apart from the programme of further nationalisations referred to previously. In late 1981 a representative of the Ministère de l'Industrie summarised the two main facets of the new policy to the writer as follows:

> (i) No longer would government aid to industry be directed mainly towards the newer science-based industries, to the often deliberate neglect of the older, more traditional industries.
> (ii) In future government assistance will be more selective, and will provide assistance, in various forms, to those cases, firms or products, in whatever industry, which it feels particularly merit support, either for economic or for social reasons.

Major policy statements[60] by Monsieur P. Dreyfus, former head of Régie Renault and now Minister for Industry, have amplified the rationale behind the above approach and its integration within the government's socialist philosophy, but have not given any more precise details of what the new policy will consist of or how it will work in practice. By early 1982 the Ministry had issued lengthy policy statements relating to the future development and restructuring of only two industries, machine tools and textiles and clothing.[61]

Notes

1. INSEE Division Etude des Entreprises, *Les Collections de l'INSEE*, Série E, no. 68 (Sept. 1979).
2. M. Baleste, *L'Economie Française*, 5th edn (Masson, 1978).
3. A. Costable, 'La Construction de Logements et l'Industrie du Batiment en France', *Problèmes Economiques*, no. 1530 (6 July 1977).
4. Ibid.
5. Baleste, *L'Economie Française*.
6. A. Azouvi, *Emploi, Qualifications et Croissance dans l'Industrie*, vol. 1, *Les Collections de l'INSEE*, Série E, no. 58 (Feb. 1979).
7. M. Moreaux, 'Bilan et Perspectives de l'Industrie Automobile Française', *Economie et Humanisme* (Sept.-Oct. 1978).
8. *World Autos Forecasts* (DRI Europe, 1981).
9. J. Tuppen, *France, Industrial Geography* (Dawson Westview, 1980).
10. Azouvi, *Emploi, Qualifications et Croissance dans l'Industrie*.
11. P. Roux-Vaillard, 'L'Industrie' in J.P. Pagé (ed.), *Profil Economique de la France au Seuil des Années 80* (La Documentation Française, 1981).
12. O. Drouin, 'Charbon: le cout de l'indécision', *Le Nouvel Economiste* (6 Feb. 1978).
13. Roux-Vaillard, 'L'Industrie'.
14. Baleste, *L'Economie Française*.
15. Tuppen, *France, Industrial Geography*.
16. L. Marthey, 'L'Industrie Chimique en France', *Notes et Etudes Documentaires*, no. 4454 (Jan. 1978).
17. Ch. Gabet, *Emploi, Qualifications et Croissance dans l'Industrie*, vol. 3, *Les Collections de l'INSEE*, Série E, no. 66 (Aug. 1979).
18. Ibid.
19. Roux-Vaillard, 'L'Industrie'.
20. 'La Situation de l'Industrie Pharmaceutique Française' (anon.), *Bulletin du Crédit National* (4th quarter, 1976).
21. G. Tussau, 'Les Industries Electriques et Electroniques', *Notes et Etudes Documentaires*, no. 4563/4 (Mar. 1980).
22. Azouvi, *Emploi, Qualifications et Croissance dans l'Industrie*, vol. 1.
23. Tussau, 'Les Industries Electriques et Electroniques'.
24. Azouvi, *Emploi, Qualifications et Croissance dans l'Industrie*, vol. 1.
25. Roux-Vaillard, 'L'Industrie'.
26. J.-C. Boulard. See also 'L'Usine Nouvelle, Perspectives de l'Industrie sidérurgique dans le monde', *Problèmes Economiques*, no. 1613 (7 Mar. 1981).
27. Roux-Vaillard, 'L'Industrie'.
28. 'Actualités Industrielles Lorraines, La Crise dans les Mines de Fer Françaises', *Problèmes Economiques*, no. 1610 (14 Feb. 1979).
29. Roux-Vaillard, 'L'Industrie'.

30. J.R. Hough, 'Government Intervention in the Economy of France' in W.P. Maunder (ed.), *Government Intervention in the Developed Economy* (Croom Helm, 1979).

31. For this expression and for further detail see R. Drago, 'France' in W. Friedmann (ed.), *Public and Private Enterprise in Mixed Economies* (Stevens, 1974).

32. By J. Chardonnet, *La Politique Economique Intérieure Française* (Dalloz, 1976).

33. J.-C. Boulard, 'L'Industrie', Ch. 6 in J.P. Pagé (ed.), *Profil Economique de la France* (La Documentation Française, 1975).

34. This period was studied in detail in *Les Collections de l'INSEE*, Série E, no. 68 (Sept. 1979).

35. Roux-Vaillard, 'L'Industrie'.

36. Ibid.

37. A. Lepas in J.P. Pagé (ed.), *Profil Economique de la France au Seuil des Années 80* (La Documentation Française, 1981).

38. This theme is repeated in Boulard, 'L'Industrie'.

39. Roux-Vaillard, 'L'Industrie'.

40. All these statistics are based on the exclusion of (i) all firms with less than 10 employees and (ii) all firms in the food and building industries. See Boulard, 'L'Industrie'.

41. Roux-Vaillard, 'L'Industrie'.

42. Boulard, 'L'Industrie'.

43. G. Legall, 'Industrie: l'héritage', *l'Usine Nouvelle* (16 Mar. 1978).

44. Ibid.

45. Ibid.

46. C. Stoffaes, 'La Grande Menace Industrielle', *Bulletin de l'ACADI* (Oct.-Nov. 1978).

47. Ministre du Commerce Extérieur, 'Les Perspectives du Commerce Extérieur Français', *Economie et Statistique* (Dec. 1978).

48. 'La Reconquête du Marché Intérieur' (anon.), *Bulletin Mensuel de la SPFG* (Feb. 1977); and N. Grange, 'Vendez Français', *L'Usine Nouvelle* (Mar. 1977).

49. R. Tendron, 'Industrie: S.O.S.', *Le Nouvel Economiste* (13 Feb. 1978).

50. Chardonnet, *La Politique Economique Intérieure Française*.

51. Hough, *Government Intervention in the Economy of France*.

52. A. Le Pors, 'Les Transfers Etat-Industrie en France et dans les Pays Occidentaux', *Notes et Etudes Documentaires*, no. 4304/5 (12 Jul. 1976).

53. Ibid.

54. Ibid.

55. Chardonnet, *La Politique Economique Intérieure Française*.

56. G. Dyas and H. Thanheiser, *The Emerging European Enterprise* (Macmillan, 1976).

57. Le Pors, 'Les Transfers Etat-Industrie en France et dans les Pays Occidentaux'.

58. Chardonnet, *La Politique Economique Intérieure Française*.

59. D. Green, *Managing Industrial Change* (HMSO, 1981).

60. See *Le Point* of 9 Oct. 1981, *Le Monde* of 14 Oct. 1981, *Le Matin* of 16 Oct. 1981 and *L'Expansion* of 6 Nov. 1981.

61. *Dossiers de Presse* (Ministère de l'Industrie, Dec. 1981).

3 AGRICULTURE

Introduction

In no other section of the economic life of the country have the problems of change, modernisation and growth been so intractable as they have been in French agriculture. No other high-level government post has been less coveted than that of Minister of Agriculture. No other aspect of intra-European relationships has caused such prolonged difficulties or occasioned so many late-night meetings at Brussels, Strasburg or Luxemburg as the development of the European Community's Common Agricultural Policy (the difficulties frequently being largely due to the iconoclastic stance of the French government's representative). The fortunes of French agriculture and the development of the Common Agricultural Policy have in fact been inexorably linked for at least the last twenty years and it is impossible to write of one without frequent reference to the other. Whilst it is easy to be critical and to write emotively of butter mountains and wine lakes, it also needs to be stated that a very great deal has been achieved at the European level in terms of progress, modernisation and stability.

No longer, hopefully, do French farmers feel the need to demonstrate by blocking roads with their tractors or giving away free produce at the roadside, and the very fact that French agriculture now makes front-page news rather rarely is in itself evidence of what has been achieved.

A Heterogeneous Sector

For many readers the stereotype of a French farm will probably be a small parcel of land, with little in the way of agricultural machinery or modern farming methods, worked by an old and rather poorly educated tenant farmer who lives in a rambling old farmhouse which may well lack such modern appurtenances as running water or even electricity. Whilst there is still some truth in such a vision, and there was even more so thirty or even fifteen years ago, it can represent no more than one side of a very complex picture. French agriculture is, in fact, most characterised by a very wide degree of heterogeneity and there is scarcely any statement one can make that would be true of the whole agricultural sector. Initially there is the wide variety of soils and climates from, say, Brittany to Provence or Aquitaine, from the rich soils of the plains around Paris to the bare slopes of the Massif Central on which farming, where it persists, can scarcely reach subsistence levels. Imposed on this is the contrast, so great as to occasion the use of the term 'the two agricultures',[1] between the large wheat and cattle farms of the north-east plains and the Paris basin and the small, poor farms of the more western and south-western regions: the former typically are highly productive and mechanised and use the very latest and most efficient farming methods, whilst the latter have in the past been typically rather unmodernised and inefficient and in some cases have approximated to the stereotype outlined above. A third aspect of diversity relates to the produce mix, although here France has no more, and perhaps rather less, diversity than many of her competitors, except perhaps regarding the very special position of viniculture within French agriculture.

Agricultural Structures

In all developed economies agriculture has ceased to be the most import-ant single 'industry' and has seen its share of Gross Domestic Product and of total employment steadily decline, usually after a fairly readily identifiable 'agricultural revolution'. In France such a 'revolution' occurred very late, if at all, and in some respects might be said to be still taking place now. By 1945 agriculture was still the pre-eminent sector in the French economy, but over the ensuing years its share in the economy steadily declined so that by the time of the 1975 Census it was contributing just over 6 per cent of Gross Domestic Product and employing less than 10 per cent of the national labour force (down from nearly 30 per cent in 1950).

Agricultural Output

Agriculture's record for the last few years is summarised in Table 3.1, which shows that agriculture's share in the national economy has con-tinued to decline, albeit unevenly, into the beginning of the 1980s. Except for the poor harvest of 1976, each year has seen total agricultural output increase (although in 1980 by only 0.4 per cent), as the right-hand column shows. The declining share can therefore only be explained by the rates of increase being lower than those recorded elsewhere in the economy. Total agricultural production reached 200,000m frs. for

Table 3.1: Agricultural Output, 1975-80

| Year | Agricultural Output | |
	As Percentage of GNP	Percentage Change on Previous Year
1975	6.1	
1976	5.9	−5.3
1977	5.7	4.8
1978	5.7	7.9
1979	5.7	8.1
1980	5.1	0.4

Source: *Rapport sur les Comptes de la Nation 1980*, vol. 2 (Les Collections de l'INSEE, Série C, no. 94-5, 1981).

the first time in 1979 as nominal values continued to rise, the greater part of the increase relating to the effects of inflation. Of this total some 38,000m frs. worth of products were eventually consumed within agriculture, leaving a net output of 162,421m frs. Table 3.2 shows the breakdown of this total value over the principal product categories, the largest being milk and cereals, but with no one category being very predominant. The animal-arable mix, at about 55-45, is now fairly stable over time after the earlier efforts in the 1960s to expand output of cereals.

Table 3.2: Composition of Agricultural Production, 1979

| | Value | |
	As Percentage of Total	Million frs.
Cereals	16.0	26,071
Fruit and vegetables	12.1	19,577
Wines	10.5	17,007
Other vegetable products	4.3	7,026
Sugar-beet	2.8	4,537
Arable total	45.7	74,218
Milk	17.4	28,327
Beef	12.6	20,485
Pork	7.4	12,002
Veal	5.2	8,517
Fowl	4.8	7,617
Other animal products	4.3	7,029
Eggs	2.6	4,226
Animal total	54.3	88,203
Total	100.0	162,421

Source: B. Vial, 'L'Agriculture' in J.P. Pagé (ed.), *Profil Economique de la France au Seuil des Années 80* (La Documentation Française, 1981).

Perhaps 60 per cent of France's land surface is devoted to agriculture of which about one-half (or some 17m hectares) represents arable land, of which cereal growing is the largest single user with some 10m hectares; grasslands, primarily for cattle, cover over 13m hectares. Gross tonnages produced are (for 1979)[2] around 44m tons of cereals (of which soft wheat represents over 40 per cent), 4.5m tons of meat (of which nearly half for beef), 3m tons of sugar, 7.5m tons of potatoes, 84m hectolitres of wine (an exceptionally good year) and some 300m hectolitres of milk. The animal population includes some 24 million head of cattle and some 11 million each of pigs and of sheep. France is by far the largest producer in Europe of cereals (more than the UK and West Germany put together) and of sugar, ranks first equal with Italy for wine production and is ahead of West Germany for both meat and milk.[3]

Provisional results for the year 1980[4] suggest that on the year total output in volume increased by only 0.9 per cent, a much smaller rise than that for the preceding two years (7.9 per cent each). There were notable increases in each of cereals (10.3 per cent), oil-seeds (96.1 per cent), milk (5.2 per cent) and fowl (8.8 per cent), but these were offset by the heavy fall of 23.4 per cent in the production of wines. After allowing for running down of stocks (particularly of wines), total deliveries of agricultural produce continued to rise at the steady rate of 4.7 per cent. Prices of agricultural products rose on average by only 5.7 per cent during a year when the national price index rose by 11.3 per cent. Therefore the purchasing power of agricultural incomes recorded a further significant decline.

Structural Change

The post-war years have seen 'a very considerable evolution'[5] as the number of farms and the number of people working on the land have declined steadily, but production of all categories of crops and animal products has recorded large increases, as a result of significant, if uneven, improvements in productivity. Thus the index for total agricultural production at constant prices (i.e. changes in volume) over a long period of years recorded an annual rate of increase of 2.6 per cent,[6] a considerable achievement from an initially outdated industry but nevertheless one much lower than the high growth rates for most French industries. It should not be overlooked, however, that this increase took place simultaneously with the shake-out of labour from agriculture so that the increase in production per worker averaged some 8 per cent per annum throughout the period.[7]

The national census of 1975 indicated that scarcely 2m people were employed on the land in France, as compared with over 5m at the time of the 1954 census. By the time of the Employment Survey of March 1981 the figure had fallen to some 1,750,000, or just under 7.7 per cent of the working population, and was continuing to decline at the rate of 1.6 per cent per annum, i.e. a slower rate of decrease than previously.[8] In 1975, of the 2m 55 per cent were 'chefs d'exploitation', i.e. self-employed farm owners or managers, whereas in 1954 the equivalent figure was only 37 per cent.[9] The number of wage-earning farm labourers fell from over 1.1m in 1954 to 376,000 in 1975. Clearly, therefore, the flight from the land has been most marked in the case of employees rather than those working on their own account and has been accompanied by a process of farms merging into larger units. Much of this change was concentrated into a relatively short number of years: according to one survey, whereas in 1955 40 per cent of farms had less than twenty hectares (about fifty acres) and only 25 per cent had over fifty hectares (123 acres), by 1971 the former figure had fallen to 26 per cent and the latter had risen to 36 per cent.[10] By 1981 the General Agricultural Census estimated figures of 18.4 per cent and 44.4 per cent respectively. There can be little doubt that the same trends have continued in the years since the 1975 Census. Table 3.3 summarises the changing size pattern of French farms over a period of nearly twenty years.[11] These statistics are not comparable with those quoted above since they were compiled on a different basis, those above relating to percentage of surface area whilst those in Table 3.3 refer to percentage of number of farms. Clearly, however, the same trends emerge from both.

Table 3.3: Size of French Farms, 1960-78

Size (hectares)	1960 (per cent)	1978 (per cent)
1 – 5	26.2	19.6
5 – 10	21.2	15.0
10 – 20	26.7	21.6
20 – 50	20.5	30.8
50+	5.5	13.0

These figures show the definite and continuing trend for farming to become concentrated in units of larger size. Much of the structural change to have affected French agriculture has come about from natural causes, including mortality and sons not wishing to succeed their fathers in running small-scale farms, rather than from the direct results of government policies.

One of the most significant causes of agriculture's greatly increased production over the post-war period has been the gradual switching from less productive to more productive types of output. Thus the growing of such crops as oats and rye-grass has been progressively abandoned in favour of soft wheat (output up 2.5 times since 1950) and maize (surface area growing maize doubled between 1966 and 1975 alone). Although France now supplies over one-third of the EEC's production of cereals, somewhat surprisingly the EEC overall is still a net importer of certain types of cereals, especially those used for animal feeds, mainly from North America.

Scarcely half of France's self-employed farmers work full-time on the land or depend solely on farming for their livelihood, the remainder having either another part-time job or some other form of income, frequently a pension. This is, of course, particularly true of the smallest farms, many of which could not otherwise support a farmer and his family. The post-war years have seen a steady trend towards modernisation and mechanisation: from having fewer than 100,000 tractors in 1950, French farmers now have over 1.4m or nearly as many as West Germany; from having fewer than 8,500 'combine harvesters' in 1950, France now has over 150,000; some 375,000 farms are now equipped to milk mechanically. French farming still lags behind her competitors in some respects, one of the most important being the use of fertilisers: French farmers use around 150 kilograms of mineral fertiliser per hectare as compared with West Germany's 250 or the Netherlands' 300. Even here, however, the regional disparities are highly significant, the large farms of northern France and the Paris basin having figures comparable to that for the Netherlands.

Comparative Yields

There are, of course, doubts regarding the valid interpretation of all these statistics, since optimal usages of equipment and inputs must depend on size of farm, soil, climate and type of product, all of which vary throughout Europe. Perhaps more valid for comparative purposes (although here again the same variations have to be taken into account) are the statistics for product yields: France's wheat yield of 4.5 tons per hectare is just ahead of those of West Germany and the UK, but significantly below the Netherlands' figure of over 5 tons; for milk, however, French cows can manage no more than 3,300 litres each per year, whereas those in most other European countries exceed 4,000.

Yields of potatoes per hectare are significantly lower in France than those elsewhere. Value added per agricultural worker in France is comparable to that in the UK, rather above that for West Germany, and well above that for Italy, but even these figures are open to question since those workers for France and the UK have much higher ratios of land per agricultural worker than, for example, West Germany. Value added per hectare (which has, of course, the same problem in reverse, i.e. how many men are available per hectare) is lower in France than in West Germany or Italy, but higher than in the UK. Again all of these figures conceal the very wide variations within the national scene: whilst France can take legitimate pride in her modernised and efficient cereal farming in the north, there can be little doubt that very many of the small farms in the west and south-west 'ont encore un retard technique important à rattraper'[12] ('are still technically way behind').

Value added per hectare in the Paris region is more than double that in Limousin per hectare and more than treble per worker. Farmers in the south and west tend to be considerably older and less well educated than those in the north, and they also have lower incomes, work longer hours, have worse housing equipped with fewer consumer durables, and have few of their children remaining at school or college for an extended education. Statistics published in 1981 show that fewer agricultural employees had cars (72.6 per cent), washing machines (77.4 per cent) or colour televisions (28.1 per cent) than almost any other category of worker in France.[13] Small wonder then that it has been the poorest regions that have seen most of the 'exode rural', or flight from the land, and that this has come largely from agricultural employees, over the years since the Second World War. This flight from the land was at the level of over 130,000 persons per year throughout the 1960s, since when it has continued at a reduced rate.

The food producing industries, directly dependent on an efficient national agriculture, have developed significantly in France in recent years, to attain a total production of 233,000m frs. (1979), spread over the whole range of consumer-oriented food and drinks. The giant 'Générale Occidentale', with nearly 15,000m frs. annual income, is the second-largest such firm in Europe, but more characteristic of this sector are very much smaller firms, scattered throughout France: 70 per cent of the firms involved have fewer than fifty employees.

Agriculture after 1974

The average incomes of all farm workers increased steadily in line with the increase in the national average wage from the end of the Second

World War to 1974. For the subsequent years, however, agriculture, being heavily dependent on fertilisers and foodstuffs, many of which were by-products of increasingly expensive energy sources, found its raw material costs rising rapidly. With the gathering pace of the recession, however, agricultural product prices did not rise in line with the increase in the cost of living. The efforts of the EEC to hold down the levels of agricultural support, the poor climatic conditions of 1976 and 1977 and increasingly severe competition for export markets from other EEC countries all combined to add to the difficulties facing French agriculture and total agricultural output in volume declined after 1974, not reaching the 1974 level again until 1978. From this mix of reasons agricultural workers' incomes ceased to rise in real terms after 1975.[14]

External Trade

Agricultural and food products combined brought France exports of 63,900m frs. in 1979 against imports of 57,200m frs., a surplus balance of 6,700m frs.; within these global totals there were large surpluses for cereals, milk products and (mainly alcoholic) drinks (nearly 20,000m frs. combined) but significant external deficits for sugar, meat, fruit, vegetables, coffee and tea. Coffee and tea alone cost France some 9,000m frs. of imports and it is arguable that this amount should not be included in accounts relating to France's agricultural and food-producing industries: if it is removed, the overall statistical result becomes a much larger surplus. Somewhat similarly, the external deficit for fruit and vegetables refers to products which can be produced more easily, or earlier in each season, in more favourable climates. Rather more worrying perhaps is the significant excess of imports of meat and meat products over exports and the fact that France is now less self-supporting for each of the major categories of meat products than she was twenty years ago.[15] On the credit side France's agricultural exports were larger than those of any other country in Europe until they were overtaken by the Netherlands in the late 1970s. France's performance for agricultural exports has greatly improved since the early 1960s and particularly since 1971: before that year the agricultural sector regularly had a net external trade deficit each year but since 1971 there have been external surpluses each year except for 1977. Agriculture has, however, still a long way to go to reach the objective specified in Plan 7 of an overall sectoral annual surplus of 20,000m frs. (supposedly by 1980). Some two-thirds of France's agricultural exports went to other EEC Countries. Provisional results for 1980 suggest that the external agricultural surplus continued to improve and that exceptionally good results were achieved by the food products sector.

French Policy Measures

Throughout the post-war period the successive plans have always laid great stress on the importance attached to the modernisation and expansion of agricultural production and active policies to aid agriculture go back even further, to the 1930s. The major protective measures have been developed at the European level, as discussed below. French domestic policies have related primarily to facilitating structural change in farming and to providing social assistance, of various kinds, to the large number of poor farming families.

'The past twenty years have seen a tremendous effort of modernisation on the farm.'[16] Such effort had commenced earlier, but may be said to have begun in earnest with what is known as the Pisani Law of 1960 (Edgar Pisani did not in fact become Minister of Agriculture until 1961, but he took the initiative in promulgating decrees to implement the law): these decrees provided, *inter alia*, for a new pension fund to encourage old farmers to retire, an agency for buying land, stricter rules for absentee landlords, and measures to encourage farmers to group together both for marketing and for shared production.[17] All of these measures were important, indeed they were all eventually to be revived and given greater effect in the Vedel Report of 1969, which echoed the EEC's Mansholt Plan providing for structural reform and long-term change. If, however, there was one of the measures that was of overriding importance, it was that referring to the establishment of an agency to buy up land. This found expression in SAFERs — Sociétés d'Aménagement Foncier et d'Etablissement Rural — which were regional bodies empowered to buy up land as it came on to the market, improve it, and then sell it selectively, often in larger parcels, to younger and better qualified farmers. This process has greatly aided the merging of farms into larger units, an essential prerequisite for mechanisation and modernisation, but it has proceeded rather slowly due to the SAFERs' shortage of funds. By 1978 SAFERs had enabled some 106,000 farms to be enlarged and had bought and sold some 15 million acres or around one-tenth of the land that had come on to the market. By 1978 they were involved annually in 26 per cent of land sales. Closely allied to the above were systems for co-operative buying and selling which again developed slowly and varied greatly from one locality to another. Some inroads were made into the large profits enjoyed by the middlemen and wholesalers and overall there were some improvements in marketing methods, but perhaps the movement lost some of its impetus after the advent of guaranteed product prices from the CAP. Where they existed, 'Groupements Agricoles d'Exploitations en Commun' could have significant results, but overall their effect was 'disappointing'.[18] Potentially of great impact were the subsidised loans for the purchase or modernisation of farms ('prêts fonciers bonifiés') but here again funds were limited, and they dwindled to a trickle after the advent to power of the Barre government.[19]

One of the final acts of President Giscard d'Estaing was to sign the 'Loi d'Orientation Agricole' ('Law of Agricultural Development') which read as a general résumé of the status of French agriculture and its problems and prospects for the foreseeable future and introduced a number of legal reforms, relating particularly to the ownership and transfer of land. The 'Loi' also provided for increased education and training for farm workers, especially the young, increased competition in agriculture, and greater integration of farming into regional economic policy.[20] Rather little happened, however, as the result of this major initiative before the Giscard d'Estaing/Barre regime was voted out of office in the elections of May-June 1981.

The 'Plan Intérimaire' issued by the socialist government in November 1981 stated that the successful development of agricultural production was essential both to reduce the country's economic dependence on imports and to assist the overall policy of reducing unemployment. Only in the context of an expansionist programme was it possible to plan for improved incomes and living standards for those engaged in farming. Increased investment would be necessary, including from public funds, the prime aims of the increased investment being to increase technical efficiency (by, for example, further regrouping of farms into larger units, and irrigation and drainage schemes) and to improve the effectiveness of agricultural markets. At the same time farmers must come to be less dependent on state intervention.

European Agricultural Policy

In the words of a member of the EEC Commission, 'The Common Agricultural Policy is seen by some people as the pièce de résistance of European integration policies. For no other sector of the economy has a common policy been developed so far as for agriculture.'[21] In the Treaty of Rome, the original document which brought the European Economic Community into being, Article 39 defined the five fundamental objectives to be assigned to the Common Agricultural Policy as follows:

(i) to increase productivity by promoting technical progress and by assuring the national development of agricultural production and the optimum utilisation of the factors of production, in particular labour;

(ii) to ensure a fair standard of living for the agricultural community;

(iii) to stabilise markets;

(iv) to assure the availability of supplies; and

(v) to ensure that supplies reach consumers at reasonable prices.

From the above it is immediately clear that not only was the wording imprecise (for example, how fair is 'fair'?) but also the different object-ives were liable to conflict with each other (for example, prices that the agricultural community would deem 'reasonable' would be liable to seem less so from the point of view of the consumers). Much remained to be done to iron out the details of a common policy and this was only achieved after several series of marathon negotiations between the member states, negotiations in which the French voice was never silent and often seemed to predominate. The result that emerged was not perfect and can easily be criticised, but that any agreement could be reached in view of the disparate needs and wishes of the original six member states was in itself no mean achievement. Broadly speaking, this was done by concentrating at first on what might be called the shorter-run problems of stable markets, uniform prices and reasonable incomes for producers. Only later, many years later, was it possible to turn to the longer-run problems of agricultural productivity, structural change and modernisation. Over-production and the generation of large surpluses such as the 'butter mountain' and the 'wine lake' might not unreasonably be cited as the link between the two: the accumulation of the vast surpluses was, with the escalating cost of the scheme, one of the two major reasons which compelled the EEC eventually to take seriously the intractable problems of productivity and structural reform.

The essential features of the Common Agricultural Policy have re-mained the same since its inception. Agricultural markets throughout the Community are artificially manipulated to ensure high prices and thus guarantee adequate incomes for producers. This result is achieved partly through the imposition of tariffs, on a sliding scale, to imports from outside the Community and partly through a system of official support buying for surplus products within the community, at predetermined support prices. These support prices are to be distinguished from the target prices which are set to ensure uniform prices for each category of product throughout the Community: in the case of soft wheat, for example, the common target price was that previously applying in the area with the least adequate supplies of soft wheat, which was defined as Duisburg in the Ruhr.[22]

When market prices in the Community fall to some 5-7 per cent below the target prices (with due allowance made for normal regional variations), support buying by the Community commences and thus prevents prices falling any further. Any imports from outside the Community have levies applied to them sufficient to bring their prices up to the internal price levels. From the point of view of the consumer, therefore, this is a regime of high prices, often considerably higher (in real terms) than applied previously, but from the point of view of the producer it is one of virtually guaranteed income and from the point of view of the Community's Commissioners (whose job it is to run the system under the direction of the Council of Ministers) it is one of stable markets and prices. Politically speaking, the achievement of such a coherent system, after many late-night sittings by the Council of Ministers, the Commissioners and the European Parliament, was a remarkable achievement. For an economist, however, it is difficult to justify a system which rewards over-production (without limit) and makes no reference to structural change or modernisation. The natural result of the system is the accumulation of surpluses, which might be termed the Achilles' heel of the CAP, and to which no completely satisfactory solution has yet been found: the surpluses are disposed of (or 'dumped') on world markets often at a huge loss, especially in the case of butter, milk and grains, so that not only were the Community's consumers faced with high internal prices, but they also had to finance the deficits on these surpluses.[23] It is, however, only fair to add that when world prices for agricultural products rose sharply in the mid-1970s in the face of acute shortages of basic foodstuffs, the EEC not only enjoyed prices below those applying in the rest of the world (the reverse of the experience throughout the 1960s), but was also able to provide extra food, especially grain, to the hardest-hit developing countries.[24]

The system as a whole is financed by payments from the governments of the member countries and therefore ultimately by their taxpayers, the allocation between these governments being determined initially as for the general budget of the Community, but latterly also by the size of each state's net imports of agricultural products from non-member states. The complexities of how these contributions have varied over the years need not detain us here except to note that initially (in 1962/3) France, West Germany and Italy contributed 28 per cent each, by 1965-6 France's contribution was the highest of any member state (32.58 per cent against West Germany's 31.67 per cent, Italy's having fallen to 18 per cent), but subsequently fell back with the contributions of France and West Germany frequently alternating in first place over the ensuing years.

Not until the 1970s did the Community seriously attempt to tackle the problems of structural reform and modernisation, without which there could be little hope of a more efficient agricultural sector appearing. With the combined aims of increasing the size and viability of holdings, reducing the number of people working on the land and converting agricultural land to alternative uses, a series of measures was introduced, including payments from the EEC's Agricultural Fund to encourage both modernisation of farm units and early retirement of farmers. It is immediately apparent that this programme of structural reform was linked to the problem of over-production, thus endeavouring to remove some of the problem of inflexibility for which the CAP has been so criticised. An important part of this process was the holding down (the reduction in real terms) of farm support prices during the 1970s.

France and the CAP

The heterogeneity of French agriculture inevitably implies that some French farmers would do better than others out of the CAP. Overall the system was designed, at least in part, to protect the small farms such as in France's west and south-west, but in so doing it guaranteed high and stable prices to the large and much more productive farms such as in France's northern plains. The latter have therefore done extremely well out of the CAP and have undoubtedly benefited more than the former.

Successive French Ministers have not been slow to represent the needs of French farmers in the various European negotiations, and time and again the success or failure of these negotiations hinged on the stance taken by the French delegate. In view of some of the foregoing comments it may seem surprising to note that French farming has traditionally been more efficient than that of her major rival West Germany, especially regarding grain production, and there seemed to be every hope, therefore, that French farmers would fare well from a united, or a more united, European agriculture, especially one geared to a system of stable prices at high levels. A more modest system of agricultural support from the national budget pre-existed in France and this had to give way to the new (higher) European support measures.

Perhaps the earliest prolonged tussle between France and West Germany occurred over the establishment of a common price for grain, on which negotiations began in 1961, but which was not finally concluded until 1967. In the face of French obduracy the West Germans reluctantly agreed to a common price for soft wheat of 425 marks per ton, even though this was significantly below the previous German level (which was the highest in Europe): the way should therefore have been open for French grain producers to make significant inroads into the German domestic market, which they duly proceeded to do. During those same years there was a prolonged hassle, renewed annually, over the relative sizes of contributions from the member states, as noted above, so much so that by 1965 the Council of Ministers requested the Commission to produce a new plan for financing the common policy. It was as a result of this move that the Commissioners, strongly influenced by Signor Mansholt, the Commissioner responsible for agricultural policy, proposed that progressively the customs duties on imports from outside the Community should be paid directly to the Commission: no longer would member states have to haggle over their respective contributions and no longer would they feel the strain on their national budgets each year (although they would, of course, have lost the revenue from their own import duties on the same products). Equally, however, the Commission would enjoy a very large income, and in all probability a corresponding shift in power, free from intervention by the member states. To General de Gaulle such a proposal was anathema and there followed the most serious split (to date) in the history of the Community: from the summer of 1965 the French boycotted Community meetings and sought (and eventually obtained) the maintenance of the national veto in the Council of Ministers, which had been due to end shortly thereafter. Under the eventual agreement, not reached until the summit at The Hague in 1969 and not fully in force until 1975, 90 per cent (i.e. 100 per cent less 10 per cent for administration) of all levies and customs duties on imported foodstuffs were to be handed over by the national governments to the European Agricultural Fund, a result remarkably close to the original proposal to which the French had taken such strong objection.

In 1968 Mansholt put forward a radical and far-sighted plan for the modernisation of European agriculture and in the following year the French Ministry of Agriculture's Vedel Report produced equally dramatic proposals: it urged that ideally by 1985 the number of farms should be reduced from 1.5 million to 250,000, employing an average

of between two and four people each; that the active agricultural population should be reduced from 3m to under 700,000; that the 32m
hectares devoted to agriculture should be reduced by 12m (1 hectare =
2.47 acres); that the minimum size of farms should be increased from
20 to 80 hectares; and that there should be rapid increases in yields and
labour productivity via active market interventions and subsidies for
structural change. These proposals were on the same lines as those of
Mansholt, although the latter set out different criteria for different
types of farming — for example minima of some 250 acres (around 100
hectares) for wheat, of 40 to 60 cows for milk, of some 150 head of
cattle for beef and veal.[25] Whereas Mansholt had to embrace all types
of farming, the Vedel proposals were, of course, framed primarily with
reference to France's backward and inefficient cattle farmers (milk and
beef). The Vedel Plan received a more ready acceptance than that of
Mansholt, but at both the French national and the European levels the
ensuing years have seen a gradual trend towards more profound structural change.

A further major crisis in the Community's affairs again related primarily to agriculture, although ostensibly at least the cause lay elsewhere;
this occurred in August 1969 when the French government suddenly and
without warning devalued the franc by 11.1 per cent. Now the Common
Agricultural Policy expresses prices in terms of the Community's unit of
account, which has a gold content equal to that of the US dollar (currently 1 ECU = 5.847 frs. or £0.618).[26] A devaluation by one member
state causes alterations in the relative national prices: in this case French
farmers would enjoy higher domestic prices whilst apparently still elig-
ible for the same level of support from Europe as previously. After an
interregnum, during which France had to agree to grant subsidies to
imports from member states and levy compensatory duties on French
exports, a further unsettled period followed from 1971 when a number
of European currencies (not including the franc) floated, causing their
relative positions against each other to change. For agriculture some
more stable system seemed essential and this resulted in what are popu-
larly referred to as green national currencies, such as the green franc or
the green pound: separate green exchange rates are used for converting
the European currency unit (ECU) prices into national currencies and
these may differ significantly from the normal commercial rates of exchange. Currently it so happens that the two are almost on a par, but
support prices in West Germany are still some 9 per cent higher than in
the rest of the Community. New green rates of exchange are now agreed
each year by the Council of Ministers as part of the annual agricultural

settlement and apply to cereals, eggs, poultry, pigmeat, wine, fish, beef, milk products and sugar.

Currently there are two major problems for France. First, the enlargement of the Community to bring in countries — Greece (now a member) and (proposed) Portugal, Spain — which are largely agricultural competitors poses a severe threat to the farmers in the southern parts of France whose local markets may be swamped by the invasion of products from these countries. These parts of France either specialise in viniculture, in which case they will face strong competition from cheap imported wines, or tend to have rather small, inefficient farms which are not well placed to withstand competition from any quarter. The former may bring back memories of the 'wine war' of 1976 when France became so incensed at the mass imports of cheap and poor-quality Italian wines that she imposed a levy of 10 per cent, in flat contradiction of the EEC's rules.

The second problem relates once again to the question of surplus production and the total cost to the Community. The agricultural support system now comprises some two-thirds of the Community's budget and the pressures for its cost to be reduced in real terms are growing more intense. It seems increasingly likely that French farmers will have to lose at least part of the very protected position that they have enjoyed for the last twenty years or so. Whether this can be achieved without a new wave of unrest or demonstrations by French farmers must remain a matter for conjecture.

The announcement in April 1981 of agreement by the EEC's agricultural Ministers on the EEC's agricultural budget for 1982 might have been thought to be good news for French farmers: in addition to the average increase in guaranteed prices of 9.5 per cent, the European Currency Unit (ECU) was revalued by 2.5 to take account of exchange rate changes, including the 6 per cent devaluation of the Italian lira. Thus price increases for French farmers were 2.5 per cent higher than the 9.5 per cent. (There had been two similar 'green' exchange rate adjustments in France's favour during 1980, of 3.6 per cent and 1.3 per cent respectively.) Nevertheless, during the discussions in Brussels some 2,000 farmers, mostly French, demonstrated outside the EEC building with the aid of eggs, vegetables, bottles and stones, in support of their demands for price increases of 15 per cent to make up for their substantial loss of real income over the preceding two years. This latter point was made clear in the preparatory document published by the Commission prior to the April 1981 meeting, which included the figures set out in Table 3.4.

Table 3.4: Agricultural Prices and Inflation Rates, 1977-82

Year	Average Agricultural Price Increase (per cent)	Inflation Rate (per cent)
1977/8	6.6	9.1
1978/9	10.5	9.3
1979/80	8.7	10.2
1980/1	6.4	11.9
1981/2	12.0[a]	11.3

Note: a. This forecast by the Commission represents the 9.5 + 2.5 quoted above.
Source: *Green Europe Newsletter* (Apr. 1981).

These figures leave no doubt as to the decline in French farm incomes in real terms. On the one hand French farmers might have been relatively pleased with the outcome since the EEC's non-agricultural government Ministers had been pressing for much smaller price increases, but on the other hand French wheat producers did not take kindly the parallel announcement that the EEC had refused France permission to sell 600,000 tons of surplus wheat to the Soviet Union.[27]

Recent Developments

As indicated above, French agriculture has suffered rather mixed fortunes in recent years. Whilst in the longer term agricultural production (in constant prices) continues to grow, the post-1960 trend of an annual increase averaging 2.6 per cent was not maintained after 1974; the years 1975 to 1977 all had total production levels significantly below that of 1974, and although 1978 and 1979 saw a significant recovery and exceeded the 1974 level, they were still below that of the trend increase. To this it is necessary to add that agricultural prices have tended to rise more slowly than the national retail price index (for 1979, 6.6 per cent against 10.3 per cent) which would also tend to depress farm incomes in real terms.

The total land area devoted to agriculture has shown a slow fall of some 7 per cent since 1960, the decrease being concentrated almost entirely in the arable sector. In those years whilst wheat production has increased by 80 per cent, eggs by 50 per cent, meat by 25 per cent and wine by 40 per cent, the production of maize has multiplied by six, but that of fresh vegetables has fallen slightly; fruits have been very uneven, with apples multiplying some two and a half times. The average size of farms in France, for what the statistic is worth, has increased from only

15 hectares to 25 hectares (62 acres) in 25 years. The same years have seen heavy investments in farm properties and equipment, and in the use of fertilisers; the quantity of the latter has more than doubled and cattle feedstuffs have multiplied by about six since 1960. Whereas the price index of the general range of purchases by farm families doubled in the years 1970-7, the price index for their own products rose by only 80 per cent.[28] The prices of fertilisers and other agricultural inputs rose particularly sharply in the years after 1970, although it also has to be said that they had declined steadily in real terms over the previous decade.

Over the period 1960-77 the prices of agricultural products slightly declined overall in real terms. During these same years the population of France rose by some 17 per cent but thanks to the increased productivity of French agriculture no extra recourse to imported foods was necessary. The balance of demand changed towards significantly more cheese, fruit and meat, and significantly less cereals and potatoes. France's external agricultural balance with its EEC partners showed an annual surplus hovering around 10,000m frs., but no longer increasing as steeply as in the early 1970s. Over the same years, strongly influenced by Community rules and directives, state aid to agriculture doubled in real terms, to reach 47,000m frs. by 1978.[29] About half of this total went towards social security payments, including pensions, over 80 per cent of the cost of which is now met by the state in one way or another. For 1980 total state aid was estimated as some 60,000m frs.[30]

The years 1978 and 1979 were much better for French agriculture after three rather mediocre years, with especially large increases (nearly 10 per cent) for cereals and other vegetable products for 1978 over 1977 and for beef and other animal products (around 7 per cent) for 1979 over 1978. It is, of course, always difficult to know how much importance to attach to year-by-year variations in agricultural products in view of climatic and other uncertainties, but at least the shortfall as compared with the previous long-term trend of an annual increase in production of 2.6 per cent was recovered. While total farm income continued to decline, as it has done each year since the peak of 1973, the rate of decrease of the number of persons working in farming was even greater, so that farm income per head rose slightly. The external surplus with other EEC countries rose sharply to 17,000m frs. by 1979 and exports to the rest of the world also increased. Whilst farmers had to contend with the same escalation of oil and petrol prices as everyone else, they faced even more rapid rises in the prices of fertilisers and animal feeds. The use of a new statistical concept, the external balance

for non-exotic agricultural products (i.e. excluding such tropical products as coffee and tea), rather reminiscent of the UK's adoption of a
'non-oil balance', gave a surplus of 19,000m frs. The number of farms
continued to decline by over 2 per year, a rate rather below that in
previous years.[31] The increases in productivity and in farm incomes for
1979 over 1978 tended to be highest in those départements in northern
France and lowest for those in the south, thus tending to aggravate the
existing inequalities within French agriculture.[32] Provisional results for
1980 and early indications for 1981 suggest that the above improvements are being continued.

Some Trends and Future Outlook

A number of trends are discernible within French agriculture which
seem likely to continue at least into the foreseeable future. Until about
1970, more and more French farmers were becoming owners of the
land on which they worked, so that about 70 per cent of farm land was
owned in this way; in the 1970s, however, this trend has been reversed
and much outside capital has been invested in agriculture and in the
land, partly perhaps because of the high levels that land values have
reached and partly because of the increased tendency for land to be
used for a variety of leisure purposes in addition to farming. As part of
the government's policy of making farming more attractive to young,
well qualified farmers, substantial government grants for the modernisation of farms and farm buildings are now available provided that evidence is produced of agricultural diplomas to professional level.[33]

One continuing trend, described as 'remarkable',[34] is the maintenance
of essentially family-based production in an increasingly modernised and
technically based industry.[35] This emphasis on the family within the
agricultural sector has received direct encouragement from a variety of
official policies, but there are now serious doubts as to whether it will
be possible to continue this emphasis in the future in the face of the
remorseless search for greater agricultural productivity. Simultaneously,
the time must come when it will be necessary to seek to slow down or
halt the 'rural exodus' if France is to be left with a stable agricultural
industry based on adequate manpower. A major policy development
resulted from the EEC Directive of April 1972 on the modernisation of
farms, which did not become fully applicable in France until 1977. Its
desiderata for a more efficient agriculture, although much less ambitious
than the original Mansholt Plan proposals, have been termed 'unrealistic'
when compared with the still backward state of a large percentage of
French farms.[36]

If there are two major hypotheses regarding agricultural developments over the next few years, they are that French farmers may have
to learn to exist without the very high level of EEC protection that
they have enjoyed hitherto[37] and the larger farming concerns especially
will have to become more orientated towards export markets outside
Europe.[38] After the turbulent upheavals of the 1960s, more recent
years have been relatively quiescent for French agriculture. Some of
the trends outlined above suggest that this could in turn give way to a
new period of unrest, with the possibility that agriculture may move
back closer to the centre of the political stage. 'Agriculture must be our
petrol', said President Giscard d'Estaing in December 1977,[39] and this
phrase serves to epitomise the crucial importance of an efficient agricultural sector within the overall context of the French economy.

In some respects French agriculture cannot yet be said to have emerged from the severe problems it encountered in the years after 1974,
as discussed above. It is a sector particularly subject to the effects of
the successive energy crises and for all the reasons discussed above the
early 1980s seem likely to be especially difficult. Much will depend on
the general progress of the French economy out of the recession and on
the policies of the socialist government which came to power in 1981.
To date, the latter have given rise to the optimistic statements quoted
above but to rather little direct or specific action. 'Un avenir incertain'
('An uncertain future'), the conclusion of one recent study of French
agriculture, remains valid today.[40]

Notes

1. John Ardagh, *The New France*, 3rd edn (Pelican, 1977).
2. *Les Comptes de l'Agriculture Française en 1979*, *Les Collections de
l'INSEE*, Série C, no. 88 (1980).
3. J. Klatzmann, *L'Agriculture Française* (Editions Du Seuil, 1978).
4. *Les Comptes de l'Agriculture Française en 1980*, *Les Collections de
l'INSEE*, Série C, no. 98 (Oct. 1981).
5. *Agriculture in France* (French Embassy, London, Ref. A/83/7/71).
6. *Les Comptes de l'Agriculture Française en 1979*.
7. B. Vial, 'L'Agriculture' in J.P. Pagé (ed.), *Le Profil Economique de la
France au Seuil des Années 80* (La Documentation Française, 1981).
8. *Enquête sur l'Emploi de Mars 1981*, *Les Collections de l'INSEE*, Série D,
no. 87 (Dec. 1981).
9. Klatzmann, *L'Agriculture Française*.
10. J.M. Albertini, *L'Economie Française* (Editions Du Seuil, 1978).
11. *Tableaux de l'Economie Française 81* (INSEE, 1981).
12. Klatzmann, *L'Agriculture Française*.
13. *Rapport sur les Comptes de la Nation 1980*, vol. 2, *Les Collections de*

l'INSEE, Série C, nos. 94-5 (1981).

14. Vial, 'L'Agriculture'.

15. Ibid.

16. Ardagh, *The New France*.

17. Ibid.

18. J. Chombart de Lauwe, *L'Aventure Agricole de la France de 1945 à nos jours* (Presses Universitaires de France, 1979).

19. Ibid.

20. P. Le Roy, *L'Avenir de l'Agriculture Française*, 3rd edn (Presses Universitaires de France, 1980).

21. J. Van Lierde, 'Recent EEC Decisions on Price and Structural Policy' in S. Rogers and B. Davey (eds.), *The Common Agricultural Policy and Britain* (Saxon House/Laxington, 1973).

22. D. Swann, *The Economics of the Common Market*, 3rd edn (Penguin Books, 1975).

23. Ibid.

24. D. Evans, *Accountant's Guide to the European Communities* (Macdonald and Evans, 1981).

25. Swann, *The Economics of the Common Market*.

26. Evans, *Accountant's Guide to the European Communities*.

27. 'Agriculture and the Budget', *European Trends*, no. 67 (May 1981).

28. Statistic by INSEE. This and other figures in this section taken from F. Houillier, 'L'Agriculture et son Evolution depuis 1960', *Revue d'Economie Politique*, vol. 88 (1978).

29. Houillier, 'L'Agriculture et son Evolution depuis 1960'.

30. Le Roy, *L'Avenir de l'Agriculture Française*.

31. F. Houillier, 'L'Economie Agricole en 1978', *Revue d'Economie Politique*, vol. 89, no. 6 (1979); and F. Houillier, 'L'Economie Agricole en 1979', *Revue d'Economie Politique*, vol. 90, no. 6 (1980).

32. *Les Comptes de l'Agriculture Française en 1979*.

33. D. Barthelemy and A. Barthez, 'Propriété Foncière, exploitation agricole et aménagement de l'espace rural', *Economie Rurale*, no. 126 (Jul.-Aug. 1978).

34. P. Manie, *Les Exploitations Agricoles en France* (Presses Universitaires de France, 1971).

35. A. Bourgeois and M. Sebillotte, 'Reflexion sur l'evolution Contemporaine des exploitations agricoles', *Economie Rurale*, no. 126 (Jul.-Aug. 1978).

36. G. Cotton, 'Continuité et changements de la politique agricole Française', *Economie Rurale*, no. 126 (Jul.-Aug. 1978).

37. J.C. Clavel, 'L'Agriculture Française dans la Communauté Européenne et dans le Monde', *Economie Rurale*, no. 126 (Jul.-Aug. 1978).

38. H. Nouyrit, 'L'Agriculture Française dans le Marché Mondial', *Economie Rurale*, no. 126 (Jul.-Aug. 1978).

39. G. Ferrière, *Les Industries Agro-Alimentaires, Pétrole Vert de la France* (Coopération-Consommation-Distribution, Mar. 1980).

40. P. Viau, *L'Essentiel sur l'Agriculture Française* (Les Editions Ouvrières, 1978).

4 LABOUR

Employment Trends

The working population in France numbered some 21,500,000 people at the time of the official survey of March 1981 and was increasing at the rate of some 200,000 per year, the highest ever rate of increase. In recent years much attention has been focused on the alarming rise in the unemployment statistics, as is discussed in Chapter 6, to the extent of sometimes overlooking that the total number of jobs available also continues to grow year by year. The rate of such increase has, however, been much slower in the period after 1973 (less than 1 per cent per year) than before (between 2 and 3 per cent each year),[1] for reasons that we have already seen.

Three main developments have affected, and are continuing to affect, the pattern of employment.

1 Structural Change

With the continued shake-out of workers from agriculture (down to an exodus of some 20,000 per year by the end of the 1970s) and the declining number of jobs in industry (at over 100,000 per year), it required the steady increase in tertiary-sector jobs (some 190,000 per year) to ensure any growth in total employment. The sharp contrast between the trends for the earlier 1970s and the later 1970s is shown in Table 4.1.

Table 4.1: Trends in Wage-earning Employment, 1969-78

	1 Jan. 1969 to 31 Dec. 1973	1 Jan 1974 to 31 Dec. 1978
Agriculture	−142,700	−105,300
All industry	+661,800	−530,000
Tertiary sector	+1,315,400	+976,100
All	+1,834,500	+340,800

Source: J.-P. Revoil, 'La Croissance lente marque l'emploi', *Economie et Statistique*, no. 112 (Jun. 1979).

The only sector of industry exempt from the declining trend for the later 1970s was, somewhat paradoxically, the food products sector, which was itself dependent on a declining agriculture.

The Employment Survey of March 1981 confirmed the continuation of the trends shown in the right-hand column of Table 4.1: over the period of twelve months to March 1981, employment in agriculture fell by 1.6 per cent, that in all industry by 2.8 per cent and that in the tertiary sector rose by 1.0 per cent. Within the industry sector each major industry recorded a fall in employment except for food products, which had an increase of 1.0 per cent.[2]

2 Regional Change

The regional pattern of employment has changed markedly in the post-war years, and especially in the years since 1960, as discussed in detail in Chapter 7.

3 The Increased Participation of Women in the Labour Force

This has become much more marked over the last twenty years. A government-commissioned report published in 1980 found that women were still disadvantaged in terms of pay and job opportunities, despite the legal requirements of equal pay for equal work and maternity leave rights.[3] One of the final acts of the Barre government was to introduce a Bill giving women workers greater legal protection and outlawing discrimination on grounds of sex or family status (although what constituted 'discrimination' was not precisely defined).[4]

A recent authoritative long-term projection of activity rates as far ahead as the year 2000 shows that for men (all males aged 15 plus) these will continue to fall slowly from an overall 69.8 per cent in 1980 to 67.8 per cent by the year 2000, whereas for women there will be a gradual increase from 41.0 per cent for 1980 to 44.9 per cent by the year 2000. (These trends would be merely a continuation of those of the previous twenty years.) The men will show a pronounced tendency towards early retirement, from age 55 onwards, whereas for women the greatest increases in activity rates will be for the 35-50 age groups.[5]

Population Aspects

The age structure of the working population changes only slowly, as Table 4.2 shows. The estimated figures for 1985 do, of course, include a mix of France's heavy losses of manpower during the Second World War, the 'baby boom' years of the late 1940s and early 1950s, the very low birth rates of the 1970s, the tendency for more young people to remain longer in higher education, and the trend towards early retirements.

Table 4.2: Age Structure of the Working Population, 1911-85 (per thousand)

Age Group/Year	1911	1931	1954	1985[a]
Less than 35 years	470	466	414	458
35-44 years	191	180	172	234
45 years and over	339	354	413	308
All	1,000	1,000	1,000	1,000

Note: a. Estimated.
Source: J.-C. Chesnais, 'La démographie de la France: situation et perspectives', *Population et Avenir* (May-Jul. 1980).

Some indication of the relative importance of the main social factors is shown in Table 4.3.

Table 4.3: Aspects of Growth of the Working Population, 1962-90 (thousands)

	1962-75	1975-90[a]
Behavioural Effects:		
Extension of education	−1,002	−242
Early retirement	−1,080	−713
Increased female working	+1,074	+1,848
Total	−1,008	+893
Demographic Effects:		
(Effects of age composition)[b]	+3,532	+2,596
Total growth	+2,524	+3,489

Notes: a. Estimated.
       b. Including immigration.
Source: Chesnais, 'La démographie de la France'.

These figures make it clear that the effects of longer education and (rather surprisingly) of early retirement were more pronounced for the years to 1975 than subsequently, whereas the trend towards increased female working is, in spite of rising unemployment, a phenomenon of steadily greater significance. Much of the reduced demographic effect would be accounted for by the effective cessation of immigration in 1976 (close on 1 million immigrant workers had entered France between 1960 and 1975 and some 350,000 members of the labour force had returned to France from Algeria in the 1960s); the effects of age composition alone, however, are sufficient to ensure that the total working population continues to increase far more rapidly than the rate of job creation. Although mitigated by such factors as reductions in the length of the working week, short-time working, increased staying on into higher education, increased early retirement and concealed overmanning by large companies, the inevitable result is mounting unemployment.[6] Prior to May 1981 the French government admitted that it did not expect unemployment to fall significantly for the next twenty years or so: even the expansionist measures (public expenditure increases and tax cuts)[7] introduced by the Mitterrand government are expected to do little more than slow down or possibly halt the rate of increase, in spite of the noticeably more optimistic pronouncements by the present regime.

Working Conditions[8]

Over the last twenty years French workers have benefited from significant improvements in working conditions in a variety of ways. The length of the average working week has fallen steadily from 45.9 hours in 1961 to just on 40 hours by 1980. The reduction has been particularly pronounced in those industries which previously had exceptionally long working hours, notably building and public works and transport, so that there has been a tendency towards the lessening of disparities, especially in the latter half of the 1970s (an INSEE study had shown the reverse to be the case prior to 1973).

Much attention has been given to the question of health and safety at work and the prevention of industrial accidents, but with apparently rather little success: the total number of accidents at work in 1979 was barely less than that of twenty years previously and the number of days lost through temporary incapacity, some 27.6 million, had stayed more or less constant for some years. It is also some eight times greater than the number of days lost through industrial disputes quoted later in this chapter.

The average working life has tended to shorten steadily over the last twenty years, both because of the increased numbers of young people staying on into higher education, up to the age of 25 in some cases, and because of the movement towards early retirement after age 55. When combined with the introduction of longer paid holidays (up to five weeks), more retraining schemes and improved sickness and maternity provision, the cumulative effect is for French people to have to work less. Inevitably wide disparities still remain.

Trade Unions

Much of the remainder of this chapter must be devoted to French trade
unions, which present a number of quite distinct characteristics not
found in the trade union movements in any other comparable countries:
'No other trade unionism in Europe is so divided and numerically so
weak as trade unionism in France'[9] or 'In most of French private industry genuine collective [bargaining] relations have scarcely been
tried'[10] are typical of the comments that have been made by various
observers on the state of trade unionism and industrial relations in
France. Most remarkable of all, in the eyes of most observers, is the fact
that no single national representative body or voice of the trade union
movement, equivalent to the UK's Trades Union Congress, exists in
France. Although this situation is not unique (it is also to be found in
Australia and in Sweden),[11] it does help to explain the lack of unity or
coherence on the part of French trade unionism: with three major and
at least two minor union confederations, usually with conflicting policy
approaches, points of view and political allegiances, it would be surprising if it were otherwise.

Historical Development

Elements of a socialist movement can be traced back as far as the revolution of 1789 and certainly by the later years of the nineteenth century
there was a relatively strong, if disunited, brand of socialism in France,
intent on both polemical argument and political action. After many
years of intermingled growth, set-backs, policy U-turns and internecine
strife, socialists of various persuasions achieved power in the Popular
Front government, formed after their major victory in the general elections of May 1936. Trade unionism developed initially as the industrial
wing of the socialist movement and can be traced as far back as 1863.
The first Confédération Générale du Travail (CGT) was set up at the
Limoges Congress of 1895 but it is from 1906, with the Charter of
Amiens, often cited as the basic text of French unionism, and the drawing up of a new constitution for the CGT, that the birth of a modern
union movement may be dated.[12] By 1914 the CGT could claim no
more than 40,000 members out of an estimated 6 million industrial
workers in France and the ensuing years saw remarkable ups and downs
in membership: perhaps 2m by 1920, down to 1m by early 1936, up to
approaching 5m during the Popular Front era, down to around 2m by
1939, up to around 5½m by 1947, then falling to some 2m in 1957.[13]

Arising out of the hostility of the leaders of the Roman Catholic

Church in France, and of many of the more right-wing Roman Catholics, to much of what the CGT stood for and especially its involvement with the socialist movement, a quite separate strand in the history of trade unionism evolved. This led to the growth of the second major confederation of unions, for avowedly Christian and denominational members, under the title Confédération Française des Travailleurs Chrétiens (CFTC); not until 1964 was the word 'Chrétiens' dropped and the title changed to Confédération Française Démocratique du Travail (CFDT) and even then a sizeable minority formed themselves into a new organisation, the CFTC (Maintenu). When the earlier splitting off from the CGT of a significant anti-Communist element into a new movement known as CGT-FO (for Force Ouvrière) is taken into account, the genesis of the present-day structure of several competing confederations, with only occasional and spasmodic attempts at mutual co-operation, becomes apparent.

The Communist Party (PCF) grew in terms of both membership and electoral share in the immediate post-war period; it joined General de Gaulle's government from October 1945, and was soon able to gain total control of the CGT, with a prominent Communist, Benoît Frachon, installed as General Secretary. Only when one takes full account of the fact that the French Communists faithfully followed whatever was the current Moscow policy, which in turn was liable to sudden changes of direction and U-turns, can one begin to understand the tergiversations and conflicting policy stances of the CGT in the ensuing years (even though the equation CGT = PCF is much too simple, since the relationship between these two bodies was both complex and subject to fluctuations). Thus when the overall policy stance dictated by Moscow was one of the utmost co-operation with the government of the day in order that the Communists within the government could exert maximal influence in a pro-Russia direction, we find the CGT denouncing strikes, minimising or resisting wage increases, privately encouraging managements to fine striking workers, or, during 1945-7, seeking to refuse wage increases offered by the Renault management to its workers.[14] After the dismissal of the five Communist Ministers from the government in May 1947, however, the Communists switched back to militant pro-strike policies and thus ended the fragile post-war unity of the CGT.

In 1958 when General de Gaulle was returned to power, the CGT made no secret of their hostility to him, the CGT Secretary, Pierre Le Brun (himself not a Communist), rejected an invitation to join de Gaulle's Cabinet as Minister of Labour, and in the vote on the new constitution tried, not very successfully, to mobilise workers to vote

'No'. The CFTC, on the other hand, adopted a policy of wait-and-see and did not issue any voting instructions to its members. In May 1968 the social unrest which had started amongst university students soon spread to workers and a large-scale demonstration in Paris on 13 May brought together the CGT, CFDT, FO, FEN (together with the National Union of Students); this has been seen as one of the very rare demonstrations of solidarity by French trade unionists, but in fact from the outset the CGT were opposed to some of the students' demands and supported the government over the maintenance of law and order. The general strike, which within a few days had been joined by some 10 million workers, was the first ever at which workers in private-sector industries, the nationalised industries and the civil service stopped work together.[15] Economic life almost ground to a halt. The veneer of unity did not last long, however: as soon as the negotiations with the government began on 25 May, the CGT were pressing for large wage increases whilst the CFDT's main demand was for union recognition in the workplace.

Following the traumatic events of 1968, both major confederations adopted expressly socialist policy statements, the CGT at its Congress of 1969 and the CFDT the following year. (Their policy approaches had in fact been converging over the preceding few years.) The CGT also urged the need for a single representative trade union organisation whilst the CFDT expressed its belief in workers' participation and in democratic economic planning (as opposed to France's 'technocratic' system of indicative planning discussed in Chapter 5). On the occasion of the socialist-Communist 'Common programme' of political aims, enunciated in 1972, the CGT immediately declared its support and actively campaigned on behalf of the programme whilst the CFDT again reserved its position.

The steady rise in the published unemployment statistics and the worsening position of the national economy in the later 1970s did nothing to aid inter-confederation co-operation. Even *within* each confederation disunity was sometimes apparent: in 1974, for example, Edmond Maire of the CFDT campaigned vigorously against Giscard d'Estaing during the presidential elections, but he later had to admit rather ruefully that probably a quarter of his own members had not supported him. The CGT has made strenuous efforts to widen its membership base, particularly towards white-collar workers, but with only slow success. The less radical Force Ouvrière was more acquiescent than either of the other two major confederations with incomes restraint and the 'contractual' approach of the government of the day prior to the elections of May-June 1981; the smaller CFTC and CGC (Confédération Générale des Cadres) usually followed its lead, as, on occasion, did the FEN (the large teachers' union). It is possible to argue that membership figures alone are an insufficient guide to the overall importance of the various confederations. The CGC, for example, includes mainly white-collar professional workers and executives in positions of some authority, who may well have more influence than is indicated by their relatively low numerical figures.[16]

Far, therefore, from the trade union movement gradually moving towards unity of policy and action, which was the expressed hope of the CGT as far back as 1919, pluralism is, in the view at least of one of the most perceptive observers, getting worse.[17]

At this point mention should be made of the long series of measures of social reforms relating either directly or indirectly to the interests of trade unions. The major landmarks to 1974 are summarised in Table 4.4. This table originates from French government sources, but in one sense it may be considered misleading in that it does not include more gradual changes such as reductions in working hours or extra weeks' holidays.

Table 4.4: Some Landmarks in Social Policy and Collective Bargaining, 1864-1974

1864 Ban on strikes lifted by law and recognition of right of combination.	1947 Institution of the statutory complementary superannuation scheme for cadres.
1864 Waldeck-Rousseau Act authorising trade unions.	1950 Creation of the minimum growth wage (SMIC).
1891 First collective agreement (in coal mines in North of France).	1955 Renault agreement linking wages for the first time with productivity increases and raising annual paid leave to three weeks.
1898 Act relating to industrial accidents.	
1910 Old age pension Act.	
1919 Reinforcement of collective agreements legislation. Act on eight-hour day.	1956 Generalisation of the three weeks' leave entitlement.
1928 First social insurance Act.	1958 Extension of complementary superannuation to all wage-earning and salaried categories.
1932 First family allowances Act.	
1936 Acts establishing the right to annual leave with pay, the 40-hour week, and instituting collective bargaining and staff delegates.	1959 Ordinance on profit-sharing.
	1962 Annual leave raised to four weeks at Renault.
	1966 Outline Act on vocational training.
1945 Ordinance on Social Security. Ordinance making joint works committees compulsory in firms with more than 50 employees.	1967 Creation of the National Employment Agency providing a better labour-exchange organisation. Ordinance on compulsory profit-sharing.
1946 The Preamble to the Constitution guarantees the right to strike.	1968 Grenelle Agreements on wages.

Table 4.4: Some Landmarks in Social Policy and Collective Bargaining, 1864-1974 (cont'd.)

1969 First agreement on security of employment, providing for joint employment commissions, the information and consultation of the joint works committee when mass redundancies are proposed, and guarantees in the event of dismissal or transfers. Generalisation of four weeks' annual leave with pay. The first 'progress contract' signed at Electricité de France/ Gaz de France.	National agreement on vocational training.
	1971 Act on continuous vocational training.
	1972 Agreement instituting anticipated superannuation for persons who become unemployed over the age of 60.
1970 Declaration of employers and trade unions on the conversion of terms of employment to a monthly basis.	1973 Creation of the Wages Guarantee Fund to pay workers the sums due to them if their employer goes bankrupt.
	1974 Redundancy compensation agreement providing for payment of 90 per cent of last gross pay for up to one year.

Source: French Embassy, London, *Facts and Figures*, no. A/108/5/75.

Trade Union Structure and Membership

For any discussion of the structure of French trade unionism to be meaningful, it must take into account both the radical divisions which exist between the various confederations and the union membership strength or weakness, in addition to actual organisational structures to be found within each confederation and its constituent unions. The inter-confederation divisions are, as has already been shown, unlikely to disappear within the foreseeable future and they necessarily weaken the unions' organisational structures at every level. Similarly, strong union organisation is rendered unattainable by the very low membership, and lack of funds, of French trade unions. It is difficult to avoid giving the impression of a vicious circle, with each cause of weakness reinforcing, and in turn being reinforced by, each of the others. An outline of the main union confederations, with their claimed membership figures and principal areas of strength, is given in Table. 4.5.

Membership of trade unions is at a very low level and this must be a root cause of union weaknesses. A major problem for any observer, however, is that no accurate or reliable statistics of union membership exist and, given all the related circumstances that have to be taken into account, it is not at all clear how any valid statistics could be assembled. It is generally agreed that no more than 20 per cent of French wage-earners are members of trade unions, but even here there is a problem of defining terms: what exactly is a 'member of a trade union'? It has long been the custom for trade unionists to be issued with membership

Table 4.5: The Five Representative Confederations, 1981

Confédération Générale du Travail (CGT). The Communist-dominated confederation; founded in 1895.

Claimed membership: 2,400,000

Most influential in steel, metallurgy, building, chemicals, mining, printing, ports and dockyards, electricity and gas, railways.

Confédération Générale du Travail — Force Ouvrière or *Force Ouvrière*. (CGT-FO or FO). Founded in 1948 from a split in the CGT.

Claimed membership: 850,000

Most influential in civil service, Paris transport, agricultural and food trade, banking, insurance, electrical engineering, building and civil engineering, clothing, leather and hides.

Confédération Française Démocratique du Travail (CFDT). Founded in 1919 as the CFTC, transformed in 1964 when formal links with the Catholic Church were severed.

Claimed membership: 770,000

Most influential in metallurgy, rubber, oil industry, textiles, electrical engineering, banking, insurance.

Confédération Générale des Cadres (CGC). Founded in 1944.

Claimed membership: 250,000

Most influential in sales (travellers and representatives), textiles, metallurgy, chemicals, banking, insurance, paper-cardboard, furniture.

Confédération Française de Travailleurs Chrétiens (CFTC). Founded in 1919; broke away and reformed as the CFTC in 1964 when the minority rejected the newly established CFDT.

Claimed membership: 200,000

Most influential in mining, banking, insurance, air traffic control, oil industry, glass, ceramics.

Source: French Embassy, London, ibid.

cards on which stamps should be affixed to correspond to the payment of monthly subscriptions. It has also long been customary, however, for not all the monthly subscriptions to be paid and stamps affixed. Even the cards of the most stable and loyal unionists would not have more than ten, out of twelve, monthly stamps, and the CGT estimated an average of eight stamps per card in 1959.[18] Some unionists never have more than a small number of stamps on their cards. During the later months of each year the local union representatives are particularly reluctant to press for payment of monthly subscriptions for fear that their members will decline to re-join the union for the following year.

The membership cards are issued by the national confederations to their constituent unions and by the latter to their members, but at each of these stages many spare cards are available in case of need. Similarly, a number of members over the course of the year receive more than one card, for example if they move house, or change their job, or transfer to a different union. In any event a membership card with no, or only a few, subscriptions paid can scarcely indicate membership in any meaningful sense. Clearly, therefore, a count of membership cards is of little use. At the other extreme a count of members with twelve monthly stamps on their cards would give a minimal figure which would be equally misleading. Dr Chatillon suggests the adoption of a norm of at least six stamps, but it seems obvious that what is needed, from the point of view of the development of a soundly based and adequately financed unionism, is a completely different system for the collection of subscriptions.

Each of the confederations issues annual membership statistics (as shown in Table 4.5), but these are clearly exaggerated claims. The figures shown may be compared with the estimates by Kendall of realistic membership figures which were:

CGT:	1.3m
CGT-FO:	500,000
CFDT:	700,000

Kendall quotes estimates of a total trade union membership of 2.7-3.0m, out of a total active labour force of some 20.5m (as shown in the 1968 Census), of whom only some 15m would have been wage-earners, i.e. a rate of unionisation of around 13.1-14.6 per cent, whereas Chatillon suggests a realistic rate of unionisation would be 20 per cent and Stewart[19] suggests 20-25 per cent. The discrepancies are clearly very wide, but they show that the density of unionisation in France is relatively low.

L'Entreprise of 8 November 1974 accepted the claimed membership figures issued by the three principal confederations and suggested that these were grouped in the following:

CGT:	37 professional federations, 95 departmental unions, 14,000 'syndicats de base' (company, factory or plant unions);
CGT-FO:	36 professional federations, 95 departmental unions, 11,000 'syndicats d'enterprise' (company, factory or plant unions);

CFDT: 40 professional federations and national unions, 99 departmental unions, 3,500 'syndicats de base'.

For what it is worth, the official definition of a member given in the CGT constitution is one who pays at least ten stamps per year and Kendall points out that on that basis the CGT's actual membership was almost exactly half of the figure officially claimed by the confederation. It is not even clear from the various figures quoted above which is the second-largest confederation. Kendall indicates the CFDT and he subsequently speculates whether the CFDT, with a tradition of more soundly based, dues-paying unions may eventually emerge as the leading organisation of the French working class. It is difficult to find any evidence to support this, and since Kendall admits that his figures are partly based on statistics supplied by the CFDT, some caution may be necessary.

Quite separate and more indirect attempts at assessing reliable membership statistics have also been made via the elections within industrial plants to the boards which formerly administered social security funds and, more latterly, to the *comités d'entreprise* (works councils) which should exist to defend the workers' interests in all firms with more than 50 wage-earners. Official Ministry of Labour statistics showed that in 1970 out of a total of 1,419,727 votes cast some 46 per cent went to CGT candidates, 19.6 per cent to CFDT candidates and 7.3 per cent to CGT-FO candidates, with all union-supported candidates taking 88 per cent of the votes.[20] It is not clear what meaning can be attached to these figures since it is evident that the vast majority of workers either did not bother, or did not have the opportunity, to vote; this would seem to support the contention that the CFDT has considerably more support than the CGT-FO but even this is not certain, since the latter's membership tends to be concentrated in the public-sector services, where comités d'entreprise do not exist.

If all comités d'entreprise and similarly elected representative bodies are taken into account, the total votes obtained by all union-supported candidates greatly exceed the number of trade unionists (ignoring problems of double-counting) and this has been taken to indicate implied confidence in the unions by those workers who are not union members. It is certainly true, as will be shown below, that union calls for a strike are often supported by many non-members.

Why are French workers so reluctant to join trade unions? This question is discussed at some length by Chatillon but, perhaps not surpirsingly, there does not seem to be any one simple answer. He asks whether French people are by nature so essentially individualistic that they are philosophically inclined against such banding together, but notes that in some occupations, for example typographers and basic grade schoolteachers, the rate of unionisation in fact exceeds 80 per cent. Similarly, he asks whether the reputed antipathy of Frenchmen to the payment of compulsory contributions makes them unwilling to commit themselves to the payment of regular subscriptions, but finds this unlikely since the contributions required are so small. More valid and fundamental causes appear to be the deep-rooted divisions within the trade union movement, which can only cause confusion among potential members, the steady improvements in wages and living standards which all workers have enjoyed since 1945 without, for the most of them, having to join unions (so that these benefits appear as 'free goods'), and the very real fear that joining a union may endanger either their prospects for advancement and their future career or their job itself, so opposed are many French employers still to trade union membership. Given such root causes, it is difficult to foresee how the unions will be able to develop into more soundly based and more representative institutions.

For a period of about six years following the social unrest of 1968 the trade unions recorded significant increases in membership, particularly among workers in private-sector firms; a considerable falling off of membership seems to have followed in the late 1970s with perhaps a new upturn in the Mitterrand era from early 1981.

Funds and Resources

The importance and influence of French trade unions, both politically and in the workplace, are claimed to be out of all proportion to their low membership figures.[21] It is true that trade union representatives sit on many national governmental and semi-governmental committees, as well as on the boards of nationalised industries. Moreover, there has often been at least one trade union representative in the government at Ministerial level. It does, on the other hand, appear undeniable that the work of the unions is severely hampered by their acute lack of funds, which is an inevitable consequence of their weak membership position. The full-time union executives are clearly rather poorly paid – so much so that in 1971 the employees of the CGT actually went on strike for higher wages – and the unions are unable to employ the services of the highly qualified specialists, for example in statistics or economics, that complex negotiations now require. They are thus at a severe disadvantage *vis-à-vis* the Patronat, the employers' organisation, who will be well supplied with all the supporting evidence they require. Lefranc, himself a French trade union leader, has written in graphic terms of the impression this created on their union counterparts from other countries:

> Foreign trade unionists view us with a degree of condescension. They have the impression that French trade unionism has not got beyond the developmental phase: whereas in Germany, the United States, and England, the unions have sufficient resources to engage the services of experts, who, covered with diplomas and loaded with figures, are capable of entering into discussions on a basis of equality on various commissions with representatives of the employees and of the public authorities.[22]

The subscriptions of members are obviously the major source of income for the trade unions, but they also receive considerable sums of money from the government, largely geared, nominally at least, towards the education and training of trade union officials. This system has developed largely since 1959, up to which year the unions, and especially the CGT-FO, received annual subsidies from their counterparts in the USA. The sums are now distributed annually by the Ministry of Labour and a major bone of contention for many years, especially on the part of the CGT, has been the basis on which this distribution is effected. The division was strongly biased in favour of the more moderate confederations, the CFDT and the CGT-FO, and not until 1971 was the CGT able to persuade the government that it should receive a greater share of the total sum available. By 1975 the direct payments from the Ministry of Labour for education and training purposes amounted to:

CGT	2,615,000 frs.
CGT-FO	2,615,000 frs.
CFDT	2,615,000 frs.
CFTC	1,100,000 frs.
CGC	900,000 frs.

Naturally the CGT still feels a grievance over the basis now used: its claim is that if funds were allocated according to size and responsibilities, i.e. per head of membership, it should receive far more than (perhaps twice as much as) the FO and CFDT.[23] One may anticipate that the socialist government elected in May-June 1981 will modify and perhaps increase these payments.

Finally, under this heading mention must be made of strike funds which are in fact minimal. Even active members have traditionally been unwilling to make the separate payments into strike funds, which in turn has severely limited the possibilities for any long drawn-out stoppage and has tended to orientate union policy towards short sharp strikes, often of only one day's duration. Strike funds are, however, rather stronger in the industrial areas in the North-East, around Lille, and in Alsace and Lorraine, in which localities the nearness of the Belgian and German frontiers respectively has always tended to exert definite influences on trade union practice. One recent study[24] suggested that the financial problems of the major confederations, and especially the CGT, had now become acute and that serious cash-flow difficulties were being experienced at the end of each month.

Organisational Structures

When writing of the organisational structures within French trade unionism, one observer notes that the 'appearance' is that the confederations' structure is 'logical, decentralised, under close membership control, and independent of political parties', whilst the reality is that

> communist controls have ended political independence, and vitiated both membership control of officials and the autonomy of union bodies close to the base (grass roots). The logic of national union structure within each federation is less important than the practice of competing unions of the three major workers' confederations, several splinter confederations, and many unaffiliated unions.[25]

The former part of this statement appears to relate primarily to the CGT, whereas the latter brings us back yet again to the rifts in the movement as a whole.

Nominally, the structural pattern provides for a considerable degree of decentralisation and local democratic control. The national confederations have little power or autonomy beyond what their member unions choose to give them and the latter are subject to all major decisions being taken or confirmed by frequent local assemblies or conventions. Diagrammatically the organisational structures of the three largest confederations may be summarised as in Table 4.6.

The local unions present an almost infinite variety of types and sizes: they may be based on the industrial plant or on the locality, whether area, city or departmental, although the overall tendency is towards being industry-based rather than craft-based. The largest have several thousand members but the smallest less than ten. The CGT prefers

Table 4.6: Confederation Organisation Structures, 1981

(i) Confédération Générale du Travail (CGT)
(affiliated to WFTU)

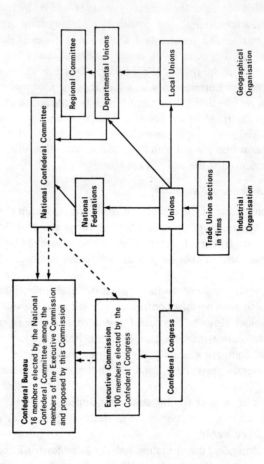

Table 4.6: Confederation Organisation Structures, 1981 (cont'd.)

(ii) Force Ouvrière (CGT-FO)
(affiliated to ICFTU and ECTU)

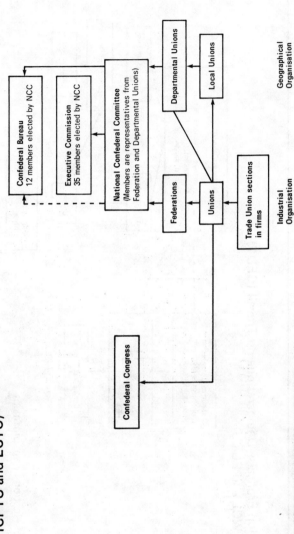

Source: French Embassy, London (correspondence).

Table 4.6: Confederation Organisation Structures, 1981 (cont'd.)

(iii) Confédération Française Démocratique du Travail (CFDT)
(affiliated to WCL and ECTU)

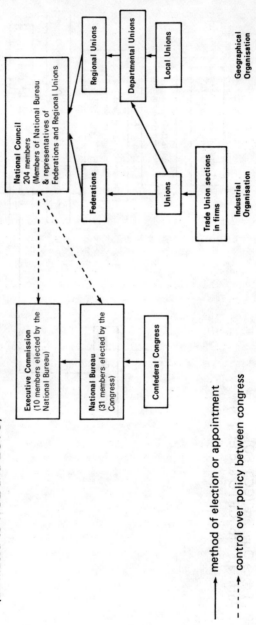

——————▶ method of election or appointment

- - - - ▶ control over policy between congress

one local (branch) per plant but the CFDT locals (branches) are more occupation-based and may include one for white-collar workers, one for engineers and technicians and one for production workers, all within a single plant. In theory at least all decisions are taken, on a strictly egalitarian basis, by the periodical general meetings of workers, but inevitably considerable executive power rests with the executive committee or general secretary: in the smaller locals the latter will be a worker on the shop floor but in the largest ones he will be a full-time salaried official. Sometimes his salary may even be paid by the firm, especially in the case of public-sector organisations.

Where the local union is not confined to one plant (and even sometimes when it is) it may embrace a number of branches, or subdivisions. Representatives of local unions meet, in connection with matters of common interest, with colleagues from the same city or from the same département. At the city level trade unions often receive assistance, financial or otherwise, such as by the provision of a building, from the local municipality. Of rather more importance than these, however, is the grouping of locals into national unions (sometimes termed 'federations' with rather a loose framework, sometimes, especially in the case of government administrative employees, termed 'syndicats nationaux'), each of which will normally have an executive board, perhaps comprised of locals' secretaries, and a national committee, elected from amongst the membership.

On paper at least ever since 1906 the CGT's policy has been to favour industrial unions at the expense of craft unions and until 1939 considerable success was achieved in, for example, mergers involving respectively practically all the railway unions, several regional agricultural unions and a number of electrical workers' unions. Some earlier opposition to this process on the shop floor seems to have been overcome, but many craft unions still remain. *Within each confederation*, a single railway workers' union and a single metalworkers' union have been achieved, but elsewhere divisions remain. Victor Feather, writing of the possible development of factory unions in the UK, succinctly remarked 'There could be a French situation of thousands of completely autonomous local and factory unions, without responsible central control or guidance or a central organisation which could advise employers nationally and negotiate authoritatively with governments.' Within the CFDT the industrial unionism question has tended to be focused on the position of white-collar workers who are far more prominent in this confederation than in the CGT.

The Confederations

The confederations themselves are most directly involved in the formulation of national policy, in direct dealings with various government
bodies and in international representative meetings. It is the confederations, too, that are seen by the general public as the voices (not always
in harmony) of the French trade union movement through contacts with
the mass media. The permanent full-time officials of each confederation
are subject to a national committee which in turn is answerable to
periodic, usually biennial, conventions or congresses. The latter are, in
theory at least, the supreme decision-making bodies, but inevitably they
can be swayed or manoeuvred by the executive. The delegates, representatives of local unions, often see the proceedings as an opportunity
to voice their feelings of dissatisfaction over developments since the
previous assembly. Barjonet[26] describes the proceedings as 'une Grande
Messe' (a High Mass – a complex church service in which the movements
of all the participants are known beforehand). In smaller biannual
meetings of representatives there are, according to the same writer 'one
or two speeches of magisterial quality, delivered by the top leaders,
received in a religious silence and followed in the midst of general in-
difference by inevitably laudatory contributions of the federation and
department chiefs'.

In the case of the CGT twelve to fourteen full-time secrétaires con-
federaux meet regularly in the Bureau Confédéral (BC), under one
secrétaire général, and in practice this body is sufficiently well organised
to be able to exercise sway over the Commission Administrative (CA)
of some 35 elected representatives. Since the whole apparatus is firmly
under the control of the French Communist Party, the question of
which committee controls which is in practice rather academic. The
general trend over the last thirty years has been for the Party to seek
more centralised control, at the expense of the local unions.

Regarding the national committees and conventions of the three
major confederations, in the earlier years the voting systems in use were
weighted in favour of smaller units and this principle has been retained
in both the CFDT and the FO. In the CGT, however, since 1946 voting
has been based on numbers represented (as in the TUC in the UK)
which does, of course, allow the large industrial centres to dominate
the proceedings.

The position of Secretary General is not as prominent as might have
been expected and within each of the confederations there has been a
tradition of hostility towards entrusting too much power to any one

such figure. In practice, however, as mentioned above, he is the most important member of the Bureau Confédéral which in turn can effectively dominate policy. Certainly the CGT Secretary Generals in the post-war period, Benoît Frachon and Georges Seguy, have been major national figures, as also, to only a slightly lesser extent, have been Edmond Maire of the CFDT and André Bergeron of the FO.

Disillusion

Finally, mention may be made of a detailed survey of the state of trade unionism in France conducted by the respected newspaper *Le Monde* and published in a series of articles on 4, 5, 6 and 7 March 1980. This survey presented a picture of disillusion with the unions, a steady loss of membership, and more unwillingness than ever to pay union dues. Examples were quoted of local union sections which had lost 50 to 60 per cent of their membership within the space of a few years. Whilst the reasons for this state of affairs were not entirely clear, they appeared to be a mix of: (i) profound disappointment among left-wing activists following the loss of the French parliamentary election in March 1978; (ii) increasing national unemployment; (iii) the deepening economic crisis and fear of retaliatory action by the employers; (iv) disillusion over what trade unions had achieved or could achieve; and (v) increased willingness by employers to involve workers in factory decision-making processes in other ways. One union official interviewed was particularly regretful that the unions lost contact with the unemployed (chomeurs): 'Trade unions have not managed to maintain contacts with the body of unemployed. Committees have been set up here and there to bring them together but these remain largely empty structures' (writer's translation).

The General Secretary of the CGT, Georges Seguy, some ten years ago accepted that the divisions in the unions' ranks were a major cause of their low membership figures, although he went on to argue that these divisions were diminishing in importance over time, a view for which it is difficult to find strong supportive evidence. A second major cause, in Seguy's opinion, was the 'lies and slanders of the enemy and his allies as to the subordination of the CGT to the French Communist Party'. Whether such disillusion has been lessened in the wake of the victories of the Socialist Party in the presidential and parliamentary elections of 1981 is considered further below — paradoxically it seems to have worsened, at least if the official pronouncements of the various confederations are to be believed.

Trade Union Policy

It will by now be apparent that the weak and divided French trade
union movement, lacking both financial resources and expert support
services, is unlikely to be a strong force in collective bargaining. Indeed,
collective bargaining in the sense of meaningful negotiations between
two parties of approximately equal strength scarcely existed before
the 1981 elections, as we have already seen. Negotiations took place
between employers and union representatives in most large factories,
but whatever might be the objective strength of the unions' case, it was
undermined by (i) their minority membership and (ii) the legal provision
for the compulsory arbitration of disputes.

With regard to the former, ever since the 'Matignon' legislation of
1936, trade union representatives have been entitled to be accorded
bargaining status even if they represent a minority of the work-force.
The Ministry of Labour lists as 'representative' 61 trade union organisations which could only muster less than 10 per cent of the total vote in
comité d'entreprise elections, when the great majority of workers do
not even bother to vote. Alone of the three major confederations, the
CFDT's view is that representation should only be accorded where the
figure reaches 10 per cent, thus providing an incentive to recruitment.
The provision for compulsory arbitration, also enacted in 1936, has
often seemed to remove the real crux of any negotiations and again to
make the unions seem impotent in the eyes of the workers. The fact
that the representatives of the CGT, under orders from the Communist
Party, have often been seen to put forward points which scarcely seemed
to be in the workers' interests did nothing to dispel the feeling of *mal-
aise*. (For example, *Le Monde* of 5 March 1980 reported union opposition to an employer's attempt to introduce flexitime for his employees.)

The disunity within the trade union movement, both vertically and
horizontally, has also chronically weakened the bargaining process. In
large-scale national negotiations, the employers' united front would
often be face to face with over one hundred trade union representatives,
by no means united in viewpoint or policy.

The structure of the employers' organisations has been described
as 'très complexe':[27] the annual listing of the names of all the various
national and local representative bodies now covers 350 pages in the
Patronat's yearbook. The largest and most important of these employers' organisations, the 'Professional Federations', are industry-
based and are established for all the major industrial sectors. The overall
Confederation, Le Patronat Français, achieves a quite remarkable degree

of strength and unity and manages to co-ordinate a single, coherent, employers' policy on each of the major issues of the day.

Following the civil unrest of May 1968 the Chaban-Delmas government decided to institute, for the first time, meaningful union-employer negotiating to settle wages in the nationalised industries, and a series of bilateral agreements followed in the years 1969 and 1970. It was the government's hope that private-sector firms would be influenced by and follow this lead, but in reality little of the sort seems to have taken place. Where collective bargaining did exist in private industry in any meaningful sense, the employers were generally able to refuse to participate either at the level of the plant or at national level, confining the proceedings to the departmental level where the union would be able to muster much less of a show of strength. Where wage levels were negotiated these were frequently fairly nominal: wages actually paid depended greatly on the degree of institutionalised wage drift which followed. The CFDT aimed at sectoral agreements, each to cover a part of an industry, but had rather little success in enforcing such a policy.

Prior to the election of the socialist government in May-June 1981, French employers continued to refuse to become involved in realistic collective bargaining whenever possible; many still had an attitude to their employees which could only be described as paternalistic. Michelin, for example, which is said to pursue aggressive anti-union policies, is said to have boasted that its workers

> belonged . . . to the Michelin company from cradle to grave. Born in a Michelin hospital, they were educated in a Michelin school, lodged in Michelin houses. When they died, the company, with pious wisdom, paid for a mass to be said for the good of their souls.[28]

Citroen and the former Simca (now within the Peugeot-Citroen group) were reported to be so anti-union that they refused facilities for posting union notices, fired workers for distributing union literature in the plant and searched workers' lockers for incriminating material.[29]

Where negotiations did take place the lack of unity on the unions' side greatly weakened their position, as the official Sudreau Report noted:

> The commitments undertaken in the name of the workers are inevitably precarious. The representative unions are not always signatories to an agreement. Each is free to participate or not in negotiations, to sign or not to sign the agreement, to associate itself ultimately (with the agreement) or to denounce it.[30]

On similar lines a recent comparative study could refer to France as having 'unilateral management regulation of work-place relations', 'the paternalistic setting of the French Works Committee' and the maintenance of a large area of unilateral control by French employers, although it went on to suggest that over time more meaningful workplace organisation was gradually developing.[31]

With regard to strikes, it follows from what has already been said about lack of an adequate financial base that prolonged major stoppages are usually out of the question for French unions. Short surprise or irritation strikes, sometimes called 'pin-prick' stoppages, are much more common. They seem both to command considerable support from non-union members and to impress employers as to the strength of the workers' feelings. One estimate is that the average support for such a strike call is around 50 per cent which would, of course, normally be sufficient completely to disrupt the productive process, even if union leaders profess to find it disappointing.[32] On the other hand, as the French periodical *Le Point* commented on a joint CGT-CFDT day-long series of demonstrations in 1975:

> The turn-out was honourable, but the factories continued to function. At the Matignon [the prime minister's residence] they observed the day with interest . . . It was not a great demonstration of force, but it was the best organised by the CGT and the CFDT for a long time.[33]

Union leaders in France continue to see these short strikes in psychological and even mystical terms. Many of the stoppages are very short: according to official government statistics, in 1952 out of every ten strikes, eight lasted less than one week, five less than one day, and two less than one hour. However, though prolonged strikes are largely out of the question, it is a rare year in which the total number of man-days lost through strikes is less than several million. Short wildcat strikes may be called even whilst negotiations with employers are in progress, partly, it seems, as a general expression of feelings on the part of the workers: 'The strike is an affirmation of class consciousness and class action. It is an act of revolt, a moment of disassociation of the worker from the capitalist system.'[34] Often it may be one of the smaller unions which issues a strike call and gains the support of both non-organised workers and members of the larger unions. By 1980 this tendency towards short-term strikes was being increasingly questioned, especially within the CFDT; on the rarer occasions when strikes of longer duration take place a major problem is lack of finance, as has been indicated above. Usually considerable sums do in fact become available from outside sources, including the Communist Party (to the CGT), municipalities, special collections in churches with the support of sympathetic priests and even bishops, and also indirectly from employers, in that employer-financed welfare facilities may continue to function. Traditionally during strikes in France picketing was never so common or taken so seriously as in the UK or the USA. Its use has, however, become far more widespread over the last ten years or so, doubtless influenced by examples of such practice in other countries.

A table of annual average working days lost over 1969 to 1978 for twenty developed countries showed France, with an average of 3,410,000 days, ranked fourteenth, well above the UK (19th, with 10,610,000 days) but below such countries as West Germany or Australia. Significantly, the average duration of each stoppage was shorter in France than in any of the other countries studied.[35] Like all fairly short-run time series, however, there is an arbitrary element: this particular series, for example, omits the massive 1968 strikes in France. Broadly similar figures for the 1970s published by the French government show that of the four European countries with working populations of over 20 million, Italy and the UK always had the worst records for total days lost and West Germany nearly always the best, with France usually in between: an exceptional year was 1978, when France lost fewer working days (2.2m) than West Germany (2.5m).[36]

Political Action

As is to be expected, all the major confederations have links with one or more political parties. As has already been indicated, these links are closest in the case of the CGT and the Communist Party, whose activities are closely enmeshed at every level. In the immediate post-war period the frequent switches of policy by the French Communist Party, at Moscow's behest, did nothing to add to the credence or stability of its union counterpart. On paper at least the aims of both CP and CGT include the outright abolition of the capitalist system, but in practice policy has often been much less radical and tempered by the opportunism of the moment. At all levels non-Communists, including some Catholics and even priests, have always been present within the structure of the CGT and their value for propaganda purposes is obvious. French trade unions have always lacked an adequate mouthpiece in the form of an effective newspaper or journal for the movement and the CGT are able to make good use of the Paris Communist daily *L'Humanité* to put forward their views. Except for a brief honeymoon

period after 1945 the French Communist Party was always excluded
from the current government coalition and thus out of power until the
elections of 1981. This fact perhaps helps to explain why the CGT failed
to develop the effective power base of a strong and active membership
in the post-war period.

The links between Force Ouvrière and the Socialist Party have never
been so close at any level. The FO's member unions include many
members of the Socialist Party, which is perhaps hardly surprising in
view of the appeal the unions of this confederation make to a broadly
left-wing but non-militant point of view. The essential reasonableness
of the Socialist Party's point of view has often been seen as its undoing:

> neither on workers' material interests nor the hope of peace can it
> compete effectively with the lack of scruple of communist propa-
> ganda. Only in its anti-clericalism does it make a comparable polemic
> appeal. Otherwise there is a mild ineffectuality, a routine and doc-
> trinaire quality, to all its attempts at opportunistic agitation.[37]

The Party is far from being in a position to control the FO and the links
between the two are mainly informal, especially via individuals who
are in executive or prominent positions in both movements. Both have
tended to appeal to white-collar and often middle-class quasi-intellectuals
as much as to workers on the factory floor. Many of the leaders of the
FO are not in the Socialist Party: many are members of no party whilst
others are scattered across almost the whole political spectrum. The
official FO banner still reads 'Against any political control'; it is, however, undeniable that the FO's morale has risen noticeably since the
Socialist Party's successes in the 1981 elections, although this did not
prevent the outbreak of renewed unrest in late 1981/early 1982, as
discussed below.

It was at one time possible to write, as did Lorwin, of quite close
contacts, coexisting with nominal independence, between the CFDT
and the MRP, the former Catholic-orientated, slightly right of centre
political party; since 1958, however, not only has the CFDT ceased to
have formal connections with church-orientated politics, it has also, as
shown above, shifted away from a confessional stance and towards the
left. Some informal contacts between the two movements remain at
ground level and some church leaders still urge on the faithful the desir-
ability of supporting the CFDT, but these links are no longer at all
strong. Even in the 1950s, when they were at their strongest, there
were frequent prolonged disputes between the two sides, for example

over such questions as state subsidies to church schools.

Despite, or perhaps because of, the nature of these party-union links, the unions have overall been able to exert rather little real influence on government policies. As one widely quoted study notes: 'Labour's role is largely a matter of public relations. The real contact is between industry and the State and these two effectively exclude the "third partner" from serious discussions.'[38] Given this process, it is hardly surprising that much of the most significant legislation that has dealt with the working-class condition has been passed in spite of the vigorous opposition of the trade unions.[39]

The sphere of politics saw one of the most noteworthy examples of disunity among French trade unions in December 1981 on the occasion of the introduction of martial law in Poland, with the strong encouragement of the Soviet Union. The CFDT, FO, CFTC, FEN and CGC, i.e. all the major national union confederations except the CGT, were unanimous in condemning the suppression of the 'free' trade union movement in Poland and organised various protest demonstrations in Paris and other major cities. The leaders of the CGT, on the other hand, were clearly embarrassed by the turn of events and were in a dilemma as to what stance to take, not wishing directly to oppose the Soviet Union. Eventually they issued a nebulous statement urging trade unionists to 'face up to their responsibilities' and condemning 'those on the Right who sought to profit from the current situation'. Many individual members of the CGT did, however, contrary to their confederation's instructions, participate in the nation-wide demonstrations.[40]

Workers' Participation and Profit-sharing

Partly, perhaps, as both effect and cause of the weak trade union situation, a complex system of workers' participation has evolved in France: on paper at least the worker is now frequently involved in the decision-making process both with his employer and with the government, although in practice the level of participation still falls short of that found in many other comparable countries.[41]

Every concern with fifty or more employees is required by law to establish a comité d'enterprise (works council) although the Sudreau Report found that over half of the companies in question had not done so. The comité is to be composed of employees elected by their fellow workers. It is required to meet at least once a month in a consultative capacity. The comité often operates alongside *delegués du personnel*, empowered to take up individual or collective claims or grievances with the management. The legal provisions relating to these and other representative provisions are extremely complex. As an example of how the intentions of the law could be avoided, one firm known to the writer divided itself into two separate fictitious legal entities, each with 49 employees, in order to secure exemption.

One of General de Gaulle's final political acts was to implement a modified profit-sharing scheme, enacted in 1967; this scheme was compulsory for all companies with 100 employees or more, whereas an earlier scheme introduced in 1959 had been voluntary. A share in profits, devised via a complex mathematical formula such as perhaps only French legislators could devise, is attributed to the employees and may then be used in various ways: only after a period of five years may it be paid out to the workers in cash. A related Act in 1973 permitting workers to purchase shares in the company in certain circumstances has had rather little effect.

The attitude of the trade unions to each of the above developments had been one of ambivalence, if not of outright opposition. The overall tendency has been to be suspicious of any such moves which have not originated within the union movement and which would do nothing to incline workers to become members. Further, the CGT, and more latterly the CFDT, have been opposed to any provisions which would tend to reconcile the worker to the existing capitalist system, as opposed to seeking its radical transformation. The consequence, that French trade unions have often been in the position of opposing developments which would seemingly be of direct benefit to the workers, has already been mentioned above. Only since the late 1970s has this stance been seriously questioned.

Some Conclusions

It is difficult to be optimistic regarding the future of French trade unionism. The root causes of the movement's internal divisions and weaknesses are deep-seated and it is difficult to see any signs of a real desire to overcome these. Opposition to the development of strong unions is manifest and well organised on the part of the Patronat and was probably still present, more covertly, on the part of the French government prior to the 1981 elections. To an Anglo-Saxon observer at least, until the trade union leaders decide that their top priority must be to put their own house in order, the outlook for a strong and united union movement in France must remain bleak. One should, however, at least mention the opposite point of view, currently emphasised by the

CGC, that the disunity of the various confederations is itself a source of strength in that it allows for the expression of a diversity of views and opinions.[42]

Conversely, with the left now in political control in France at both presidential and parliamentary levels, will the rival confederations see significant gains in membership and/or will political influence be used to effect structural changes, especially towards greater unification?

The initial social reforms carried through by the Mitterrand government, notably the 39-hour week, a fifth week of paid holidays, increased power for works councils, more access to company information and improved collective bargaining methods, were all well received by the unions. Further, since these reforms were achieved by decree rather than by legislation, they came into force more speedily than many had expected. The introduction of realistic collective bargaining has been a major element in the Mitterrand regime's policies and meaningful negotiations between employers and unions have been taking place right across France – for the first time ever in many instances.

Nevertheless, 'the labour organizations are as deeply divided under the socialist regime as they were under its conservative predecessor.' The CGT, for example, refused to negotiate on the 39-hour week because it wanted a 38-hour week introduced immediately, the CFDT issued a detailed point-by-point attack on the government's proposals and the FO and CFTC provoked a series of conflicts and stoppages and the number of days lost through industrial action rose sharply. A major aim in all this seemed to be the wish to be seen as maintaining some independence from the socialist government.[43] At the same time unrest from workers on the shop floor, connected principally with the continuing high rates of both inflation and unemployment, was by early 1982 showing signs of increasing and was often leading to spontaneous stoppages.

Over almost every aspect of its new economic and social policies the Mitterrand government has insisted on active discussions with representatives of all the major trade union confederations. Never before have the unions been so courted and never before have they had such an opportunity to put their own house in order, achieve at least a semblance of unity with the aid of the new social measures, and aspire to a massive increase in membership. By early 1982, however, all the signs were that none of this would happen. The endemic inter-confederation squabbles appeared to be worse than ever before.

108 _Labour_

Notes

1. J.-P. Revoil, 'La Croissance lente marque l'emploi', *Economie et Statistique*, no. 112 (June 1979).
2. *Enquête sur l'Emploi de Mars 1981*, *Les Collections de l'INSEE*, Série D, no. 87 (Dec. 1981).
3. *European Industrial Relations Review*, no. 76 (1980).
4. *European Industrial Relations Review*, no. 86 (1981).
5. O. Marchand and N. Balland, *Projection de Population Active Disponible 1975-2000*, *Les Collections de l'INSEE*, Série D, no. 79 (Oct. 1980).
6. Revoil, 'La Croissance lente marque l'emploi'.
7. *Guardian*, 1 Oct. 1981.
8. This section draws on R. Cessieux, 'l'Emploi' in J.P. Pagé (ed.), *Profil Economique de la France au Seuil des Années 80* (La Documentation Française, 1981).
9. G. Martinet, *Sept Syndicalismes* (Editions Du Seuil, 1979).
10. V. Lorwin, *The French Labour Movement* (Harvard University Press, 1966).
11. E. Owen-Smith, *Trade Unions in the Developed Economy* (Croom Helm, 1981).
12. G. Lefranc, *Le Syndicalisme en France*, 10th edn (Presses Universitaires de France, 1978).
13. W. Kendall, *The Labour Movement in Europe* (Allen Lane, 1975).
14. Ibid.
15. Lefranc, *Le Syndicalisme en France*.
16. *Le Figaro*, 7 Nov. 1980.
17. Lefranc, *Le Syndicalisme en France*.
18. S. Chatillon, *Pourquoi la Division Syndicale?* (Economica, 1978).
19. M. Stewart, *Trade Unions in Europe* (Eyre and Spottiswoode, 1974).
20. G. Adam *et al.*, *La Négociation Collective en France* (Paris, 1972).
21. Stewart, *Trade Unions in Europe*.
22. G. Lefranc, 'Histoire et évolution récents du syndicalisme français', *Vie Sociale* (Aug. 1970) (writer's translation).
23. Chatillon, *Pourquoi la Division Syndicale?*
24. *L'Express*, 6 Dec. 1980.
25. Lorwin, *The French Labour Movement*.
26. A. Barjonet, *La CGT*, quoted in Kendall, *The Labour Movement in Europe*.
27. J.-D. Reynaud, *Les Syndicats en France* (Du Seuil, 1975).
28. Kendall, *The Labour Movement in Europe*.
29. J. Lesire-Ogrel, *Le Syndicat dans l'Entreprise* (Du Seuil, 1967).
30. Sudreau Report: *Rapport du Comité d'étude pour la reforme de l'entreprise* (1975).
31. D. Marsden, *Industrial Democracy and Industrial Control in West Germany, France and Great Britain* (UK Department of Employment, Social Science Branch, Research and Planning Division, Research Paper no. 4, Sept. 1978).
32. Reynaud, *Les Syndicats en France*.
33. *Le Point*, no. 158, 29 Sept. 1975, quoted in M. Schain, 'Corporatism and Industrial Relations in France' in P. Cerny and M. Schain, *Politics and Public Policy in France* (Frances Pinter, 1980).
34. Lorwin, *The French Labour Movement*.
35. S. Creigh, N. Donaldson and E. Hawthorn, 'Stoppage Activity in OECD Countries', *Department of Employment Gazette* (Nov. 1980).
36. *Tableaux de l'Economie Française, edition 1981* (INSEE, 1981).

37. Lorwin, *The French Labour Movement*.

38. J. McArthur and B. Scott, *Industrial Planning in France* (Harvard University Press, 1969).

39. M. Schain, 'Corporatism and Industrial Relations in France', in Cerney and Schain, *Politics and Public Policy in France*.

40. 'La CGT Isolée', *L'Aurore*, 14 Dec. 1981.

41. T. Kennedy, *European Labour Relations* (Lexington, 1980).

42. For a somewhat longer study of French trade unions with fuller references, see J.R. Hough, 'France' in Owen-Smith, *Trade Unions in the Developed Economy*.

43. C. Hargrove, *The Times*, 16 Dec. 1981.

5 ECONOMIC PLANNING

Historical Development

In the view of many observers the single most interesting aspect of the French economy in the years since the Second World War is its sustained experience with economic planning, an experience without parallel in any other Western developed economy. The main focus of this chapter will be on French planning as it exists today and as it has existed in recent years, but it will initially be necessary to set this in the context of the genesis and earlier development of the planning process.

So great was the devastation of France by 1945, with an estimated 2 million buildings damaged or destroyed, 91,000 factories inoperative, the railway network virtually paralysed and many major roads unusable,[1] that some co-ordinated plan seemed necessary for the country's recovery. Much has also been written of the prominence of socialist and Communist sympathisers, including those who had been members of the Resistance, and it is true that there was at least a general climate in favour of a planned or interventionist approach to economic policy as evidenced, for example, by the wave of nationalisations that took place in the late 1940s. By 1946 a general planning office (Commissariat Général du Plan) had been set up under Jean Monnet, who was to become known as the father of French planning, with a small administrative staff and an avowed intention of working through, and in conjunction with, existing Ministries and other official bodies. This approach has remained essentially the same throughout the intervening years: despite the great changes that have taken place in French economic planning and despite the enormous complexity of the task it now has to undertake, the Commissariat still had a staff of less than one hundred people at the time of its incorporation into the new Ministry, responsible for both planning and regional economic policy, formed in 1981 by the new socialist government.

The main work of developing the successive plans was, and is, done by a series of interlocking commissions on which sit representatives of various national government bodies, local government associations, professional groups, trade unions and other particular interests. This process has now continued, with considerable changes, for over 35 years, from an initial Plan 1 to the present Plan 8. The planning is nominally indicative

110

in character, as opposed to the centrally planned economies of Eastern Europe, but in fact has the support of a whole battery of financial incentives, legal restrictions and other provisions, so that it is very much more than the pure version of indicative planning found in economics textbooks, such as the UK adopted in the ill-fated 'National Plan' of 1965. It is also true that the state is in a position to take direct action to secure the implementation, at least in part, of the current plan in view of the size of the public sector in France and the state's ownership or part-ownership of many private companies, and the ways in which these are, at least on occasions, used to further general economic policy.

Chronology of the Plans[2]

Plan 1 was drawn up to cover the years 1947-50 but was subsequently extended to 1953. It was essentially a simple document which set out to give high priority to what were seen as the country's basic needs in the early stages of reconstruction, i.e. coal-mining, steel, agricultural machinery, electricity, transport and cement. There was no pretence at any underlying theory or sophisticated strategy, merely the aim of restoring the economy to pre-war levels of activity in the shortest possible time. The fact that building permits, import licences and financial credits were all allocated strictly in accordance with the targets specified in the Plan serves to emphasise the point made previously that economic planning in France has always been rather more than 'indicative'. The precise targets specified in the Plan were all achieved and were often exceeded by a considerable margin. France in Plan 1 was doing little more than the UK over the same period, but the UK did not put her post-war reconstruction programme into a unified plan: it is possible to speculate whether, had she done so, her economic experiences in the succeeding years might have followed a different course.

Plan 2, which covered 1954-57, was more diverse in both nature and aims: it set detailed production and investment targets for the whole of manufacturing industry, which was given much greater priority. Modernisation of French industry was to be achieved via a programme of rationalisation and removal of protection and restrictive practices. The Plan aimed at total growth for the period of 25 per cent, but in fact the achievement was just on 30 per cent. Paradoxically this very successful out-turn led to considerable doubts and criticisms regarding the planning process: how meaningful, commentators asked, were planning targets which could be exceeded by such a wide margin? A further problem was that the expansion of the economy led to higher rates of inflation and a financial crisis, related to both inflationary wage claims in a situation of very full employment and to pent-up consumer demand after many years of deprivation.

Nevertheless planning continued, and Plan 3 (1958-61) has been called the first attempt at an integrated and coherent national programme. Much more attention was paid to the collection of abundant data and to economic forecasting techniques, then in their infancy. Growth targets were set for all sectors of the economy and detailed production and investment objectives calculated for all major industries. Detailed consideration was given to industrial development with particular reference to the need to reduce imports, stimulate exports and thus improve France's external balance. Plan 3 was considerably wider in its perspective than Plan 2 and incorporated estimates of the effects of changes in the size and structure of the national population, of scientific and technical progress, of the creation of the European Communities, and of links with France's former colonial territories. It was proposed to proceed in two stages, first with the restoration of monetary stability and, second, with growth of 20 per cent by the end of the period. The out-turn corresponded very closely to these objectives, with the aid of the return to power of General de Gaulle and the devaluation of the franc at the end of 1958: from having balance-of-payments deficits each year from 1956 to 1958, France was to have surpluses each year from 1959 to 1965. Thus 1959 can be seen as a major turning-point in the French economy.[3] With the ending of bottlenecks from the immediate post-war years and with the removal of both political instability and the balance-of-payments constraint, the stage was set for a quite remarkable decade during which France achieved an annual growth rate of 5.7 per cent, a record which no other comparable country, not even West Germany, could match.

Both Plan 4 (1962-5) and Plan 5 (1966-70), therefore, were implemented during boom years and this was naturally reflected in the ever more ambitious scope and growth forecasts in each. Plan 4 set the strictly industrial and economic targets against other aims which were avowedly social, regional, and even political in nature. Thus whilst emphasis was placed on the need for an intensified export drive to offset the growing liberalisation in world trade and on the further modernisation of French industry, targets were also specified for projects of a more social nature, such as schools and hospitals, and on the needs of the relatively disadvantaged, such as low wage-earners and old people. Although Plans 2 and 3 had included references to the plight of the poorer regions of France, in Plan 4 this was taken more seriously, especially the need to attract industry and employment towards the underdeveloped western half of France. Overall, Plan 4 aimed at growth of 24 per cent by 1965, which was almost exactly matched by the out-turn of 24.1 per cent.

Plan 5 is sometimes referred to as 'the high-water mark of French planning', although it can be argued that plan 6 was equally extensive in scope: they were the most ambitious of all the Plans and were followed by a period during which French economic planning went into some-what of a decline. Plan 5 covered the years 1966-70 and aimed for total growth over the period of 27.5 per cent, i.e. broadly in line with the country's recent experience. The Plan was extremely ambitious in its aim of achieving national 'concertation', or meshing together of the requirements of and products from all France's industrial sectors into a complex Leontief input-output table. Further, monetary values were included in the Plan for the first time and were related to both embryo-nic price controls and implied estimates of the rate of inflation. The Plan anticipated the ending of tariffs between EEC member countries on 30 June 1968 and the consequent increase in competitiveness which French industry would have to face, and it also gave much more atten-tion than previously to problems of regional inequalities (as discussed in Chapter 7).

The mounting criticisms of the planning process in France, which will be discussed below, in some ways led to some retreat from the degree of complexity represented by Plan 5, and from certain points of view Plan 6 (1971-5) is a less ambitious document. For example, the detailed 'concertation' which was carried to its peak in Plan 5 was not pursued in such detail in Plan 6. In certain other respects, however, for example in its social and regional objectives, Plan 6 was even more far-reaching than Plan 5. One recent commentary notes: 'the apparent paradox that the sixth plan, which was compiled using far more sophisticated mathemat-ical techniques than its predecessors, finally contained fewer numerical targets.'[4] Perhaps overall Plan 6 should be seen as being as ambitious as its immediate predecessor, albeit in rather different ways. The position is further complicated because a reading of the plans themselves tends to exaggerate this notion of a 'decline', since from Plan 6 onwards it has been increasingly the practice to withdraw much of the detail and the statistical data from the plan itself and to include these in voluminous appendices which are published separately. Plan 6 specified 'six basic Options' which were developed into '25 objectives': a mixture of eco-nomic and social in nature, they included, *inter alia*, references to the achievement of a sustained and orderly growth rate, increased com-petitiveness and share in international trade on the part of French firms, improvements in the areas of education, research and employment, and increased budgetary subsidies for social and economic purposes. The planners realised the need for greater flexibility and included a system of 'clignotants' ('warning lights')[5] to indicate deviations from target values requiring corrective action by the government.[6]

Plan 7 (1976-80) has to be seen as 'the beginning of the end' of the previously very ambitious approach to economic planning. It set out '25 priority programmes', which were described by the government as being both original and absolutely operational.[7] They were said to represent a departure from the setting out of broad generalities and a concentration instead on quite specific areas requiring early attention: an example was France's notoriously inefficient telephone system, the modernisation of which was given high priority. A good example of both the single-mindedness of the system in concentrating on such 'black spots' and the successful results achieved is provided by the out-turn in this case: in 1975 to have a telephone installed in Paris involved a wait of eighteen months; by 1980 this had been cut to two weeks. Some 80 per cent of households now have a telephone and the number of public phone booths has nearly trebled.

On the other hand, the references to the adjustment of industry to international competition and the restoration of balance-of-payments equilibrium read much as in previous plans, and these were particularly stressed in a mid-way report which was published in September 1978.[8] The latter represented an updating of the objectives of the Plan, but with no very sudden or dramatic changes of direction. Working conditions, employment policy, development of new towns and improvement of urban transport were all assigned priorities in the Plan, which showed a detailed breakdown of the global sum of 206,000m frs. (in 1975 values) over all such items.

By the time of the current Plan 8 (1981-5) the status of economic planning (to be discussed below) had in some ways stabilised, but in other ways there was a further decline, for example no detailed quantitative macro-economic objectives were included. In other ways Plan 8 can be seen as a continuation of its predecessor with less of the tendency towards either expansion or decline of the planning process which had been a characteristic of much of the period since 1945. Plan 8 set out its principal objectives in 'six options', specified as:

(i) to reduce dependence on outside sources of energy and raw materials;
(ii) to develop industrial competitiveness;

    (iii) to strengthen the agricultural and food sector;
    (iv) specific policies for employment;
    (v) to consolidate social protection while containing its cost;
    (vi) to improve housing and the living environment.[9]

It is not difficult to see (ii), (iii) and (vi) as a direct continuation of policies that have appeared in some form or other in every Plan back to Plan 2; (iv) clearly relates to the problem of large-scale unemployment which is a comparatively new phenomenon for France and which is discussed at some length in Chapter 6; (v) refers to relatively recent concern in France over the escalating cost of the welfare state and the fear that this was getting out of control. The policy approach of the Barre government is clearly discernible here. To take one example on the social front, the Plan specifies the need to curb the growth of the number of doctors, of whom there were 77,000 in 1976 and would be 150,000 in 1985.

Most important of all, however, for France at the present time is (i) — the series of oil crises in the latter 1970s emphasised all too clearly France's degree of dependence on imported energy, probably more so than any of her immediate competitors. The Plan notes that three-quarters of the country's energy consumption is supplied by imports of oil, gas and coal and comments starkly, 'there is reason to fear that the energy crisis lies before us at least as much as behind us.' The Plan's objective is to reduce the import bill by 15,000-20,000m frs. (in 1985 values) by 1985 — apparently a very ambitious aim but one capable of realisation in view of the complex policy programme of rapid development of nuclear energy, diversification of energy sources, energy-saving measures and substantial price rises for energy where appropriate. France's attempts at insisting that Britain's oil and gas fields in the North Sea must be considered as a European Community asset, which have occasioned so much surprise and resentment in the UK, perhaps appear more understandable when viewed from the point of view of a France virtually lacking any such sources of her own.

Finally, late in 1980 the French government added a seventh option — a major increase in research and development expenditure, from 1.8 per cent of GNP to 2.5 per cent.

The 8th Plan has been termed 'the first truly strategic plan'.[10] This is because as compared with its predecessors it gives much more attention to long-term trends and their economic and social implications: examples are the development of new production methods based on microprocessors and the slowing down of economic growth throughout the Western world, both of which are highly significant for the major problem of unemployment with which France is now faced. Indeed, in preparatory documents[11] for Plan 8, this problem of achieving high and stable levels of employment in a situation of low world economic growth was seen as the third major challenge to confront the French economy since 1945 (the first being post-war reconstruction and the second being entry into the European Common Market). Indeed the first draft of the various statistics to be included in Plan 8 had to be amended after being violently opposed by the trade unions on account of the high levels of unemployment forecast. The Plan gave demographic predictions up to the year 2030, forecasts of the working population up to 1985, and estimates of France's energy requirements up to 1980. A degree of flexibility is retained with the provision of alternative indicators for certain variables.

An important element in the 8th Plan was the extent to which it will be possible to combine wage moderation with a high level of savings or, as expressed by the late Sir Andrew Shonfield, 'The thinking behind the 8th Plan appears to be based on the expectation that French wages will prove to be fairly inelastic in respect of a further moderate increase in demand and activity.'[12] It was by no means clear that this would prove to be the case, even before the further 'oil shocks' of 1981.

By the latter part of 1981, partly as a result of the coming to power of the socialist regime in May/June 1981 and partly because of economic developments since the drawing up of the 8th Plan, a revised and updated version of the Plan's major proposals was required and was published as a 'Plan Intérimaire' ('Intermediate Plan'), with the sub-title 'Strategy for 2 years, 1982-83'.[13] This Intermediate Plan specifies the first and foremost economic problem, which must take precedence over all other eventualities, as the need to reduce the national level of unemployment which was specified in the document as having reached 1,850,000 and was forecast as likely to exceed 2,400,000 by 1986. (In fact the level of unemployment had reached 2,100,000 by the time the document was published at the end of November 1981 and by then all expectations were that the level forecast for 1986 would be achieved very much more quickly, perhaps before the close of 1982.) The Intermediate Plan focuses on both the social problems and the economic waste resulting from this high level of human inactivity.

The Intermediate Plan aims to create 400,000 to 500,000 jobs within two years and thus reverse the upward trend of unemployment, the key instrument in this process being an expansion of the public sector. Apart from the programme of nationalisations, public expenditure will be increased, particularly in ways leading to modernisation of capital and equipment. The nationalisation of those banks hitherto in the private sector was seen as a vehicle for making available the finance required for this programme. In view of what is written elsewhere in this chapter, it is of considerable interest that the Intermediate Plan states that the economic planning process will be renewed and reinforced, although no details are given beyond the statement that the government has decided that Plan 9 will commence on 1 January 1984, i.e. at the conclusion of the Intermediate Plan. This makes Plan 8, in its original form, the shortest-lived of all French plans.

The Intermediate Plan aims for the simultaneous expansion of consumption, investment and exports and replacement of imports by nationally produced goods. In this way it is hoped to reduce both unemployment and inflation without causing any increase in the external deficit. As one prominent economist said to the writer in Paris in December 1981, 'It is an ambitious proposal – no one has ever been able to do this before – I wonder if we can?' The raising of the minimum wage (SMIC), expansion of the home construction programme, extra subsidised loans to industry, creation of new jobs in the public sector and increased welfare state benefits (as part of a planned deficit for the 1982 budget) and increased investment in domestic energy production with particular reference to coal are some of the main elements in the new policy.

Quite apart from the economics, no one who has read the Intermediate Plan can fail to be struck by its overtly political tone, to a far greater extent than any preceding Plan. Thus considerable space is devoted to attacks on liberal and conservative economists, to a discussion of 'the mistakes of the past' and to the justification of further nationalisations. The key word in all this appears to be 'solidarity', which recurs throughout the 300-page document. There can also be no doubt that the Intermediate Plan was prepared on a very different basis as compared with its predecessors. There are few statistical tables or other detailed forecasts and there is no evidence of any use of econometric modelling. As to whether all this provides an indication of the future shape of economic planning in France it is, of course, too early to say.

Analysis

A rather bald outline of the chronological development of planning, as given above, whilst necessary for an appreciation of how French economic planning has arrived at its present position, cannot suffice for an understanding of the forces acting on the planning process and how these changed over time. A number of excellent analytical studies of French economic planning have now been published and it will be convenient to review these here.

Initially, however, it perhaps needs to be emphasised that 'planning' in France is not a static or fixed concept: it has changed greatly, one might almost say out of all recognition, in the period of over 35 years since its inception: its star was in the ascendant for the first approximately 25 years since when it is undeniable that it has suffered some decline in status. It also needs to be stressed that any attempt to compare a 'planned' French economy with an 'unplanned' UK economy is partly misleading, since a number of aspects of economic or social policy are, with suitable local variations, common to both. Thus both countries have had their own versions of policies relating to their poorer regions, to controls on monopolies and restrictive practices, to redistribution of income and wealth, to protection of the environment and to long-term measures to correct the external balance: in France all such measures have been included in the current Plan, whereas the UK has had no such plan into which to incorporate them.

A very useful analysis of France's experience with economic planning was given by Holmes and Estrin,[14] who showed that change was endemic in the planning process from the earliest years, due, at least in part, to the unusual situation in which the Commissariat found itself: with no juridical or independent existence of its own it had to operate by persuasion and was more successful in some spheres, and with some official bodies, than with others. Throughout the 1950s, which these writers characterised as 'the heyday of French planning', the planners' techniques and data were still poor and 'the precise figures were probably relatively valueless', but nevertheless planning was successful. The reason for this was that it succeeded in persuading the French people, including industrialists and governments, that the post-war boom could and would continue into years of sustained high economic growth. This conclusion, which verges on saying that the effects of planning were psychological rather than directly economic, matches the view of perhaps the most extensive study then made by French economists of the French economy to the early 1970s.[15]

By the 1960s and early 1970s, which Holmes and Estrin characterised as 'the years of decline', the increasing complexity of the French economy coincided with serious doubts as to what planning as such had achieved or could achieve and the still growing ambitions of the planners, to produce a new mood of pessimism and even disillusion, so that 'by the end of the 6th Plan people began to wonder if there was any point in continuing with a 7th Plan.'[16]

A comparison of the rates of growth of Gross Domestic Product forecast in the successive plans and those eventually achieved is set out in Table 5.1

Table 5.1: GDP Growth Rates: Plan Targets and Out-turn, 1952-80 (per cent)

	2nd Plan 1952-7	3rd Plan 1958-61	4th Plan 1962-5	5th Plan 1966-70	6th Plan 1971-5	7th Plan 1976-80
Target	4.4	4.7	5.5	5.7	5.9	5.9
Out-turn	5.4	3.8	5.8	5.9	3.7	3.9[a]

Note: a. 1976-9 (Plan and out-turn data for the 8th Plan are not strictly comparable because of changes in national accounting conventions.)

Nominally these figures indicate a close match between target and out-turn for the whole of the period of some twenty years preceding the oil crises and consequent world economic depression of the 1970s. For Plans 2, 4 and 5, the out-turn actually exceeded the already ambitious targets. The out-turns for the 1970s look mediocre in comparison with the targets, but were considerably better than those achieved by most comparable countries. In any event such global comparisons tell us rather little about the success or otherwise of economic planning as they frequently concealed wide divergencies at the level of different industries or sectors of the economy. It is perhaps more significant that in 1967 the percentages of all large firms (those with more than 5,000 employees) reporting that the Plan forecasts did have a significant effect on their investment and production decisions were over 50 per cent and over 33 per cent respectively.[17]

'Decline' of Planning

That there was some decline in the role and status of planning after about 1970 is undeniable. Indeed, at a seminar attended by the writer at the London School of Economics in 1976, Monsieur Jean Ripert, Head of the Commissariat, readily admitted as much: he went on to emphasise, however, that observers who exaggerated this 'decline', or who foresaw no future for the Plan or the planners, were mistaken. He saw the Plan as having stabilised at an admittedly less ambitious level than previously and said the change could be summarised as being from 'concertation' to 'consultation', i.e. from ceasing to try to enmesh the precise input and output statistics of all the major industries to more of a discussive process aimed at identifying priorities and removing bottlenecks. Frequently, said Monsieur Ripert, he was still asked for his advice on major economic policy decisions on a day-to-day basis – and where he was not asked he still found ways of giving his views, which would be related to the context of the current Plan. Certainly his view that the plan had stabilised at a level of status and activity at which it would remain for the foreseeable future appears to have been borne out by the events of the ensuing years.

The causes of the decline in French planning can be ascribed to a combination of a number of different factors:

(i)   There was increasing awareness of the fact that, as the French economy grew in complexity and particularly in openness to external influences, it was increasingly impossible to achieve the detailed 'concertation' at which planning in its zenith had aimed.

(ii)   Increasingly, significant discrepancies were recorded between the Plan's forecasts and the out-turns; in some instances, particularly relating to exports and imports, the forecasts systematically underestimated. What was the point, commentators asked, of targets which were exceeded by wide margins? This point certainly seems to have led to a revised concept of economic planning, although whether the latter necessarily has to be seen as a 'decline' is, perhaps, partly a question of semantics.

(iii)   On a number of occasions, including in 1963, 1968 and 1974, the Plan's targets had to be set aside on account of the exigencies of short-term demand management or stabilisation policy, and thereafter attempts to get back on course presented difficulties. Of what use, the critics asked, were target variables which were simply set aside each time the economy ran into difficulties in the short term?

(iv)   Increasingly economists questioned whether the planning process had not had harmful side-effects such as increased collusion and the growth of restrictive practices and pricing agreements between firms. Given the widespread nature of such restrictive practices and protective agreements in France for many years, on balance it seems unlikely that the planning process led to any significant increase.

(v)   The events of May 1968 had a cataclysmic effect on France and led to a wave of questioning over the problems of French society and the direction in which the economy was heading, which was fuelled by the alarming rise in the unemployment statistics. Was the country right, critics asked, to concentrate so much on economic growth to the apparent neglect of harmful effects on society? The question was not, perhaps, aimed specifically at the Plan, but inevitably planning became involved in the ensuing upheaval.

(vi)   Political considerations have undoubtedly influenced planning, although not always in the ways that had been anticipated. Thus Valery Giscard d'Estaing, as Minister of Finance, was seen to be quite 'anti-planning', yet when he came to power as President of the Republic he made no attempt further to relegate planning – and similarly when Barre became Prime Minister. Even after the coming to power of the socialist President Mitterrand it was at first not certain that he would take active steps to secure an enhanced role for the planners. Perhaps the overall effect of the interaction between the political and economic dimensions has been to increase the feeling of uncertainty, but also there can be little doubt that for the politicians the specification of precise targets and forecasts was a cause of later embarrassment when these were not met and provided ammunition for the opposition of the day.

(vii)   Finally, and perhaps most important of all, it gradually became apparent that no 'proof' that economic planning was responsible for the exceptional success of the French economy in the post-war period was available, or could ever be available. Increasingly it was suggested that in the early years high growth rates had been the direct result of post-war reconstruction and subsequently had been stimulated by the release of resources from the declining agricultural sector and by such external influences as joining the European Common Market. This point has been put forward by a number of university economists seeking rigorous justification for economic planning, in contrast to the generally more practical approach of economists within the government service, including within the planning Commissariat itself.

Clearly none of the above arguments are in any way conclusive, but taken together they did serve to create, at the very least, a feeling of less optimism about what planning could achieve. The spirit of self-examination which ensued is epitomised in the title of the book *Quelle Planification pour la France?* (*What Sort of Planning Should France Have?*) by P. Pascallon.[18] It is, however, also significant in the context of the criticisms noted above that Pascallon's assessment of the future of economic planning in France was essentially positive and optimistic: his conclusion was that planning gives France both control of and hope in the future, to a greater degree than she would otherwise have. This conclusion is in essence identical to that of Monsieur Gabriel Mignot[19] in an authoritative review of the place of planning in economic policy in the wake of the world crisis of the latter 1970s. All of these assessments do, of course, pre-date the new policy approach of the socialist government after June 1981, which has already been referred to above.

Planning's New Role

Having moved away from earlier concern with detailed micro-economic projections, planning did in some respects take on a more general character. Holmes and Estrin suggested that it had acquired two new roles for itself, one economic, the other political. On the economic side the Plan now gave much more attention to predicting macro-economic variables and served as a framework within which the government could set its medium-term economic policy. The Plan 'has become more aggregative and more concerned with macro-economic consistency than with micro-economic coherence'.[20] The same writers concluded: 'there is a certain logic to the re-emergence of planning in France as a major feature of economic policy-making', a conclusion which is in line with those noted above.

At this point it is instructive again to refer to the views of Monsieur Jean Ripert, head of the Commissariat Général du Plan,[21] who saw three major features of planning in its new and somewhat reduced role. First, consistency: by bringing together representatives of a wide spectrum of French industry, government and society, and by comparing and contrasting their expectations for the ensuing few years, conflicts and bottlenecks came to light and could be studied and eliminated, even though this process stopped short of the 'concertation' referred to above. The statistics dealt with could not be considered as 'firm' as they had been in, for example, Plan 5, and in any event some of the outcomes were completely outside the control of the Commissariat.

Secondly, the democratic process: with its own staff still numbering less than one hundred, the Commissariat was obliged to, and chose to, involve wide representation from outside. Almost all the civil service had been involved in some way or other in the formulation of the latest

Plan and a total of 19 committees and 15 working parties had ensured very wide participation. The dovetailing of 'vertical' committees (looking at particular sectors such as major industries) with 'horizontal' committees (looking at more general problems across all sectors, an example cited being income distribution) ensured that the work of the various committees was put together into one harmonious whole.[22] In this regard Monsieur Ripert quoted with approval the statement by Professor Massé: 'The planning process is more meaningful than the plan itself.'

Third, realism: the planners now aimed at being more realistic than previously in the light of the many problems now facing the French economy — this led, for example, to accepting that there were no short-term solutions to the problem of large-scale unemployment. Similarly, in view of the evident difficulties in accurately forecasting for the later years of the Plan, alternative assumptions — one labelled 'optimistic', the other 'pessimistic' — were included throughout. Monsieur Ripert cited as the main weakness in the whole planning system the question of how to deal with the last two or three years of each planning period: the government of the day had usually been unwilling to admit that the targets specified in the Plan were now in need of amendment even where these had evidently become unattainable; in his view there was a need for periodic revision of the original targets in the light of subsequent amendments. The subsequent introduction of the 'Intermediate Plan' as discussed above seems particularly relevant here.

Professor Massé has written recently that, whilst we shall never see a return to the notion that France can, by means of an all-embracing Plan, largely determine the country's economic future, a definite role remains for the Plan. The latter must make it easier for industrial and commercial companies to react to economic events, pave the way for less dependence on imported energy sources and for an improved domestic employment situation, and thus help to build a strong economic future. In his view, to abandon planning in its new role would be a fatal mistake.[23]

In the words of a recent authoritative study, 'planning continues to provide the framework within which our economic and social policy is set.' The bringing together of representatives of all the major participants in the economy, the specification of the major medium-term economic objectives and the orientation of public expenditure towards these ends remained highly significant in the eyes of the same authors who concluded: 'the principal characteristic of French planning is undoubtedly the collective discussion which it organises every five years between the major socio-economic spokesmen and the government on the country's major development problems.' The specification of the country's principal priorities was bound to give rise to tensions, but planning must be seen as a significant achievement which led to a reasonable degree of effective action.[24]

The Economic Model

From Plan 5 onwards, at the plan's developmental stage, detailed forward projections were produced by an economic model known as FIFI (modèle physico-financier). FIFI, which was developed from an earlier model of Professor R. Courbis, was a model of some 2,000 equations covering in great detail links between economic participants in each of seven major branches: agriculture; food industry; energy; manufacturing; transport and communications; housing construction and public works; services and trade. Projections were made forward to the final year of the Plan, to give estimates at that point and not the trajectory over time.[25] Prior to FIFI, previous simpler models had been used for background work on earlier plans, but FIFI was subsequently described as 'the centrepiece of the planners' technical apparatus'.[26]

Courbis' original model commenced with Keynesian-type equations, but FIFI departed from these in certain significant respects, partly regarding the close substitutability between the products from French industry and imported goods, which in turn made use of the (increasingly unrealistic) assumption of a fixed exchange rate for the franc. Output of tradeable competitive goods, aimed at the total world market, was determined by capacity which itself was a function of past investment, largely derived from self-financing out of profits.[27] Some of the assumptions of the model, especially those of exogenously determined prices and wages fixed by a Phillips Curve relationship, had to be seen as increasingly unrealistic as time went by. The planners' attempts at predicting world inflation rates were obviously fraught with difficulty and subject to a wide margin of error and the escalation of total national unemployment, which broadly coincided with much higher rates of inflation than previously, appeared to cause one central part of the model to break down completely. Nevertheless FIFI did retain a high degree of flexibility.[28] A major policy implication of the model was that, due to the close interdependency between the French and extra-territorial markets, the government could not manipulate national demand via fiscal policy in order to regulate the level of unemployment. This conclusion fitted fairly well with the general approach of the majority of French economists until around 1970, but was much less suited to the gradual tendency towards Keynesian-type intervention which became more characteristic of French macro-economic policy thereafter, as discussed in Chapter 6.

These were some of the reasons that led to FIFI being replaced by the new DMS model (for 'dynamique multisectoriel') from the commencement of Plan 8 (it had first been used for some of the work on Plan 7's 'mid-way report' of September 1978 which was mentioned above). DMS is a very ambitious, all-embracing model, which has been cited by the head of the planning Commissariat as one of the most significant macro-economic models developed in the Western world. Perhaps its chief characteristic is that of rolling forecasts for each of the ensuing five to eight years, the forecasts being automatically revised as new information comes to hand, rather like a system of moving averages. DMS is, as its name implies, not only dynamic but also multi-sectoral, i.e. it incorporates estimates for all the major sectors of the economy and achieves coherence between these and the global macro-economic variables. There are eleven sectors for industrial and commercial companies plus separate ones covering, for example, nationalised industries, households, government, credit and the rest of the world. The model comprises some 1,900 equations, of which 250 are cited as 'behavioural'; around 400 exogenous variables cover such factors as demographic variables, fiscal and monetary policy, agricultural changes and the international environment. Most calculations are based on the method of ordinary least squares, i.e. multiple regression, and on extrapolations from the previous 15-year period, with subsequent adjustments. The model's forecasts are revised annually, with particular reference to rates of accumulation of physical capital, availability of financial capital, spare capacity and rates of profitability for each industrial and commercial sector. The model then provides a direct (and perhaps over-mechanistic?) connection between levels of industrial profits and future price changes, on the basis that companies seek to achieve stable net incomes in real terms. Within the model, variables receive a series of minor corrections until internal coherence is achieved.[29]

Clearly any model can only be as good as the assumptions it embodies and from this point of view it is easy to criticise either FIFI or DMS. Overall, however, they have served the French planners well and have consistently produced forecasts of the major economic variables that were remarkably close to the eventual outcomes, as was seen above. Not, as Liggins[30] emphasises, that that proves anything either way about the success or otherwise of French planning: to answer such a question would require micro-economic data of (i) detailed decisions taken by French firms and (ii) how these were affected, if at all, by the current

Plan. For the most part such information does not exist, especially for the last fifteen years or so.

Assessments of Planning

Not surprisingly, there has been a very large number of books or other studies seeking to assess, in whole or in part, the effectiveness of French economic planning, and some of the most recent and most useful of these have already been cited. Briefer references will be made here to the other main works of interest, some of which must now seem rather dated and perhaps primarily of historic interest. A number of the works already cited emphasised the creation and sustaining of a climate of optimism and orientation towards economic growth which in turn un-doubtedly had a stimulating effect on investment, thus helping to bring about the very growth that was the main target variable. Carré, Dubois and Malinvaud[31] developed this point at some length and suggested that its effect was undoubted, even if it could not be measured in any precise way. Holmes and Estrin[32] linked the same point to the size and stability of the public sector and to the buoyant effect of setting down on paper details of future public-sector expenditure: private-sector firms had then been able to go ahead and plan in advance for the required capacity, in the safe expectancy that those orders would be forthcoming. Mignot[33] developed much the same point, but more cautiously linked it with the inevitable forecasting errors that had crept in, and with a series of detri-mental side-effects which he saw as having ensued. These, he argued, were related to adverse working and environmental conditions, to the worsening of inequalities in society, to potential inefficiencies resulting from the growth of the public sector and to the lack of attention given to social and cultural development alongside the high economic growth. Mignot suggested, as also did Deleau and Malgrange,[34] that in view of the increasing complexity of the French economy and particularly its openness to foreign trade, the planners would in future have to be both less ambitious in their growth targets and more flexible in their setting of precise targets. From this relatively recent series of assessments, there-fore, the overall conclusion might be summarised as one of cautious optimism, in the sense that French economic planning has undoubtedly had a major impact on the country's economic development and has created a climate in which high rates of growth were much easier to achieve, but without losing sight of the obvious difficulties, especially those that have arisen in more recent years.

What might collectively be termed a previous generation of assess-ments of French planning were published in the 1960s and were rather more diverse in their conclusions. J.W. Hackett,[35] in his considered praise of the achievements of French planning, drew a sharp contrast between the co-ordinated consultation and long-term approach which were the basis of the French system and the stark lack of any equivalents in the UK; the only major cloud on the horizon was the suspicion that membership of the European Economic Community might of itself limit the areas within which such national planning was free to operate. At about the same time Vasconcellos and Kiker[36] published a detailed statistical study which strongly suggested, although it could not prove, that planning had been responsible for significant improvements in productivity and therefore economic growth.

Sometimes eulogistic conclusions are also to be found in Harlow[37] ('Planning has made government-owned industries operate with more independent judgement ... and has strengthened the sense of security of the private sector'), Vasconcellos and Kiker ('the available data attest to the post-war success of the French economy — the result of French planning'), Cohen[38] ('planning has provided cheap funds for investment projects'), Pagé[39] ('planning is needed to foresee and organise the considerable changes required in our society's systems of production and consumption'), Cotta[40] ('planning has given the private sector the means of better co-ordinating its intentions and making better use of investment opportunities'), and Ullmo[41] ('planning has contributed to a modification of expectations and more basically of the attitude of businessmen compared with the Malthusian behaviour ... which characterised the pre-war years').

Adverse assessments, however, are given by Du Boff[42] ('the plan as a philosophy is at a dead-end: its economic, social and political unity has been disintegrating ... the integration foreseen by the EEC is incompatible with national economic planning') — who also quotes with approval the statements by Giscard d'Estaing when Minister of Finance ('le plan, c'est l'inflation') and Gilbert Mathieu[43] ('the plan has been sacrificed on the altar of stability') — Sheahan[44] ('the planners greatly under-estimated the potential growth of the French economy ... planning was only saved because of the general climate of expansion and investment'), the strongly worded comment by Vera Lutz[45] ('France's high growth rate was in no way connected to the Plan ... planning has never worked, either in France or elsewhere'), and more recently Diana Green[46] ('measured in terms of performance (as compared with its stated objectives), clearly planning in France leaves much to be desired. For example, it is difficult to demonstrate that planning has resulted in more efficient investment'). Green even goes so far as to suggest that planning would be progressively emasculated (unless the left achieved a major political victory which at that time seemed increasingly unlikely) a view which could hardly be in greater contrast to that of Latham-Koenig[47] ('it is partly thanks to the vision of these plans that France is, next to Japan, the industrialised country which has restructured most rapidly and successfully its industrial sectors').

It may, of course, be objected that such short quotations cannot hope to capture the full flavour of what are frequently complex arguments or of views which were in many instances hedged with qualifications or reservations. Nevertheless they do serve to show that the conclusions of apparently independent observers, some in France, some overseas, have often been in sharp contrast – perhaps especially so in the case of the earlier studies. It is perhaps not surprising that there should be disagreement over whether French planning has been responsible, wholly or partly, for the remarkable success of the French economy in the postwar years, since such a question is, as we have seen, virtually impossible to answer. The weight of evidence seems to fall in favour of planning having significant successes to its credit, particularly regarding the creation and maintenance of a psychological climate favourable to high rates of economic growth – and certainly a numerical count of 'pro' and 'anti' informed observers would result in a majority for the former. Notions of French planning being progressively further downgraded could probably be safely discounted even before the victory of the left in the elections of 1981, the status of the Plan appearing to have stabilised. After those elections the future of the planning process must at the very least be the maintenance of the status quo – and could well be rather more.

As indicated previously, the Intermediate Plan issued in 1981 specifies a new period of renewal and expansion for the planning process, although quite what form this may take is not yet known. One of the first acts of the socialist government after the elections of May/June 1981 was to transform the planning Commissariat into a Ministry, or at least the major part of one: the new 'Ministère du Plan et de l'Aménagement du Territoire' combined the functions of economic planning with those of regional economic policy. Whatever form economic planning may take in the future, therefore, it seems certain to have a strong regional emphasis. The new Minister, Monsieur Rocard, has set up a 'task-force' to consider the future of planning, under the chairmanship of Monsieur Attali. A detailed exposé submitted to this task-force, and shown to the writer in Paris in December 1981, suggested that among the major questions to be tackled were the specification of objectives and priorities, the place of econometric modelling and statistical fore-casts, the time-scale to be envisaged, the interaction between national economic planning and regional development plans, and the role of the newly enlarged public sector. Whatever shape of economic planning may emerge, the planning process looks set for a major role in the formulation of economic policy for the foreseeable future.

Appendix

Further details of the economic models prior to DMS used as part of the process of drawing up the later plans to Plan 7, together with an indication of the stage of development of these models, were given by Professor Courbis,[48] who wrote of 'a network of large macro-economic models, to which are connected peripheral models'. FIFI, the central model, was being supplemented by a model with a multinational emphasis, entitled MOISE, whilst the new model REGINA (for regional-national) was also becoming operational.

FIFI was·a short-term forecasting model which analysed industries, by major branches, the economic activities of households and those of government departments. Interdependent forecasts are produced by volume and by value, with the aid of estimates of price movements and the position of the financial sector. The setting was that of an open eco-nomy, so that both industries' competitiveness and the level of aggre-gate demand were important for determining production levels in the 'exposed' sectors — but not in those sectors still classified as 'sheltered' — although this distinction was gradually weakening over time.

MOISE added in the multinational dimension by simulating the effects of commercial exchanges with each of the world's major eco-nomic zones (20 in all), each of which was the subject of a separate in-corporated model. Here the effects of monetary and economic policies for each zone were included. REGINA aimed at including the spatial dimension by dividing France into five major regions and each of these regions into rural, small towns and major conurbations: the major ob-jective was to see the effects of each aspect of national development at the regional level. The 'peripheral' models, of which there was a large number, sought to amplify in much greater detail the outline details afforded by the models already mentioned.

The role of all these forecasts in the planning process was threefold:

(i) to throw up general problems arising from the development of

the French economy over the period in question;
(ii) to analyse the incidence of potential economic policies under discussion; and
(iii) to provide a quantitative basis for the work of the various planning commissions.

The team of economists working on the development of the models saw their essential role as aiding the making of informed choices and rejected any suggestion that they were in any way taking over the government's task or infringing the democratic process.[49]

Notes

1. H. Clout, *The Geography of Post-war France, a Social and Economic Approach* (Pergamon, 1972).
2. Detailed accounts of the development of the successive plans are given in each of Clout, *Social and Economic Geography of France*; A.G. Gruchy, *Comparative Economic Systems* (Ch. 6, 'The French Planned Economy') (Houghton Mifflin, 1977); and D. Liggins, *National Economic Planning in France* (Saxon House, 1975).
3. Gruchy, *Comparative Economic Systems*.
4. M. Cave and P. Hare, *Alternative Approaches to Economic Planning* (Macmillan, 1981).
5. 'Clignotants' is not easy to translate precisely; in its original meaning it refers to the warning lights on a car to indicate, for example, electric failure or lack of oil pressure.
6. P. Holmes and S. Estrin, *French Planning Today* (University of Sussex, Economics Seminar Paper Series 76/4).
7. 'Priority Programmes of the Seventh Plan', *News from France* (French Embassy, London, Sept. 1976).
8. 'Rapport Sur l'Adaptation du VIIème Plan', *La Documentation Française* (Sept. 1978).
9. 'The Six Options of the Eighth Plan', *News from France* (French Embassy, London, Dec. 1979).
10. A. Latham-Koenig, 'A French lesson for Britain', *The Times*, 5 Dec. 1980.
11. *Huitième Plan-Options* (La Documentation Française, 1979).
12. Sir Andrew Shonfield, 'The 8th Plan, Assumptions and Constraints', *Revue Economique*, vol. 31, no. 5 (Sept. 1980).
13. *Plan Intérimaire, Stratégie pour Deux Ans, 1982-1983* (La Documentation Française, 1981).
14. Holmes and Estrin, *French Planning Today*.
15. J. Carré, P. Dubois and E. Malinvaud, *La Croissance Française* (Du Seuil, 1973), now published in English as *French Economic Growth* (Oxford University Press, 1975).
16. Holmes and Estrin, *French Planning Today*, p. 7.
17. Cave and Hare, *Alternative Approaches to Economic Planning*.
18. P. Pascallon, *Quelle Planification pour la France?* (Les Editions de l'Epargne, 1979).
19. G. Mignot, *La Planification et la Politique Economique* (Collège d'Europe,

Cahiers de Bruges NS 35, 1976).
20. Holmes and Estrin, *French Planning Today*, p. 33.
21. From his lecture to a seminar at the London School of Economics, October 1976.
22. The suggestion in Holmes and Estrin, *French Planning Today*, p. 10, that this approach had been dropped therefore appears incorrect.
23. P. Massé, 'Repenser le Plan', *Revue Economique*, vol. 31, no. 5 (Sept. 1980).
24. B. Gamby and J. Balladur, 'Les Institutions Economiques' in J.P. Pagé (ed.), *Profil Economique de la France au Seuil des Années 80* (La Documentation Française, 1981).
25. M. Deleau and P. Malgrange, 'Recent Trends in French Planning', paper given to World Congress of the Econometric Society, Toronto, 1975.
26. Holmes and Estrin, *French Planning Today*, p. 15.
27. Deleau and Malgrange, 'Recent Trends in French Planning', p. 11.
28. Holmes and Estrin, *French Planning Today*, p. 16.
29. CGP/INSEE, *Pour Comprendre le modèle économique DMS* (La Documentation Française, 1979) and INSEE, 'Une représentation de l'économie Française: le modèle DMS', *Revue Economique*, vol. 31, no. 5 (Sept. 1980).
30. D. Liggins, *National Economic Planning in France* (Saxon House, 1975).
31. Carré, Dubois and Malinvaud, *La Croissance Française*.
32. Holmes and Estrin, *French Planning Today*.
33. Mignot, *La Planification et la Politique Economique*.
34. Deleau and Malgrange, *Recent Trends in French Planning*.
35. J.W. Hackett, 'Britain and France, Two Experiments in Planning', *The Political Quarterly*, vol. 37 (1966).
36. A. Vasconcellos and B. Kiker, 'The Performance of the French Economy under Planning', *Economics of Planning*, vol. 8, no. 3 (1968).
37. J.S. Harlow, *French Economic Planning* (University of Iowa Press, 1966).
38. S.S. Cohen, *Modern Capitalist Planning, the French Model* (Weidenfeld and Nicolson, 1969).
39. J.P. Pagé, 'Les Institutions Economiques et la Planification' in J.P. Pagé (ed.), *Profil Economique de la France, Notes et Etudes Documentaires*, nos. 4241-4 (Dec. 1975).
40. A. Cotta, 'La Croissance de l'Economie Française', *Analyse et Prévision*, vol. 11, no. 1.2 (1966).
41. Y. Ullmo, 'The National Context France' in J. Hayward and M. Watson (eds.), *Planning, Politics and Public Policy* (Cambridge University Press, 1975).
42. R. du Boff, 'The Decline of Economic Planning in France', *Western Political Quarterly*, vol. 21 (Mar. 1968).
43. G. Mathieu, *Le Monde*, 21 May 1964.
44. J. Sheahan, *An Introduction to the French Economy* (Merrill, 1969).
45. Vera Lutz, *Central Planning for the Market Economy* (Longmans, 1969).
46. Diana Green, 'The Seventh Plan – the Demise of French Planning', *West European Politics* (Feb. 1978).
47. A. Latham-Koenig, 'A French Lesson for Britain', *The Times*, 5 Dec. 1980.
48. R. Courbis, 'Un Processus collectif du choix: l'example de la planification française', *Revue d'Economie Politique* (May-June 1977).
49. The whole of this chapter has benefited from an extended discussion the writer had in Paris in December 1981 with Monsieur B. Cazes of the Commissariat Général du Plan.

6 MACRO-ECONOMIC POLICY

French macro-economic policy differs markedly from that in other countries such as the UK and has developed in quite different ways over the post-war period. Whereas until quite recently it was valid to refer to a gradual convergence of policy approaches in the two countries,[1] this is no longer the case and at the time of writing it would be necessary to refer to a marked divergence.

Theoretical Approach

Economists in the UK are by now so used to thinking in terms of the overwhelming influence of John Maynard Keynes on the development of economic policy — and the labelling of successive stages of development as, for example, pre-Keynesian, neo-Keynesian, post-Keynesian — that it comes as something of a cultural shock to find that until very recently the development of economic policy in France ignored Keynes completely. Where scholarly books or journal articles referred to Keynes at all, which was in itself quite rare, they did so to refute the main tenets of a Keynesian approach. That approach is here taken to mean initially fiscal intervention to manipulate the level of aggregate demand, subsequently developed in the era known as neo-Keynesian to refer to fine tuning of the economy, primarily by fiscal means but with the aid also of monetary instruments, to control some mix of the four objectives of full employment, price stability, balance of payments equilibrium and economic growth. The post-Keynesian phase is taken to mean disenchantment with Keynesian-type intervention and switch of emphasis towards a monetarist approach.

Thus one of the most detailed studies of macro-economic policy, by an eminent French economist Professor De Lattre,[2] ran to six volumes, but made no mention of Keynes: the discussion of the central government's budget deficit, for example, analyses the threefold effects on the loan market, on the floating of new stock issues and on the expansion of the money supply. Nowhere are there any references to the expansion of aggregate demand or potential effects on the level of unemployment, on economic growth, or on the balance of payments. Such an approach is clearly very much on the lines of what in the UK would be regarded as the classical or pre-Keynesian approach. By contrast, the same study does refer in some detail to Professor Milton Friedman and his monetarist approach, emphasising the importance of control of the money supply as the main, or even the only, economic variable of interest.

The same approach to macro-economic policy was embodied in a series of articles to which a special issue of one of the most authoritative economic journals, published by the Ministry of Economy and Finance, was devoted.[3] Given that the main emphasis of the Keynesian approach was towards using tax changes as instruments of policy, it is not surprising that the three detailed studies included all refer to different aspects of such possible changes. First, Brochier[4] discussed at some length whether interventionist fiscal policy in the sense in which it has been applied in the UK could be utilised in France and concluded that it could not, at least without great difficulty, even commenting that no direct French translation of 'fiscal policy' existed: he could see little prospect of relating the chosen policy instrument specifically to the problem in hand (for example the level of investment), envisaged fatal time-lags in any attempt at fiscal intervention, viewed tax changes as much more effective in reducing consumption than in expansion, and concluded that institutional aspects of the French tax system considered it particularly unsuitable for such usage. Second, Goux[5] considered specifically the use of consumption taxation, which in the French context means Value Added Tax, and came to similarly pessimistic conclusions: the natural tendency of consumption to switch to alternative substitute goods, the tendency for consumers to adjust their consumption/savings ratios, the impossibility of taking specific or selective action in certain sectors and the inability to forecast relative price changes would all combine to render consumption taxation a quite inefficient instrument. Third, Fréville[6] found that, quite apart from adjustment effects broadly similar to those already mentioned (variations in working hours, changes in marginal propensities to consume, anti-symmetrical results), the institutional arrangements relating to the French income tax system rendered it particularly unsuitable. These latter aspects related to the very low rates of taxation (among the lowest in any developed country), the lack of any deductions at source or equivalent of the UK's PAYE (Pay As You Earn) and the long time-lags before the payment of tax. Whilst there has been an important subsequent modification, in that 'provisional' advance payments of tax are now required and are the subject of regular deductions from wages and salaries, these are unlikely to alter the general tenor of Fréville's conclusion.

All three of these economists, therefore, each writing from a different point of view, wrote in what can only be described as anti-Keynesian terms. Whilst the points they were making were not new, and many of them have appeared in one form or another in scholarly assessments of stabilisation policy in the UK,[7] in the instances cited they were being given far greater emphasis. Overall the writers are united in their conclusions, which are in accord with those of Professor De Lattre noted previously. It is, in the circumstances, not without interest that by 1976 another of the leading French economic journals should have published a special issue[8] explaining in detail to its readers the elements of Keynesian macro-economic policy, so great by then was the interest in a Keynesian interventionist-type approach (just when, incidentally, across the Channel disenchantment with Keynes and increased interest in monetarism were gathering pace).

The Development of Policy

This rather extensive theoretical preamble has seemed necessary for any understanding of the development of macro-economic policy in France, particularly for any readers influenced by the UK's own experiences in the post-war period. It has served to show that French policy commenced from a quite different orientation, as summarised by Professor De Lattre: 'The Budget is not normally used in France to regulate the economy with a view to full employment.'[9] This position may be taken to have remained fairly static for at least twenty years after 1945: fiscal and monetary policies did, of course, exist, not in any Keynesian interventionist sense, but primarily to provide financial support for the objectives of the current Plan and these will be considered in detail below.

From the late 1960s or early 1970s, however, signs of change could be discerned although it is not at all clear, and observers are by no means in agreement, as to exactly when such change occurred. Coffey[10] is confident that late in 1970 there took place the first Keynesian-type policy intervention in the economy, known at the time as 'Opération Jeunes': with the published unemployment statistics reaching 800,000, a level which at that time seemed catastrophic, and with unemployment of young people and school-leavers a particularly serious problem, the government decided to:

(i)   subsidise, to the extent of 50 per cent, the costs of firms engaging young workers, in 26 of France's more needy départements;

    (ii) increase public investment in education and housing; and

    (iii) raise the national minimum wage (SMIC).

Coffey comments: 'all these measures mark a most important departure from former French practice.' Other writers are less certain: Professor Maillet,[11] for example, recounts a series of measures from 1968 onwards, including varying the discount rate 16 times in six years, all of which were clearly intended to alter the direction in which the national economy was heading. Since the instruments used were primarily monetary and since the target objective was to lower the rate of inflation, can we still refer to such measures as Keynesian? Professor Maillet clearly thinks we can, since he subsequently refers to continuing to utilise measures which are 'd'inspiration plutôt keynésienne'.

Once the issue appears to savour of the semantic there is probably little point in pursuing it; we should, however, note the comment on France in the authoritative review published by the European Communities Commission: 'From the period 1967 to 1970 the general government budget was used extensively as an instrument of short-term stabilisation policy'[12] and the view of Hansen that the budget was being used to deflate the economy as far back as 1964 and 1965.[13] Whatever the rights or wrongs of this debate, it is clear that by the early 1970s French policy-makers had moved much more closely towards a Keynesian-type position. They were to retain it until September 1976, when the newly appointed Prime Minister, Raymond Barre, embarked on a new economic strategy which represented a significant departure from previous policies.[14]

The Barre Years (September 1976-May 1981)

By 1976 the economic euphoria in which successive French governments had basked, as a consequence of the continuous high growth rates and apparent success of the planning process, had given way to a situation in which France faced problems similar to those in her competitor countries: a combination of accelerating inflation, rising unemployment and a deteriorating balance of payments. France had been very hard hit by the onset of the oil crisis and in addition economic policy in 1975-6 had been directed primarily towards raising demand on account of the sharp rise in the unemployment statistics, rather than to curb the new phenomenon of a high rate of inflation; by the end of 1975 the government's budget deficit had leapt to 43 billion frs. and the growth of the money supply was approaching 20 per cent, which it was to reach by mid-1976.

Raymond Barre was perhaps unique among Western premiers in being not only a former professor of economics but also a noted writer and the author of one of the most widely used economics textbooks for French students at university level. President Giscard d'Estaing referred to his Prime Minister as 'the first economist in France'.[15] It was no great surprise, therefore, when his government adopted a more monetarist approach to the economy's problems, including a strict monetary policy to control the money supply, combined with the removal of government controls on industry wherever possible. For the first time a target was set for the growth of the money supply on the basis of a progressive reduction from the 1976 figure of 14 per cent to an objective of 12½ per cent for 1977, i.e. slightly less than the expected growth in nominal Gross Domestic Product, and the restoration of a budget balance. Simultaneously an immediate price freeze was announced, to cover most goods until the end of 1976 and the major nationalised industries until April 1977.

The immediate results were disappointing, with inflation for 1977 finalising at 9.5 per cent compared with 1976's 9.2 per cent and, with an increased majority for the coalition government in the general election, by April 1978 Barre felt able to embark on a 'Phase Two' operation which 'amounted to nothing short of an about-turn in French economic and industrial policy'.[16] The strategy now became more specifically long-term, with the emphasis on industrial profitability, investment and competitiveness: industrial prices were freed from all controls for the first time since 1939, via a three- or four-stage progression commencing in July, the government's financial aid to 'lame ducks' was radically reduced, so that 'companies in traditional industries, which cannot make ends meet, will be allowed to go to the wall.'[17] As Barre was quoted as saying in the French business magazine *L'Expansion*, 'we must not hesitate to get rid of the dead wood in sectors in which we are badly placed.' The nationalised industries were instructed to aim at financial self-sufficiency, it being understood that substantial increases in the prices of their products would be necessary. State subsidies to the nationalised industries, running at an annual 30 billion frs., were to be substantially reduced, although it was recognised that this would take two or three years to achieve.

Privately the government admitted that both inflation and unemployment would continue at high levels for the foreseeable future, but their hope was that the combination of tight control of the money supply and a strict exchange rate policy to keep import costs down would pave the way for success in the medium term. Perhaps with hindsight more importance should have been attached to the fact that the vagaries of the French electoral system would give Barre only three more years before the presidential election would be due.

By April 1981, shortly before the election, it was possible to see the Barre record over the period of four and a half years as very mixed. The success rate in holding down the growth in the money supply was poor: for 1979 the target of 10 per cent resulted in an out-turn of 14.3 per cent. Not that the target had, in any event, been set as monetarist doctrine would require, i.e. in relation to the growth of real output: it had simply been set a couple of percentage points below what was likely to happen otherwise.[18] Unemployment rose steadily over the period to reach 1.6 million, showed no sign of having peaked and was forecast to reach 2.5 million by 1985; inflation had obstinately refused to fall, stabilising at around 10 per cent. It must be remembered, however, that the shortage of domestic energy resources was a more acute problem for France than for most of her competitors. Further, since France had survived this period with an average economic growth of 3 per cent each year, and had records for both unemployment and inflation which were very much better than those of the UK, Barre could claim considerable credit for the overall achievement. Industrial competitiveness and export performance are both slower to respond to change and more difficult to measure, but did show significant signs of improvement over this period, as in the examples cited by Blake:

> Public spending is being used aggressively to boost industries such as telematics, the word the French have invented to describe the cross-breeding of computers and telecommunications. Huge investment in nuclear power is pressing ahead to cut down the country's dependence on imported oil, thus making the economy less vulnerable in future.[19]

As the latter quotation implies, it is by no means easy to assess the standpoint of Barre from the point of view of economic doctrine. Despite his adopting a more monetarist approach than his predecessors, as mentioned above, it would be a misleading over-simplification to view him in purely monetarist terms. Barre saw himself as a threefold combination, part monetarist, part classical economist and part Keynesian, and he considered that elements of all three approaches were to be found in the policies espoused by his government: he was a monetarist in that he sought to control the money supply, as mentioned above, a classical economist in his advocacy of free wage bargaining and a Keynesian in his willingness to vary, for example, social security payments and levels of investment of public-sector firms in the light of the overall needs of the economy. Thus by early 1981, in the months before the elections in which it was voted out of office, the Barre government was running a budget surplus as one means of curbing inflation.

It has also tended to be overlooked that in some areas of economic policy Barre advocated strong, almost *dirigiste*, government action, hardly an approach likely to appeal to economists of purely monetarist persuasion. Thus in a speech introducing the 8th Plan, Barre confessed that his anti-inflation measures had not been successful but attributed the reason for this to the entrenched network of protective measures, restrictive practices and general lack of free competition. His government had proposed strong action to curb the latter, but had been unable to secure the approval of members of parliament, on whom, Barre stated, the responsibility for failing to bring inflation under control must therefore rest. In a quite different sphere, however, Barre was in favour of the continuance of an artificial market situation, namely the rationing and allocation of credit, believing this to be beneficial to the path of economic growth as provided for in the Plan.

Barre has also not been given adequate credit for his success, despite the reservations of President Giscard d'Estaing, in persuading the trade unions, and especially the CFDT, to resume participation in various negotiations with the government and particularly in the planning process at the time of the elaboration of Plan 8.[20]

The Socialists in Power

In the event the pluses indicated above did not weigh with the electorate as heavily as the minuses in an election, or rather a series of elections, in 1981 which, it could hardly be doubted, were dominated by economic events. The sweeping to power of President Mitterrand, with an absolute socialist majority in the French parliament, was always a predictable reaction from a nation which after some thirty years of economic success found it doubly difficult to adjust to notions of economic crisis. It was soon clear that for the new regime economic policy would be directed towards the achievement of social goals such as the reduction of inequalities in society and the elimination of mass unemployment. Tax increases for the rich, rises in public expenditure for social purposes and an increase in the national minimum wage were all announced after the new regime came to power and are detailed elsewhere in this book (see Chapters 1 and 9).

President Mitterrand himself is on record as saying that he has never been very interested in economics and for him one economic policy is much like another. It is therefore rather paradoxical that, immediately after assuming office, he announced that reducing the level of unemployment must be one of the major aims, if not the major aim, of his administration and that the combined effect of his various early policy measures was 'his attempt at Keynesian reflation'.[21] At the same time initial reaction was that, on the economic front, they were considerably more moderate than had been feared.[22]

Soon after the elections of May-June 1981 it became clear that the socialist government was determined on economic expansion at the expense of deficits on both the government's budget and, if necessary, the balance of payments; with the aid of specific measures aimed at encouraging exports and curbing imports, however, it was hoped that any balance of payments deficit would be limited in amount or temporary or, preferably, both. By the end of 1981 the combined effects of the fiscal and monetary expansion and the devaluation of the franc in October had made the hoped-for increase in real output without inflation look rather doubtful. In the words of one end-of-year commentary:

> Reflation in isolation was a deliberate gamble, in defiance of the monetarist attitudes in Germany, Britain, and the United States. As the year ended, production had picked up without a spurt in inflation, but most of this was replenishing run down stocks, not the new investment on which success will ultimately depend.[23]

By late 1981 it was also apparent that widely differing attitudes to macro-economic policy existed within the government with, broadly, the President and the more left-wing Ministers urging optimism and continued expansion whilst more cautious Ministers, labelled as moderates or on the Social Democrat wing of the Socialist Party, were insisting that deflation and restraint were needed if the country was to avoid further devaluations during 1982.

Policy Instruments

The above look at the development of macro-economic policy, with emphasis on the more recent years, was necessary for an understanding of the context in which detailed policy measures have to be considered. Similarly, an examination of the detailed instruments of policy, and how these have evolved, is also required.

Monetary Policy

As stated previously, the emphasis during most of the post-war period, throughout the successive policy developments as outlined above, was on the use of monetary control instruments, which cannot be adequately studied without some understanding of the details of the French financial system.

As mentioned in Chapter 2, and as the writer has described in detail elsewhere, the government owns or controls much of the financial sector including many companies operating in the banking, financial and insurance markets in France and generally exercises overriding control throughout the financial sector. At the centre of the system is the Bank of France, which operates much like any other central bank such as the Bank of England. Although it is not formally liable to act as lender of last resort to the commercial banks, it has in fact accommodated the banks in the traditional way, with the obvious motive of ensuring stability in the banking sector.[24] Theoretically the National Credit Council and the Banking Control Commission share with the Bank of France in central control functions, but in practice the responsibility rests with the Bank. In the country's financial structure deposit-taking institutions, including the deposit banks and the postal giro system, occupy a dominant position due to the reluctance of the French public to invest in longer-term contractual savings agreements such as life assurance. Until recent years the deposit-taking institutions played only a minor role in the provision of funds for lending, since most of their assets were channelled to the Caisse des Dépôts et Consignations (the very large central financial institution nominally independent but effectively controlled by the Ministry of Finance), most credit being provided by the longer-term credit institutions. Over the last decade or so this position has gradually changed, with increased participation by the deposit banks. A separate category of investment banks still exists, but after reforms in 1966 the distinctions between these and the deposit banks lessened significantly and many of the former decided to change their status to the latter. Deposit banks now account for more than 90 per cent of the liabilities of all registered banks to the non-financial sector, and of these over half of the business is in the hands of the three largest, which are nationalised institutions, the Banque Nationale de Paris (the largest bank in France), the Crédit Lyonnais and the Société Générale.[25]

The control ratios applied to French banks have for some years distinguished clearly between prudential controls and monetary and credit controls, a distinction that was introduced in the UK only with the reforms of the 1980s. The monetary and credit control ratios applying currently are:

(i)   reserve requirement: 2 per cent of resident sight deposits plus ½ per cent of most loans, to be deposited with the Bank of France;

(ii) supplementary reserve requirement: supplementary balance with the Bank of France required if loans grow by more than the permitted rate (which is varied from time to time) over a specified period;

(iii) portfolio ratio: at least 7 per cent of deposits to be held in non-liquid assets (medium-term loans and bond holdings);

(iv) other specific ratios for such areas as hire-purchase credit and leasing operations (each 10 times capital and reserves) and property guarantees (20 times). On the prudential side detailed and frankly onerous official intervention and control is endemic throughout the financial system: to cite one example, the government exercises minute control over the wording of insurance policies and the rates of premium charged and requires the insurance companies to lodge complex 'technical reserves' with the Caisse des Dépôts: that none of these controls exist in the UK is a constant source of wonder to their French counterparts. A recent report from a non-controversial source said the controls applied to banks were 'cumbersome and complex and impair the operational flexibility of banks'.[26]

To revert to the mainstream of this section, monetary policy has made extensive use of the banking sector, as in most other comparable countries, to control the availability of credit and thus both the level of aggregate demand in the economy and the allocation of credit for specific purposes. In this connection it is necessary to understand that a major difference between monetary policy in France and that in other comparable countries such as the UK relates to the way in which monetary policy, in the controlling of aggregate demand sense, has been subordinate to a selective credit policy, throughout the period since 1945.[27] This credit policy has been designed to channel funds available for credit towards those objectives to which priority was given in the current Plan. The dominant institution in this process is the Caisse des Dépôts, which channels savings from all the main savings institutions, postal giro and other sources, much of the total passing via 'the Treasury Circuit' to selected borrowers on preferential conditions and at low rates of interest. Monetary policy in the conventional sense has also been circumscribed by economic policy decisions to:

(a) keep interest rates low; and
(b) permit relatively high rates of inflation, again both designed to
     assist with the achievements of the investment and other targets
     designated in the plan. Similarly, access to the capital market,
     for example for major new share issues, is controlled with the
     same objectives in view.

More importance has, therefore, been attached to the allocation of
credit than to control of its total volume, but this should not obscure
the fact that France has undoubtedly had an active monetary policy
(as distinct from credit policy) throughout the post-war years and that
monetary instruments have certainly played a more important role than
fiscal or other instruments. Only in more recent years, and especially
under the Barre administration, was there a trend towards allowing
market mechanisms to achieve the desired ends with less direct intervention by the authorities. The big three nationalised (prior to 1981)
banks are subject to the same controls as all the other deposit banks
and do not enjoy any special privileges. Controls on interest rates still
exist, but have been applied less rigidly since the liberalising reforms of
1966; before that date even the opening of a new branch of a bank had
to be approved by the authorities. Whether the further bank nationalisations announced by the Mitterrand government in 1981 will significantly
affect the above is not yet known.

Monetary policy has been through a succession of phases designated
by the authorities by such labels as 'liberal', 'restrictive', 'neutral' or
'expansionist',[28] with durations varying from less than two to over four
years. Variations have been effected via the following instruments.

(i)   Changes in interest rates are used, the Bank of France having
       jurisdiction over the rate of re-discounting, to which other
       rates are closely related in the normal way. Here it is important
       to remember that since the French financial sector has never
       been so exposed to external influences as has that of the UK,
       the French authorities have always retained control over their
       domestic rates of interest, as opposed to those in the UK which
       for most of the post-war period have been determined or in-
       fluenced by international events.
(ii)   Direct limits on bank lending: throughout the 1960s credit
       ceilings were in operation, but by the early 1970s these had

been replaced by the system of supplementary reserve requirements on excessive growth in lending, as already described, closely analogous to the 'corset' in the UK. Whereas, however, the latter led to 'disintermediation' or the growth of equivalent credit outside the main clearing banks and was thus ineffective in curbing aggregate demand in an inflationary situation, in France this does not seem to have occurred and the prevention of credit growth was achieved,[29] presumably because subsidiary financial markets are less well developed in France.

(iii)   Selective credit controls: the authorities have long been anxious to encourage the expansion of bank finance in such areas as housing and aid for exports, and have applied specific limits to more speculative types of lending.

(iv)   Open market operations: these have been widely used to restrict bank lending via the level of bank liquidity and working of the control ratios, primarily through operations in the short-term money market; these have become of rather less importance over the last decade or so, due to the effectiveness of (ii) above.

(v)   Variations in the control ratios: the control ratios have been varied from time to time, the effect of an increase being to require the banks to maintain a larger percentage of their funds with the Bank of France, much like the system of special deposits (not to be confused with the quite separate supplementary deposits) in the UK.

(vi)   Money supply: official accounts of the successive stages of monetary policy[30] include references to the rate of growth of the money supply from 1970 onwards and, as indicated above, during the years of the Barre regime this became the main target variable of monetary policy, with a perceptible relaxation after the election of President Mitterrand in 1981. The pursuit of a monetarist philosophy involved combining attempted rigour in the central government's accounts with the selective use of most of the instruments enumerated under (i) to (v) above.

(vii)   Strict control of international capital flows have applied continuously throughout the years since 1945, justified initially by the needs of the credit allocation policy and latterly by the effects on the growth of the money supply (using the wider definition, equivalent to the UK's 'domestic credit expansion').

(viii)   Control of hire-purchase credit: much as in the UK, controls on the terms of hire-purchase credit agreements, specifying the minimum percentage initial cash payment and the maximum period of the loan, have applied and have been varied from time to time.[31] Their relative importance has been rather greater in France than in the UK, since alternative sources of finance are available rather less easily.

Fiscal policy for short-term stabilisation purposes has always played a role subsidiary and supportive to monetary policy, broadly the reverse of the experience in the UK. Reference has already been made above to the trend towards a Keynesian-type approach which by the 1970s came to involve variations in both taxes and public expenditure for demand management purposes. Both faced difficulties: the former with income taxes so low and with an unwillingness to see frequent variations in the main expenditure tax, VAT, and the latter with virtually all public expenditure being predetermined in the plan. The central government's budget was also used for specific allocative purposes which were not always in harmony with the requirements of general macro-economic policy. An earlier study of the use of fiscal policy for stabilisation purposes found that whilst there had been such intervention occasionally from quite early on in the post-war period, perhaps even as early as the mid-1950s, throughout whenever there was a budget deficit the main concern of the Ministry of Finance was always over the monetary aspects of financing the deficit. An attempt at an econometric calculation of the extent to which the expansionary effects of the budget cycles were correlated with the economy's growth rate cycles found only a weak relationship.[32] This result seems hardly surprising, since the budget has been rather little used for that purpose.

Before the lifting of controls on most industrial prices by the Barre regime, as outlined above, an extensive system of price controls had existed in France for many years, partly to serve as explicit restraints on rates of price increases and partly to act as implicit control on wage and salary rises. In the earlier years of the post-war period attempts at formulating specific guidelines for wage increases met with little success, hence the recourse to implicit restraint via price control policy.[33] Direct price controls applied to the broad mass of industrial products as well as to more specific categories such as agricultural products and nationalised industries' prices. Under both Plan 5 and Plan 6 attempts were made to negotiate a system of relating permission to raise prices to productivity agreements and to the more direct involvement of workers in the management of firms but, partly due to the weakness of and divisions within the trade union movement (as discussed in detail in Chapter 4), such negotiations largely came to nought. They did, however, pave the way for a new phase of macro-economic policy which on the face of it (and perhaps more in theory than in practice) was almost unique in comparable countries in recent years.

The Contractual Approach

Widely seen as one of the most significant innovations in the field of economic policy in recent years, the 'contractual' approach to relationships between the government and other parties in the economy developed in the mid-1960s and continued to be of significance until the mid-1970s.

The notion was developed of a 'contract' — usually a formal written document — between major participants in the French economy with in each case the government as the leading and usually the dominant partner. A report by one of the leading French economic journals on this development saw the contracts as 'a major transformation of capitalism',[34] but although there were some grounds for such optimism it was also possible to take a more sceptical view.[35] The objective of the 'contract' was to set out the rights and obligations for both, or all, the parties concerned, usually on the basis of a compromise agreement incorporating concessions by both sides.

The first such initiative came in 1965 with two series of contracts, both of which related (as also did most of the subsequent ones) to the government's concern over the current rate of inflation and the need to reduce the rates of price and wage increases: 'Contrats de stabilité' (contracts for stability) were concluded with private-sector firms and employers' organisations and replaced the previous near total strict control of prices by a somewhat more flexible system under which firms could raise prices of some products if they compensated by lowering prices of other products. At the same time 'contrats de progrès' (progress contracts) were negotiated for the public sector between the government (also in this case acting as employer) and the relevant trade unions, essentially to control the rate of wage increases: the latter could not exceed the current rate of inflation unless they were financed via improvements in productivity. By the following year, 1966, the above had given way to two new series: first, 'contrats de programme' (programming contracts), which covered not only prices but also investment, productivity, relocation and professional training: price increases were only granted if the firms concerned gave certain undertakings under these other headings; these contracts eventually covered the whole of industrial production. Second, 'programmes d'action concertée' (programmes for concerted action), essentially plans for the radical modernisation and reorganisation of France's older and often out-of-date industries through joint action by the government and by the firms concerned, commenced with the iron and steel industry and subsequently spread to engineering, furniture-making and even electronics. The programmes included such measures as closing down or converting old factories, the redeployment or retraining of personnel and the provision of cash grants by the government.

By 1969 a new type of 'contrats de programme' was concluded with the major nationalised industries, with the objective of giving the latter greater financial responsibility: each industry was to aim at a minimum of financial self-sufficiency unless exceptionally it was agreed that some specific service should be run at a loss for social or other reasons; tariffs were to be raised, sharply in some cases, to cover at least current running costs and part of capital costs and detailed statements were made regarding investment, profitability, productivity and loans. Each contract was for a period of four or five years, after which it would be revised and renewed. Two years later 'contrats anti-hausse' (contracts against inflationary increases) embodied direct and strict price controls in the wake of what was seen at the time as an escalation of inflation: price increases for manufactured goods were to be limited to 1.5 per cent for the ensuing half-year, no price increases at all were to be permitted for services and in exchange, as it were, the government undertook to hold down those public-sector charges bearing directly on firms' costs.

The following year, 1972, under the label 'programmation annuelle' (annual programming), the above 'contracts' (if that is what they were) were reinforced and extended to cover most medium- and large-size firms, and also to permit price increases to cover rises in the costs of raw materials. Finally, in 1974, these were further tightened under the designation 'accords de programmation annuelle controlée' (agreements for controlled annual programming) when, *inter alia*, a 100 per cent tax was proposed on any increase in profits as a result of inflation. As the writer has commented elsewhere, 'the veneer of a contractual agreement had by now worn rather thin':[36] by 1974 there could be little pretence that this so-called 'contractual approach' to economic policy was anything more than the direct imposition of a price control policy by the government. That this was implicitly admitted by the government was clear from the fact that they made no attempt to continue the approach after that date. There had therefore been a fairly clear development over the period of ten years, from being perhaps initially a genuine effort to evolve a partnership approach based on mutual concessions and advantages to a situation in the 1970s in which the gathering storm of the successive oil crises and their repercussions throughout the world's major economies overtook all such domestic events.

The Unemployment Statistics

There have been frequent references in the above sections to problems arising from the inadequacy of the French statistics relating to unemployment: unfortunately an adequate and reliable statistical record of unemployment does not exist in France and there is no one statistical series which can be taken as a sufficient indicator of the unemployment situation. Unemployment statistics do, of course, present difficulties in other countries but at least one can usually think of any deficiencies as being fairly consistent over time; even this has not been so in France. The number of people unemployed may be indicated in the following ways:

(i)   Some are in receipt of financial aid from the state or from semi-public bodies such as ASSEDIC (but there is a considerable problem of overlap since in November 1974 59 per cent of those receiving state aid from ASSEDIC also received direct aid from the state).

(ii) Others, registered with the Agence Nationale pour l'Emploi, are summed in the 'Demandes d'Emplois en fin de Mois' (DEFM). These statistics are readily available, since they are published each month by the Ministry of Work and are therefore widely used. Only during the 1970s, however, has the Agence Nationale pour l'Emploi opened regional offices throughout France so that its statistics began fully to reflect the true national situation. As one authoritative survey put it: 'A few years ago these figures were much criticised since the offices of the Agence did not extend to many geographical areas. Today this is no longer the case since the Agence has opened many more offices, and many more people now register.'[37]

(iii) Survey enquiries are held via annual interviews of a sample of the population, in which people declare whether they are seeking a job, the resulting statistics being termed 'Population Disponible à la recherche d'emploi' (PDRE). Similarly, the 'Population

Marginale Disponible à la recherche d'un emploi' (PMDRE) includes 'Marginal' cases such as those seeking part-time work and
those who say they seek work but in fact have taken no steps to
obtain a job.

Some indication of the state of confusion may be gained from the
following figures for March 1974:

Recipients of state unemployment aid	150,000
Recipients of ASSEDIC aid	156,500
DEFM	438,900
PDRE	440,400
PDRE and PMDRE (often termed 'chomeurs' − the unemployed)	781,800

An official study[38] of the relationship between the above statistical
series found that PDRE was usually greater than DEFM, with a fairly
stable ratio over time of 1.6, due largely to the fact that certain people,
especially women and young workers, do not register with the Agency:
the ratio became distorted, however, because during times of high unemployment a greater proportion of those out of work do register,
whereas some of those included in DEFM are omitted from PDRE, for
example if the sample survey misses them. A breakdown of the DEFM
figure of 438,900 quoted above shows some 277,000 included in
PDRE, 63,000 included in PMDRE, and some 99,000 not included in
either, largely people who have obtained a job and not told the Agency.
One measure of total unemployment is 'PDRE + 50 per cent of DEFM',
which gives some idea of the degree of approximation involved. In his
excellent short book on unemployment in France, J.M. Fahy[39] concluded that 'the various measures in use gave, for December 1974,
figures varying from 195,700 (ASSEDIC) to 1,100,000 ('PDRE + 50%
of DEFM') without it being possible to say where the correct figure
really lies.' Most authorities agree that this problem has gradually lessened since the mid-1970s as, in particular, the two main statistical series,
PDRE and DEFM, have moved much closer together. Unemployment is
now a major problem in France as in other countries: the total of unemployed rose steeply in the early 1970s, although there is even doubt
about the size of this rise since the increases in the published figures coincided with the opening of the Agency's regional offices; it had reached
some 2.1m by early 1982 and seemed likely to fall only slowly, if at
all, for some years to come. The direct effect on government macro-

economic policy could scarcely be doubted even before the elections of May-June 1981. The high priority given to unemployment by the Mitterrand government since that date has already been referred to above.

Macro-economic Policy for 1982

The socialist government's macro-economic policy for 1982 was set out in the 'Financial and Economic Report' which accompanied the 1982 budget, submitted to parliament in late 1981.[40] The background situation was described as being one in which France's productive capacities were not being fully utilised, there was large-scale unemployment, and the index of industrial production for the latest twelve months for which statistics were available showed a worse trend for France than for any other comparable country except the UK, as indicated in Table 6.1.

Table 6.1: Index of Industrial Production, 1980-1

Country	1980 (1st Half-year)	1981 (1st Half-year)
West Germany	118	117
Italy	134	130
UK	110	102
USA	126	129
Japan	142.5	144.5
France	118	112

Source: OECD.

The index for France had fallen by six points, a drop exceeded only by the UK.

With a working population increasing steadily by some 200,000 per year, some considerable expansion would be required merely to prevent the unemployment total reaching even higher levels. At the same time high priority must be given to reducing the level of inflation, even though the target rate of growth of the money supply of 10 per cent prescribed by the previous regime must now be seen as 'unrealistic'. Direct action would also be necessary to control both prices and wages (it was the latter reference that was to incur the wrath of the trade unions). As a stimulus to economic activity the government's budget deficit would be planned to rise to some 2.3 per cent of Gross Domestic Product, an unprecedented event in post-war France, although it was hoped to mitigate any harmful effects of this deficit by simultaneously reducing interest rates. Critics pointed out that the 'mitigation' indicated here must refer to the cost to public funds; from the point of view of the effect on inflation, presumably lower interest rates and a massive budget deficit would both work in the same direction.

By July 1982 family allowances would have increased by some 50 per cent since the government took office, the minimum state old-age pension would be raised to 2,000 frs. per month from 1 January 1982 and other social security benefits would have similar increases. Increased public expenditure, particularly relating to investment, would also contribute to the expected budget deficit, which would, however, be offset somewhat by higher taxes applying to the more wealthy members of society. Total budgetary expenditure forecast for 1982 showed an increase of 27.6 per cent on the forecast for 1981 and some forms of aid to industry were more than doubled.

The reference to the balance of payments appeared to have been deliberately worded as to be so vague that it would be capable of more than one interpretation: 'the deficit on the current account of the balance of payments will be a smaller percentage of the Gross Domestic Product in 1982 than it was in 1981.' It was hoped to hold the increase in the index of consumer prices to 12.9 per cent for 1982, compared to a forecast 13.5 per cent for 1981.

For all the above reasons the 1982 budget can lay claim to being one of the most exceptional, perhaps the most exceptional, of the post-war period from a number of points of view. It undoubtedly marks a major turning-point in France's macro-economic policy, in line with the earlier pronouncements of socialist Ministers since the 1981 elections. How the economy responds over the coming months, and to what extent the potential problems can be kept under control, will be of considerable interest.

Notes

1. J.R. Hough, 'French Economic Policy', *National Westminster Bank Review* (May 1976).
2. A. De Lattre, *Politique Economique de la France, Les Cours de Droit* (Paris, 1972).
3. 'L'Impôt au service de la politique conjoncturelle', *Statistiques et Etudes Financières*, supplément (April 1968).
4. H. Brochier, 'Les Instruments Fiscaux de la Politique Conjoncturelle' (Fiscal Instruments of Stabilisation Policy), *Statistiques et Etudes Financières* (April 1968).

5. C. Goux, 'L'Impôt sur la consommation est-il un instrument efficace de politique conjoncturelle?' (Is the tax on consumption an efficient instrument of stabilisation policy?), *Statistiques et Etudes Financières* (April 1968).

6. Yves Fréville, 'L'Imposition des revenus des Ménages et la Conjoncture' (The tax on households' incomes and stabilisation policy), *Statistiques et Etudes Financières* (April 1968).

7. e.g. J.C.R. Dow, *The Management of the British Economy 1945-60* (Cambridge University Press, rev. edn, 1970).

8. *Les Cahiers Français* (Mar.-Apr. 1976).

9. De Lattre, *Politique Economique de la France*.

10. P. Coffey, *The Social Economy of France* (Macmillan, 1972).

11. P. Maillet, *Réponses Nationales à la Crise: France* (Cahiers de Bruges, NS 35, 1978).

12. European Communities Commission, *The Trend of Public Finance in Member States* (Econ. and Fin. Series No. 11, Brussels, Jan. 1976).

13. B. Hansen, *Fiscal Policy in Seven Countries* (OECD, 1969).

14. 'The Barre Plan – Freeing the Economy', *Barclays Bank Review* (Feb. 1980).

15. D. Blake, 'French economic policy under test', *The Times*, 6 Apr. 1981.

16. R. Mauthner, 'Barre's prescription for an ailing economy', *Financial Times*, 27 Apr. 1978.

17. Mauthner, 'Barre's prescription for an ailing economy'.

18. Blake, 'French economic policy under test'.

19. Ibid.

20. The whole of this section has greatly benefited from an extended discussion the writer had with Mr J.P. Milleron of INSEE in Paris in December 1981.

21. W. Schwarz, 'Can Mr. Mitterrand keep his state of grace?', *Guardian*, 7 Sept. 1981.

22. C. Hargrove, 'The moderate radical in charge of the French economy', *The Times*, 24 June 1981.

23. W. Schwarz, 'Mitterrand's Socialists seize De Gaulle's Fifth Republic', *Guardian*, 31 Dec. 1981.

24. D. Vittas, *Banking Systems Abroad* (Inter-Bank Research Organization, 1978).

25. Vittas, *Banking Systems Abroad*.

26. Ibid., p. 122.

27. D.R. Hodgman, *National Monetary Policies and International Monetary Co-operation* (Little, Brown, 1974).

28. 'La Politique Monétaire en France', *Notes et Etudes Documentaires*, nos. 4214/5, 16 Sept. 1975.

29. Vittas, *Banking Systems Abroad*.

30. 'La Politique Monétaire en France', *Notes et Etudes Documentaires*, nos. 4214/5, 16 Sept. 1975.

31. 'France: Monetary Policy' in *Monetary Policy in the Countries of the EEC, OECD* (European Communities Monetary Committee, 1972).

32. Hansen, *Fiscal Policy in Seven Countries*.

33. L. Ulman and R. Flanagan, *Wage Restraint* (University of California Press, 1971).

34. *Les Cahiers Français* (Mar.-Apr. 1977).

35. J.R. Hough, 'Government Intervention in the Economy of France' in W.P. Maunder (ed.), *Government Intervention in the Developed Economy* (Croom Helm, 1979).

36. Hough, 'Government Intervention in the Economy of France'.

37. *Le Nouvel Observateur* (Faits et Chiffres, 1975).

38. *Economie et Statistique* (1975).

39. J.M. Fahy, *Le Chômage en France* ('Que Sais-Je?' series, Presses Universitaires de France).

40. *Statistiques et Etudes Financières*, nos. 383-4 (Oct.-Nov. 1981).

7 REGIONAL ECONOMIC POLICY

Within the national economy the problem of regional imbalance has been acute for at least the last fifty years and in origin goes back to the nineteenth century or even earlier. As the industrial and commercial life of the country progressed, much of the development took place in or around an approximate triangle extending from Paris north-eastwards towards Lille and the coast and eastwards towards Alsace and Lorraine, and there were further important pockets of prosperity in the Rhone-Alps region, around Lyons, and along the Mediterranean coast eastwards from Marseilles. Approximately, therefore, a line drawn from the Paris to the Marseilles regions would divide France into a prosperous eastern half, which contained most of the country's industrial and commercial centres, and a western half which was typified by Professor Gravier in his phrase 'Le désert français'.[1]

There can be little doubt that during the course of the twentieth century the problem of regional imbalance steadily worsened until at least the 1960s, and in some respects more recently still. From about 1960 the traditional problem of the underdevelopment of the western and south-western parts of France has had to be set alongside the much newer and in some ways even more intractable problem of regional decay in those areas, especially in the north-east corner of the country, heavily dependent on industries now in decline, especially coal, steel, shipbuilding and textiles.

The Regions

The Paris region is much the most prosperous area of France, however this is measured. The capital and its peripheries contain the most important markets and the most significant supply of labour and as a consequence have had an undue concentration of population and economic activity.[2] The inexorable growth of the capital needed to be slowed down or even reversed if some of the worst aspects of over-concentration were to be avoided. The outer parts of the Paris basin, such as Champagne and the area around Orléans (known as the Centre region) were formerly noted as particularly suffering on account of the attractions of the capital[3] itself but, as will be seen below, this position has substantially been reversed in recent years.

The Nord region around Lille was historically one of the more prosperous regions due to its heavy industries: the presence of seams of coal
and iron ore and proximity to markets in Belgium and Germany acted
as a natural magnet for industrial development. More recently, the continued decline of the region's main industries, including textiles, has led
to decline and decay. With a generally aged social infrastructure the
region seems to have few attractions for potential employers and there
is every indication that the region's acute problems may take many
years to overcome.

Approximately due eastwards from Paris and close to the German
border lie the regions of Alsace and Lorraine, which are usually for
convenience considered together although, as will be seen, there are
important differences between them: a heavily industrialised region
with again heavy dependency on iron and steel, coal and textiles. Inevitably, therefore, the area has shared some of the problems experienced
by the Nord region, although generally to a lesser extent. There has
certainly been industrial decline, but abundant seams of both coal and
iron ore remain much richer than those further north. Strasburg is an
extremely prosperous centre, with its share in the affluent incomes and
expenses generated by the European Parliament.

Travelling south-westwards from Strasburg would bring one to the
Rhone-Alps region, around Lyons and Grenoble, which is now second
only to Paris in prosperity. Its natural resources, attractive climate,
excellent communications and proximity to the affluent markets of
Switzerland all combine to make this an extremely attractive location
for prospective employers. Light industries predominate. Outside the
towns there is a very successful agricultural sector.

Further south lies the Mediterranean coastline, neatly divided into
two by Marseilles: to the east of this local capital lies the famed French
Riviera, successful not only as one of the most attractive tourist locations in the world but also a magnet for American and other foreign
companies seeking to locate offices in France. West of Marseilles lies
the Languedoc area, which traditionally was one of the poorest regions
in France, but which has been transformed in the last twenty years by
substantial industrial development and by an increasingly successful
tourist sector.

Languedoc has to its north the regions of Auvergne (around Clermont-
Ferrand) and Limousin (around Limoges) and to its west Midi-Pyrenées
and Aquitaine, all of which have much in common as poor and problematic areas. The difficult terrain and harsh climate of the Massif Central

were in the past relieved by successful industrial centres at Clermont-Ferrand, Limoges and Decajeville, but these too now have the problems of severely declining industries. The south-west corner of France gives the impression, still, of being almost untouched by economic development save for the very successful aerospace industry at Toulouse, the development of the natural gas deposits at Lacq-Pau (although whether the latter have brought much benefit to the local region is a moot point) and the thriving port of Bordeaux. Even agriculture has been only moderately successful. For some years hopes have been expressed that Spain's entry into the European Common Market would lead to a trade boom in this south-west corner of France, but to date these show little hopes of being realised.

Further north from Bordeaux the 'desert' continues all the way to the Brittany peninsula: the latter and its environs, traditionally dependent on a rather low-quality agriculture and with rather little industry, have attracted much attention. More recently there has been some spectacular progress[4] in attracting industry to the region, sometimes on a very large scale.

The Problem

Whilst it is easy enough to present such a Cook's tour of the major regions of France, it is very much more difficult to specify exactly what is the nature of the country's regional economic problem. The UK has had regional problems of its own and, although doubtless varied and complex in nature, these have always been presented primarily in terms of high local rates of unemployment. In percentage terms unemployment has always been high in, for example, the north-east of England or Scotland, and whenever national unemployment rates were rising local rates in such localities would rise even more rapidly. The focus of regional economic policy, therefore, has always been to reduce the local rates of unemployment.

In France the situation is quite different. As was shown in Chapter 6, French unemployment statistics have been very problematic and for some twenty years after 1945 they indicated, rightly or wrongly, that France had extremely low levels of unemployment. The prime focus of regional economic policy could not therefore be on a problem of local unemployment because, by and large, such a problem either did not exist or was thought not to exist. There were, of course, pockets of unemployment in various localities and there were some fears that

industrial changes might exacerbate these: it is certainly true that references to unemployment appeared in the official rhetoric relating to
regional economic policy.[5] For the essence of the regional economic
problem in France, however, we must look elsewhere.

We need, in fact, to consider the situation in which the regions in
question find themselves and how this is developing over time. For
broadly the whole of the western half of the country, this situation
may be summarised as follows: traditionally the principal source of
employment in the locality has been the agricultural sector, a sector
typified, as was shown in Chapter 3, by small-scale inefficient farms,
heavily reliant on a narrow range of products. Slowly, sometimes very
slowly, these have given way to larger, more mechanised and more
efficient units on which only a smaller labour force has been required.
At approximately the same time, young people, perhaps heavily influenced both by periods away from the region either whilst in higher
education or, in the case of the males, by compulsory military service,
and by the lack of a modern social infrastructure or other facilities in
the locality, have either sought to leave the countryside to seek employment in the larger towns in the region or left the region altogether to
move elsewhere, and especially to Paris. Since the available labour remaining in the area tended to be the older, less well educated and less
highly trained, there were few incentives for any prospective employer
to move in. The inevitable tendency could only be for the overall problem in the regions, as thus outlined, steadily to worsen. At the same
time the excessive concentration of both population and resources in
the Paris area became more and more acute.

From the above it will be apparent that the framing of precise objectives for regional economic policy is, in these circumstances, a matter
of some difficulty. If the policy objectives have not been clear, even
more problematic has been the question of attempting to verify whether
or not the policy is being successful: what statistical series would we
ideally need and are these available? Are the problems so complex that
no one, or more, series of statistics could hope to provide an answer?
This question will need to be dealt with, below, at some length.

The report on regional economic policy,[6] issued as part of the preparatory work for Plan 8, stated that the objectives of regional policy
could be summarised as 'the reduction of economic disparities' and
went on to suggest that such disparities manifested themselves primarily
via:

(i) demographic trends, with particular reference to the continued drift of population from rural to urban areas and especially towards the capital, Paris;

(ii) patterns of industrialisation, as indicated, for example, by the rates of creation of new jobs and, latterly, levels of unemployment, in each of the major regions of France;

(iii) standards of living, as evidenced by levels of income, patterns of household expenditure and distribution of consumer durables;

(iv) related matters such as transport, communications and education.

This summary retains the degree of complexity indicated above and does not aid the question of how to assess the results of regional policy. Nevertheless it is probably the clearest statement issued to date of what French regional policy is trying to achieve.

The Development of Policy

Hansen[7] traces interest in the general question of regional imbalance and the dominance of Paris as far back as 1724 and doubtless even earlier references could be found. Certainly by the mid-nineteenth century there could be no doubt that Paris had added overwhelming financial predominance to its existing position as the centre of political authority, culture, education and communications. Whereas in the UK official reports on the problems of the depressed areas were being published before 1939, in France no action of any note came until the 1947 study by Gravier, referred to above, which was produced independently of any government machinery. His detailed and dramatic account of the imbalances across France was largely responsible for alerting public opinion and paving the way for subsequent developments, even though these were to follow only slowly.

Professor Lajugié, writing in 1964, suggested that the development of regional policy could be broken down into three distinct phases:[8]

(i) 1945-54: emphasis on controls of development of certain regions rather than incentives to encourage expansion;

(ii) 1954-7: promotion of decentralisation of industry from Paris region; and

(iii) 1958 onwards: regional development set in context of policies aimed at increasing national economic growth.

Any such attempt to dichotomise an ongoing development of policy is inevitably arguable, and it is not difficult to point to individual policy measures which contradict the classification suggested above. Hansen points out,[9] for example, that the first major effort to control the implantation or extension of private industry in the Paris region did not come until 1955. Overlapping and sometimes conflicting strands of policy can be detected throughout the period, although Lajugié's scheme clearly conveys something of the flavour of the successive phases of regional policy and can be accepted as being useful in that sense. Chardonnet[10] suggests that from the outset the state was endeavouring to achieve a mix of objectives. Whatever the rights or wrongs of this particular debate, it clearly is of importance that, as Lajugié points out, it was not until 1954/5 that 'an endeavour was made to replace empirical and fragmentary efforts with a systematic and coherent policy involving much more considerable technical and financial means.'[11]

Some decentralisation from the Paris region to the south-west and Toulouse was aided by the government in the 1930s but, so far as can now be detected, purely for strategic reasons. Within the Ministry of National Economy a series of studies of regional problems was made over the years 1943 onwards but little, if anything, happened as a result. By 1950 the Ministry for Reconstruction and Housing produced a more general study of regional issues entitled, rather ambitiously, 'Pour un plan national d'aménagement du territoire', but again, since no legal or statutory powers existed, little happened. It was not until 1955 that the first official restrictions on industrial building in the Paris region were imposed.

Prior to this some limited financial assistance for firms wishing to decentralise — i.e. to remove all or part of their operations out of the Paris region — became available in 1950, through the establishment of a National Fund for Regional Development, but with strictly limited resources: some £370,000 in 1950, increased to some £740,000 in 1951, sums which were scarcely likely to have any noticeable effect on regional redistribution. A number of other minor measures followed during 1950-3, including some paper provisions which were never applied in practice.[12] Probably the only real effect was some contribution towards the awakening of public interest and paving the way for future developments.

These developments came from 1954 onwards with a series of legislative measures which, collectively,

   (i) enacted controls on the construction or extension of industrial (but not commercial) buildings in the Paris region; only where the firm could demonstrate strong need would dispensation be granted;

(ii) introduced investment grants for firms setting up establishments in certain Critical Zones or areas designated as being in need of assistance, mainly in the poorer regions of the west and south;

(iii) inaugurated a complex system of loans, interest subsidies, tax concessions and manpower training and mobility grants to firms decentralising from the Paris region to any other location in France, i.e. *not* restricted to the Critical Zones; and

(iv) divided the country into 22 planning regions, each embracing a number of France's administrative departments, from 1956, although it was not until 1964 that a Regional Development Commission was set up for each region.[13]

These and various other more minor provisions[14] were in force by 1957. In the ensuing years further measures followed apace as the need for regional policy to be treated with greater urgency became more and more apparent. From 1958 onwards much more detailed coverage of regional development policy was included in successive plans, as was shown in Chapter 5, and this gave at least the appearance of regional developments being projected well in advance, on a long-term basis. As part of this planning process some regionalisation of expenditure projections had been included in each central government budget since 1964.

A notable administrative move came in 1963 with the creation of DATAR (Délégation à l'aménagement du territoire et à l'action régionale) to co-ordinate regional economic policy, in face of the plethora of Ministries and other official bodies concerned with various aspects of regional policy.

Levels of Regional Aid

By 1974 regional policy provisions had developed into a complex schedule which in essence remained unchanged from that date until the change of government in 1981. It may be summarised[15] as follows.

A. Following the reforms of 1972 and 1973. A Prime de développement régional (regional development grant) replaced the previous grants: given for new factories or extensions which create employment, in whole of a Zone A, which includes the regions of the West, South-West, Centre and Corsica, the mining and iron-ore areas and the frontier regions of the North and North-East.

Other locations (provided they are outside the Paris and Lyons areas) may exceptionally receive regional development grants to aid particular problems.

The classification of Zone A was to be reviewed at the termination of each Plan.

Three zones with different rates (i.e. extensions of the previous zonal divisions):

(i) *Zone à taux maximum* (maximum rate zone): grants of 25 per cent (new factory) and 20 per cent (extension) — including most of the urban areas classified as 'priority' in 1964: Cherbourg, Brest, Lorient, Nantes-St Nazaire, La Rochelle, Rochefort; Bordeaux, Toulouse; Limoges, Brive; but with additions in South-West of Bayonne, Castres and Millau, and in Corsica the Ajaccio and Bastia areas; in North and North-East the coal and iron-ore areas, plus various other locations in Brittany and Nièvre.

(ii) *Zone à taux majoré* (higher rate zone): as before, 7 départements in the West: rates remain 15 per cent (for new factories), 12 per cent for extensions.

(iii) *Zone à taux normal* (normal rate zone) (12 per cent for new factories or extensions): corresponding to previous (iii) but with certain additions in North, North-East and Corsica.

B. A decree of 5 July 1974 added to the 'prime' (grant) a 'surprime' (additional grant) of 5 per cent which could even be doubled in exceptional circumstances: the financing of this additional grant comes from the *European Regional Development Fund*, created in 1975.

Grants are only given where the minimum investment is at least 300,000 frs. and the number of jobs created at least 30. They are calculated on the amount of the investment, but may not exceed 15,000 frs. per job created (for new factories) (12,000 frs. for extensions). Eventually the state takes back half the grant through the tax system, as and when the investment is amortised, since the grant is included in the calculation of the profits tax. The grant is normally automatic for investment up to 10 million frs.

C. In addition to grants, 3 other forms of aid from the State.

(i) Tax reductions, at varying rates, *given everywhere except in Lyons and Paris regions.*

(ii) Firms decentralising out of Paris can claim reimbursement of

60 per cent of their costs of relocation.

(iii) Aid for retraining of personnel, from the Fonds National de l'Emploi; also their removal and other expenses and for provision of housing.

D. In addition, local authorities may provide land cheaply for industrial sites or for housing. Where firms obtain loans from the Sociétés de Développement régional (SDR), the latter will frequently take a shareholding (not exceeding 35 per cent) in the firm: this in turn leads to further tax and other concessions. Certain other concessions to the regions, for example gas and electricity tariffs, were slightly lower for some firms in West until 1974. Since 1958 there has been a policy of concentrated 'industrial zonings', aided by loans from the FNAT (Fonds National d'Aménagement du Territoire), which was later renamed FNAFU (Fonds National d'Aménagement foncier et d'urbanisme), but its role was reduced after 1964. From 1972 the SCET (Société centrale pour l'équipement du Territoire) aids the locality to set up a mixed company to run the 'zoning'.

Also from 1972 a separate 'prime de localisation des activités tertiaires' was set up for the tertiary sector: given for all West, South-West and parts of North and North-East.

In November 1981 the socialist government announced major changes in the above system, with particular reference to the introduction of two new forms of regional aid plus certain other measures, to replace the system of incentives previously in force:[16]

(i) a Prime régionale à l'emploi (regional employment grant), which may be applied in rural areas or in urban areas with fewer than 100,000 inhabitants. It is up to the Regional Council for each region to determine the amounts, conditions and relevant sectors applying to such grants;

(ii) a Prime d'aménagement du territoire (regional policy grant), directly to replace, *inter alia*, the previous Prime de développement régional and Prime de localisation d'activités tertiaires. Grants will be made by each Regional Council with the aid of funds provided by the state. By early 1982 precise details of amounts and methods of financing had not been published, except for the statement that these grants would certainly total considerably more than their predecessors. Only in exceptional cases, such as very large investments exceeding 25 million frs.

(£2.5m), would decisions regarding grants be taken centrally by the Ministry in Paris.

In addition the following further measures were announced.

(i)   DATAR's total budget for regional policy measures, including the grants indicated above, would amount to 1,300 million frs. in 1982, an increase of some 55 per cent over 1981.

(ii) Local authorities were given additional powers to intervene in the economic activities in their areas in a variety of ways, such as by granting subsidies for new industrial buildings, up to specified ceilings.

(iii) For all public-sector organisations, no additional locations would be permitted in the Paris region and such organisations would be expected to be more active in transferring jobs to provincial locations.

(iv) Where personnel agreed to move to new locations, the grants available to them for moving members of their families and for rehousing were both improved.

(v)   The three regions in the South-West corner of France, which faced some of the most acute regional problems, were to benefit from a special fund of 300 million frs. (£30m), to be set up immediately.

(vi) The tertiary sector, the only sector of the economy where employment is currently expanding, is to receive special government attention from the point of view of the objectives of regional policy.

Taken together, these measures clearly represent a very considerable new regional initiative on the part of the socialist government which was perhaps only to be expected in view of its commitment to the 'decentralisation' of political and other power. Whilst the writer was in Paris in December 1981 a representative of DATAR emphasised to him that the new measures should be seen as a major turning-point in regional economic policy in France, whilst at the same time retaining a certain degree of continuity with the previous system. A noteworthy innovation is that levels of aid may in future be expected to vary very widely from one region to another. As with many other official pronouncements after the elections of May-June 1981, the key word used to describe the aim of the proposed changes was 'solidarity'. What the results of all these measures may be it is as yet too early to say.

The Planning Regions

The 22 planning regions are shown on Figure 7.1 and the larger zones for Regional Development Studies (ZEATs), the basis for the regional breakdown of budget statistics, are shown on Figure 7.2.

Figure 7.1: The 22 Planning Regions

—— Regional areas
LILLE **Regional capitals**
Amiens **Chief town of each region**
///// **Oream areas**

If there is one aspect of the development of policy, as summarised above, that has aroused more discussion and tension than any other, it is the designation of, and drawing of boundaries for, the 22 planning regions and the problem areas for financial incentives. The latter were designated in a rather *ad hoc* fashion and had to be varied as the result of political pressures.[17] Only gradually did more objective social and economic criteria, such as demographic trends and level of economic development, come into use. Similarly the planning regions were essentially a grouping of a number of administrative departments, dating from Napoleonic times. Not surprisingly, therefore, the boundaries of the new regions often ignored major economic developments, hinterlands of large cities or modern lines of communication, and they led to many disagreements between the competing administrative authorities within each region.

Figure 7.2: Zones for Regional Development Studies (ZEAT)

It must also be emphasised that regional policy measures were developed with reference solely to manufacturing industry and only as an afterthought, in the early 1970s, was a series of measures relating to the tertiary sector promulgated. This point is of considerable importance in view of the continued growth of tertiary-sector jobs in France and helps to explain the apparently continued growth of large office blocks in and around Paris, at least until the mid-1970s. Hull suggests that even by 1976 very few tertiary jobs had relocated with the aid of financial assistance from the French government and that the national pattern of tertiary-sector employment had remained largely unaffected. As in the UK, only very gradually did French policy move towards the concept of 'growth poles', i.e. the designation of specific localities (often 'black spots') within regions at which development would be concentrated, and even now this approach has not been taken very far.

For a fuller discussion of these and other questions relating to the ways in which policy developed, the interested reader should consult Allen and MacLennan or Hansen.

Assessment of Results

As might be inferred from the preceding pages, any assessment of the results of regional economic policy in France is extremely problematic. No single policy aim has ever been stated nor, given the complex mix of circumstances in the various regions, is it easy to see how any one such aim would have been possible; regional policy has been trying to achieve different objectives in different regions at different times. All of this is in marked contrast to the situation relating to regional economic policy in the UK, which has always been focused on the local rate of unemployment as the target variable of interest: broadly speaking, the success or otherwise of regional policy was assessed in terms of the variations in the local rate of unemployment as compared with the national rate.

In France, however, as was seen in some detail in Chapter 6, for much of the post-war period, including the years during which serious interest in the problems of the regions was developing, not only were the available national statistics recording unemployment at remarkably low levels, but also the statistics in question were very unsatisfactory. Apart, therefore, from isolated 'black spots' or localities where quite exceptional circumstances prevailed, local unemployment statistics were of rather little use for assessing regional policy results; only in the latter 1970s, with the sharp increase in the published unemployment statistics, may this situation have changed.

We therefore need to turn to other statistical series that seem relevant and useful. It must be emphasised, however, that, whatever may be the changes and trends that may be deduced from these various statistics, we are unable to attribute these directly to regional policy: we have no evidence of cause and effect and it is impossible to prove such a relationship. Indeed, as will be seen, for at least some of the trends we may infer just the opposite of the above, i.e. it may seem unlikely that they were caused or influenced by regional policy measures. We may therefore be confined to attempting some assessment of the amelioration or deterioration of the economic and social problems of the regions over time, quite divorced from any existing policy measures. At least, however, such an assessment may indicate whether increased policy measures may be required in the future to assist the regions in question, or whether some of the existing provisions and controls may be relaxed. We will revert to this aspect of the problem below.

Population Statistics

As already noted, a focus of considerable interest has been the large-scale movement of population within France, with particular reference to the drift of population from all of the remaining regions of France towards Paris. This population drift is not easy to measure and it is not recorded in any annual statistics; it can, however, be extracted from the periodic national census data. Censuses took place in 1954, 1962, 1968 and 1975, and from the information available for those years we may deduce the between-census trends with reasonable confidence even though the periods in question are not of equal duration. (No such information is yet available for the post-1975 period.) Inevitably such population drift needs to be considered in conjunction with the total rate of population increase or decrease from natural or other causes, and to some extent the existing population structure, in each region, for obvious reasons: concern over drift of population away from a particular region would obviously be mitigated if the region in question had a high rate of natural population increase.

Tables 7.1 and 7.2, therefore, need to be read in conjunction. They show, for the principal regions of interest from the point of view of regional policy, the census data statistics for total regional population and inter-regional migration flows, together with percentage calculations to assist in interpreting the figures. Figures for the remaining ten regions are available from the census data but have not been included here.

Table 7.1: Total Population by Region, 1954-75 (Selected regions only)

Selected Regions	Area (as percentage)	1954 Census (thousands)	Percentage Increase p.a., 1954-62	1962 Census (thousands)	Percentage Increase p.a., 1962-8	1968 Census (thousands)	Percentage Increase p.a., 1968-75	1975 Census (thousands)	As Percentage of France
Paris region (as percentage of France)	2.2	7,317 (17.1%)	1.97	8,470 (18.2%)	1.51	9,238 (18.6%)	0.97	9,863 (18.8%)	18.8
Centre	7.2	1,758	0.07	1,858	1.18	1,990	1.13	2,147	4.1
Nord	2.3	3,375	1.05	3,659	0.71	3,815	0.39	3,918	7.4
Lorraine	4.3	1,956	1.52	2,194	0.60	2,274	0.36	2,332	4.4
Alsace	1.5	1,218	1.02	1,318	1.18	1,412	1.04	1,515	2.9
Pays de la Loire	5.9	2,319	0.77	2,462	0.81	2,581	1.02	2,765	5.3
Bretagne	5.0	2,339	0.21	2,379	0.62	2,468	0.75	2,598	4.9
Aquitaine	7.6	2,209	0.58	2,312	1.07	2,460	0.50	2,546	4.8
Rhone-Alps	8.0	3,630	1.34	4,019	1.71	4,431	1.13	4,781	9.1
Auvergne	4.8	1,247	0.26	1,273	0.51	1,312	0.19	1,330	2.5
Provence-Cote d'Azur	5.8	2,415	2.06	2,813	2.81	3,288	1.64	3,665	7.0
France	100	42,780	1.06	46,414	1.18	49,698	0.82	52,541	100

Note: The percentage increases are simple averages.
Source: Census data (INSEE).

Table 7.2: Annual Net Migration Flows by Region, 1954-75 (Selected regions only)

Selected Regions	1954-62	(Number) 1962-8	1968-75	(As percentage of region's population at end of each period) 1954-62	1962-8	1968-75
Paris region	+88,788	+60,900	+12,514	+1.2	+0.7	+0.1
Centre	+ 2,550	+12,033	+12,486	+0.1	+0.6	+0.5
Nord	- 2,513	- 3,066	-15,928	-0.1	-0.1	-0.3
Lorraine	+ 6,313	-11,550	- 9,714	+0.3	-0.5	-0.4
Alsace	+ 3,213	+ 6,116	+ 6,529	+0.3	+0.5	+0.4
Pays de la Loire	- 5,250	- 1,817	+ 4,329	-0.2	-0.1	+0.1
Bretagne	- 8,425	- 2,083	+ 5,871	-0.4	-0.1	+0.2
Aquitaine	+ 5,563	+16,133	+ 6,414	+0.3	+0.7	+0.2
Rhone-Alps	+27,425	+37,417	+21,028	+0.7	+0.9	+0.4
Auvergne	- 188	+ 3,417	+ 14	-	+0.3	-
Provence-Cote d'Azur	+42,950	+65,033	+42,614	+1.7	+2.2	+1.2

Source: Census Data (INSEE).

The preponderance of the Paris region in both sets of statistics is emphasised by the first line in each table: the huge scale of the movement of population into the Paris region in the earliest part of the period is indicated by the figure of 88,788 per year, but the figures for the later periods show the very large decreases by the later years. Similarly, the rate of increase of the region's total population, initially 1.9 per cent per year, decreases steadily to 0.97 per cent per year; whereas for the 1954-62 period the Paris region had a rate of population increase which was greater than those for all other regions (including those not shown in the tables), with the exception of Provence-Cote d'Azur, and which was nearly twice the national average; by 1968-75 the Paris region's figure was very much closer to the national average and had been 'overtaken' by several other regions. However, as Table 7.1 shows, the percentage of the population of France in the Paris region (18.8 per cent) continues to increase, albeit at a slower rate, and the region's population rate of increase (0.97 per cent per year) was by the end of the period still in excess of the national average (0.82 per cent). Therefore, no simple conclusion that the problems of population imbalance in the Paris region have been overcome or are being overcome is possible and it will in fact be necessary to examine below more disaggregated statistics for the region.

The rates of population increase (Table 7.1) and the rates of population loss or gain through migration (Table 7.2) for the disadvantaged regions of France present considerable variations. For the two regions on or near the Brittany peninsula, Bretagne and Pays de la Loire, not only has the rate of population growth per year steadily increased over the period (from 0.21 per cent and 0.77 per cent to 0.75 per cent and 1.02 per cent), but also the net annual exodus of population over 1954-62 (-0.4 per cent and -0.2 per cent) was reduced to much lower rates by 1962-8 (-0.1 per cent and -0.1 per cent) and then converted into positive in-flows by 1968-75 (+0.2 per cent and +0.1 per cent). From the population point of view, therefore, the problems of the North-West corner of France greatly improved over the period as a whole. The same cannot be said of the South-West, represented by Aquitaine, but here the figures are much more difficult to interpret due to the influx of over 1 million French settlers returning from Algeria around 1962, many of whom settled in the southern regions of France, including Aquitaine: clearly this would have distorted the 1962 census figures. About all that can be said with any certainty is that the 'normal' rate of population increase, 0.58 per cent per year for 1954-62 and 0.50 per cent for 1968-75, showed a slow fall and the annual rate of migration moved from 0.3 per cent for 1954-62 to 0.2 per cent for 1968-75. The latter figures, however, again pose problems due to the considerable incidence of people of retirement age moving southwards, including into Aquitaine, from the more northerly parts of France, including the capital; the figures may therefore conceal the continued exodus of those in the younger age-groups on whom the future of the region must depend. Certainly Aquitaine continues to have the appearance of one of the least populated (and, as we shall see below, least affluent) parts of France, with only 4.8 per cent of the country's population in 7.6 per cent of the territorial area.

The same point regarding influx of people of retirement age applies even more forcefully to the Provence-Cote d'Azur region, which includes France's famed Mediterranean coastline east of Marseilles and its hinterland, and which has long been such a 'reception' area. This is why Table 7.1 shows the region as having higher rates of population growth than any other region shown (and they are in fact higher than in any other region in France) and around twice the national average. Similarly, in Table 7.2 the annual migration flows into the region have remained high throughout the period. This region is, of course, one of the most prosperous in France and seems certain to remain so, even though it is largely unaffected by regional policy measures. The Rhone-Alps region, centred on Lyons, the second-ranking metropolitan area of France, is also a prosperous region with, in Table 7.1, rates of population increase which are always high and which are consistently in excess of the national average. Similarly, migration into the region, attracted by the exceptionally good employment record and attractive working conditions, has always been at high levels, as shown in Table 7.2: by the 1968-75 period more people were being attracted into this region than to the capital.

The Centre region, just to the south-west of the Paris region, has benefited considerably from firms and their work-force moving ('decentralising') out of Paris, and this is recorded, especially for the 1960s, in the improved rates of population growth and positive migration flows. Auvergne remains thinly populated, consistently has the lowest rates of increase shown in Table 7.1, and has very little in the way of migration flows: one could be forgiven for concluding that many of her young people have, by now, left.

Finally, the statistics for Nord, Alsace and Lorraine are in some ways the most interesting of all. They show that at the time of the 1954 census all three regions had high rates of population growth and that over 1954-62 they were net recipients of migration movements with only Nord (the region based on Lille) having a deficit figure. In the ensuing years, however, in the case of both Nord and Lorraine the rates of population increase dipped sharply below the national average, which was itself declining; at the same time both these regions saw steady rises in the rates of migration out-flows, to reach the high levels shown for 1968-75 — 15,928 and 9,714 annually. As the old staple industries of these regions declined and local unemployment rates started to rise, it seems clear that their former workers were attracted elsewhere. Of the three regions only Alsace remained apparently free from such problems.

From the population statistics recorded in the periodic censuses, therefore, it has been possible to extract a good deal of information relating to the changing situations in some of the most crucial regions. It is now necessary to supplement this with data from other sources.

Although no authoritative data are available for the post-1975 period, provisional estimates published by INSEE[18] suggest that the relative orders of total population growth rates for each region, as shown in Table 7.1, stayed approximately the same for the period 1975-80, when France shared the Europe-wide experience of severe falls in birth rates. All regions were estimated to have had sharp falls in their rates of population increase, with two regions, Lorraine and Auvergne, actually having net population decline. The largest annual increase continued to occur in Provence-Cote d'Azur, with an estimated 1.64 per cent per annum. Paris, with 0.38 per cent per annum, showed one of the sharpest declines from the previous period. A number of regions, including Nord, were estimated to have had very nearly static populations. One must hazard the guess that such regions will be registering population decline in the early 1980s. Birth and mortality tables, published separately in the same volume, showed that the Paris region continued to have figures well above the national average for the former and well below for the latter. Estimates for inter-regional migration flows must be even more tentative, but they suggested that for the period 1975-80 the total of such migrations had greatly diminished for all regions, perhaps as a consequence of the economic recession. The Paris region was estimated to have a net migration out-flow and the only region estimated to continue to benefit from large-scale inward migration was Provence-Cote d'Azur.

The Paris Region

Given the dominance, historically apparently ever increasing, of Paris and its hinterland in the French economy generally and in the question of regional inequalities in particular, some assessment of the current position of the Paris region seems inescapable. Fortunately, for this section it is possible to draw on a detailed study of the 'balance' between Paris and the provinces recently published by INSEE[19], which draws on data from a wide variety of sources, including refinements of some of the census data considered above. Although this report uses statistics which are not directly comparable to those considered above, since they were compiled on a somewhat different basis, it is able to break down the net global figures for migratory flows into Paris to show that:

(i)   the number of persons migrating from other parts of Metropolitan France into the Paris region has actually continued to rise fairly steadily throughout the period in question;

(ii) the above trend has been offset by a much more rapid rise in the number of people moving out of the Paris region *to locations elsewhere in Metropolitan France*, so that for 1968-75 the net balance was a significant out-flow;

(iii) this effect was masked in the global figures considered previously by the large number of immigrants into the Paris region from locations overseas (including those technically defined as being part of France);

(iv) there are significant age differences in the respective flows, as indicated by Figures 7.4 and 7.5: whereas amongst migrants into Paris the age range 20-30 predominates, amongst migrants out of Paris the age distribution is much more varied with significant although very much smaller peaks at around ages 30-35 and at retirement age.

Figures 7.4 and 7.5 show clearly both the differences in age structure and the fact that, over time, whereas the inward flow has remained fairly constant, the outward flow has increased significantly. Again the implications for the future of the region, and especially for the age structure of its population and consequent effects on future birth rates, are obvious. In fact, when the two series are put together there is a net in-flow for the 20-30 age group but a net out-flow for all other ages.

The geographical provenance of those moving into the Paris region has changed significantly: whereas in the earlier part of the post-war period the major source was the western and south-western regions of France, post-1968 the largest positive net balances have been from the Nord and Lorraine districts. Persons moving out of the Paris region have largely gone either to the southern coastal areas or have moved rather short distances to neighbouring regions. Of all internal migration movements within Metropolitan France, whereas pre-1962 just over 40 per cent involved moves into the Paris region, by the post-1968 period the figure was only 31 per cent. All these movements have to be set against the background of the significant overall fall in the birth rate in all the countries of Western Europe, including France, in the later post-war years. Within France, however, until the mid-1970s this decline occurred less sharply within the Paris region than elsewhere, no doubt due at least in part to the age-structure figures mentioned above. This result from natural causes undoubtedly contributed to the figures showing that, of the total French population, an ever-increasing percentage are congregated in the Paris region. From about 1975 onwards, later statistics suggest that this long-term trend has now been reversed and that the birth rate has now fallen more sharply in the Paris region than elsewhere.

Figure 7.3: Migration Flows into Paris Region, by Age, 1962-75

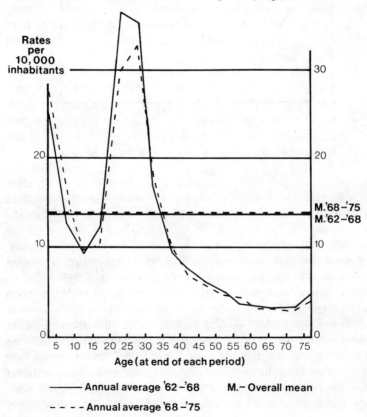

Figure 7.4: Migration Flows out of Paris Region, by Age, 1962-75

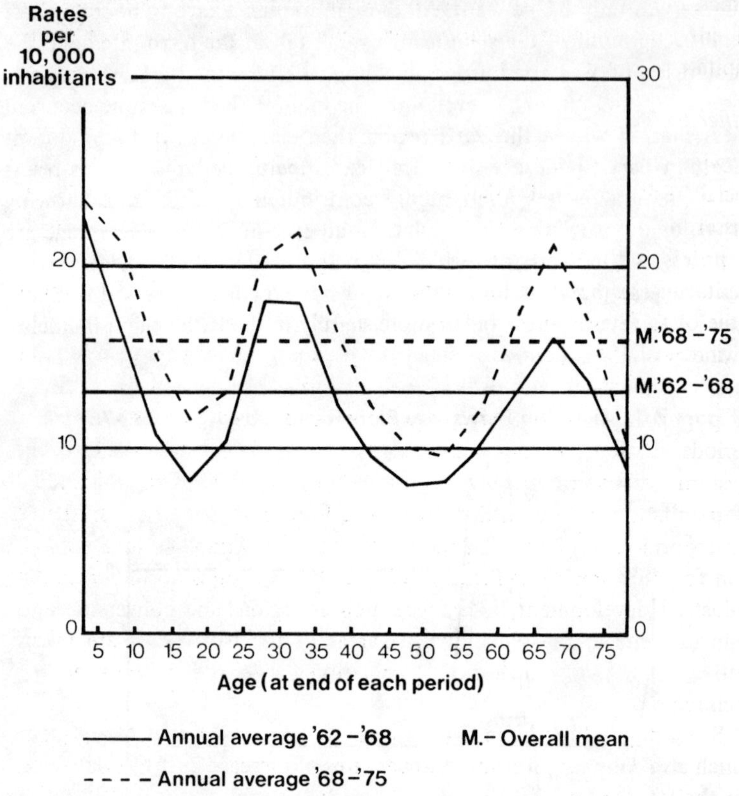

Annual average '62–'68   M.– Overall mean
- - - - Annual average '68–'75

A hopeful indicator, from the point of view of some measure of lesser regional inequality, relates to regional employment statistics and rates of growth. In the post-1968 period for the first time the rate of growth of *industrial* employment in the provinces (11.2 per cent over the seven-year period) exceeded that for the Paris region (9.5 per cent). The same is not true, however, when *all* forms of employment are taken into consideration, due to the continued tendency of white-collar jobs to be attracted to locations in or near the capital. Throughout France jobs for female workers have grown much more rapidly than those for males, but whereas pre-1968 the rate of increase of female employment was significantly higher in the Paris region than elsewhere, by the post-1968 period this gap had been substantially narrowed (2.0 per cent per annum against 1.9 per cent for the remainder of France). Overall activity rates for females in the Paris region remain substantially in excess of those for other regions with the exception of the 18-23 age group for which they are lower, presumably on account of the much higher rates of entry into higher education for young women in and around the capital.

Other Indicators

A wide-ranging attempt at a prognosis for the future economic and social health of the French regions was given in an official study by Passeron,[20] published in 1978, which was generally optimistic in tone. It noted that the decline in net population movement towards the capital had to be set in the context of the relative decline in the growth rates of all large French towns and the relatively greater attractiveness in the post-1968 period of small towns, of around 5,000 people, and rural communities: both the latter categories experienced net in-flows of population in contrast to the large-scale 'rural exodus' of earlier periods. Passeron's projections suggest that the western and south-western regions of France will continue their post-1968 favourable rates of population growth whilst Nord and Lorraine on the one hand and Auvergne and Limousin on the other will all continue to lose population for the foreseeable future. Once the Plan's proposals for continued industrial development in France's poorer regions and conversion and re-investment in the old industrial areas of the North-East are taken into account, more optimistic population forecasts are produced for each region.

Such population trends are related to the growth of employment which also shows significantly slower rates of increase in the Paris region for the later (post-1968) years and for the projection up to 1980. For the earlier years, and especially pre-1962, much the most important effect relates to the decline in agricultural jobs with those regions solely or heavily dependent on agriculture being hardest hit. By the post-1968 period the movement out of employment in agriculture had largely ceased and the predominant effect, within a total national employment continuing to rise until around 1974, was the growth of jobs in the tertiary sector, i.e. largely white-collar service jobs. The regions to have benefited have been primarily those in and around the Paris basin, i.e. just outside the Paris region itself, and along the Mediterranean coast. It is particularly important that for the post-1968 years the rate of growth of tertiary-sector jobs in the Paris region dipped below the national average for the first time (1.5 per cent against 1.7 per cent) and is fore-cast for the period up to 1980 to fall much lower (0.7 per cent against 1.7 per cent). Since 1974 the total number of industrial jobs has virtually stagnated, after the rapid expansion of the late 1960s and early 1970s, and regional effects have been rather small, save, for example, for certain regions tied to particular industries which continued to have sizeable increases (electricity, cars, chemistry) or decreases (raw materials producers). The total number of jobs in industry was forecast to decrease up to 1980, in each of the Paris, Nord, Lorraine and Provence regions; only in Rhone-Alps, the prosperous region centred on Lyons, were industrial jobs forecast to show a significant increase.

Those indications can be updated by means of Table 7.3, which was published in one of the preparatory documents for the elaboration of Plan 8.

Table 7.3: Net Creation of Jobs in Manufacturing Industry by Major Regions, 1954-79 (thousands of jobs)

	West[a]	Paris Region	East[b]	Total
1954-62	138	108	133	373
1962-8	199	-82	16	132
1968-75	355	-48	204	511
1975-9	-83	-108	-167	-351

Notes: a. 'West' includes the following ZEAT: Paris Basin, West, South-West.
b. 'East' includes the following ZEAT: North, East, Centre-East, Mediterranean.
Source: Commissariat Général du Plan, *Rapport du Comité Aménagement du Territoire* (La Documentation Française, 1980).

It divides France into 'West', 'Paris region' and 'East' and shows that, for the period to 1975, the growth of jobs in manufacturing industry was much larger in the 'West' than in the 'East', whilst the Paris region recorded an uninterrupted decline from 1962 onwards. For the period 1975-9, however, when the shake-out of jobs from manufacturing industry was taking place and unemployment was rising steadily, the above figures suggest that the effects of the recession were, from this point of view, felt less in the Paris region than elsewhere in France. Statistics from a different source for the year 1979 alone, however, suggest that the fall in jobs in manufacturing industry, expressed as a percentage of all such employment in the region, was more acute in the Paris region than in almost any other region in France: Lorraine had the highest fall (4.1 per cent) followed by the Paris region and Nord-Pas-de-Calais (2.3 per cent each), the next largest being Haute-Normandie with 1.9 per cent.[21]

According to Passeron, the overall message for any region seeking to improve its employment situation was clear: it must attract into the region jobs in the tertiary sector, the only sector of the economy in which employment trends are still on the increase. Passeron suggests that the Paris region has been gradually 'de-industrialising' as firms have 'decentralised', or moved elsewhere, and he sees this process as an essential component of successful regional policy. Such optimistic trends have, however, once again to be set against contra-indicators such as activity rates which are still far higher in the Paris region (48.0 per cent for 1974) than in any other region (national average = 41.1 per cent, lowest = Languedoc, 33.7 per cent), with the projected 1980 figures showing only very small differences from the 1974 actuals. The next-highest rates were to be found in other regions in the Paris basin (Basse-Normandie, 43.1 per cent, Haute-Normandie 43.0 per cent, Centre 41.6 per cent), or the prosperous Rhone-Alps region (41.9 per cent). Over time some trend towards greater equalisation can be discerned, but only very slowly.

Rates of unemployment have not, as we have already seen, traditionally been a significant variable for French regional policy and even Passeron's work could only make use of unemployment statistics for 1975 when the total (PDRE) amounted to some 740,000, i.e. less than half of the total for the early 1980s and about one-third of the level reached by early 1982. Subject to all the reservations relating to French unemployment statistics, as discussed in Chapter 6, the statistics did give some preliminary indications of the regional significance of the increasing unemployment of the early 1970s: expressing rates of unemployment as percentage of economically active population, the figures indicated that throughout the period up to 1975 the rate was higher for the Paris region (4.60 per cent in 1975) than for all other regions of France except for Provence-Alps-Cote d'Azur (6.23 per cent) or Languedoc (5.38 per cent); and given the exceptional age structure and high incidence of both unemployed persons and seasonal work for the tourist industry in both the latter regions, their figures must be subject to reservation. The figure for the Paris region was, however, increasing more slowly, over the 1968-75 period, than that for any other region than Nord, suggesting perhaps that the gathering economic crisis was starting to bite more deeply in the provinces than in the capital.

It is now possible to update the above by the inclusion of regional unemployment statistics for the economic planning regions to the end of 1980, as shown in Table 7.4.

This table shows clearly that the largest *number* of unemployed people are in the Paris region; this is both always the case and inevitable, just as in the UK the largest *number* of unemployed are always to

Table 7.4: Unemployment (DEFM) by Region, 1980

	Number (average for year)	Percentage Increase on Previous Year	As Percentage of Working Population
Paris region:			
Ile-de-France	271,451	4.3	5.9
Paris Basin:			
Champagne-Ardenne	37,845	8.7	7.8
Picardie	51,809	12.6	8.7
Haute-Normandie	59,530	11.4	9.6
Centre	46,797	14.7	6.1
Basse-Normandie	41,051	14.1	9.2
Burgundy	34,501	13.5	6.5
North:			
Nord-Pas-de-Calais	129,567	9.5	9.9
East:			
Lorraine	54,657	2.0	6.8
Alsace	25,048	10.8	4.4
Franche-Comté	23,650	22.4	6.2
West:			
Pays de la Loire	79,715	8.2	8.4
Brittany	72,124	8.1	9.0
Poitou-Charentes	43,540	5.2	9.0
South-West:			
Aquitaine	74,135	6.4	8.8
Midi-Pyrénées	60,497	7.5	8.9
Limousin	14,662	6.1	6.5
Centre-East:			
Rhone-Alpes	109,614	6.2	6.2
Auvergne	32,391	11.3	7.6
Mediterranean:			
Languedoc-Roussillon	57,183	4.0	10.5
Provence-Alpes-Cote d'Azur	124,942	4.4	9.9
Corsica	5,926	4.2	
All France	1,450,635	7.5	7.5

Source: *Rapport sur les Comptes de la Nation 1980*, vol. 2 (les Collections de l'INSEE, Série C, no. 94-5 (1981).

be found in London and the South-East. When the figures are expressed more meaningfully in *percentage* terms, the second column shows that the Paris region, with 4.3 per cent, continues to have one of the lowest rates of annual increase in unemployment over the previous year, although no longer the very lowest. It tended to be the more prosperous regions of the country, as for example those in the Paris Basin, that had the higher rates of increase of unemployment, on the year, with some of the poorest regions, in the South-West for example, having rates of increase below the national average of 7.5 per cent. Column 3 shows the unemployment statistics as percentage of each region's working population and here the picture differs sharply from that given by Passeron, as mentioned above. The Paris region, with 5.9 per cent, has one of the lowest figures, being bettered only by Alsace (4.4 per cent); unemployment rates are highest in the prosperous Mediterranean areas, where seasonal work and early retirement are important factors (those who retired early will often find it worth while to register as unemployed). Elsewhere the poorest regions of the West and South-West almost all have rates of unemployment well above the national average and the prominent region of industrial decline, Nord-Pas-de-Calais has, as would be expected, an exceptionally high figure (9.9 per cent). The rank order correlation between columns 2 and 3 would be weak, showing that the relative positions are in a considerable state of flux over time. All the rates of increase on previous year shown in column 2 are considerably less than their 1979 equivalents, which had a national total of 16.1 per cent. Overall, therefore, there is *some* evidence of the poorest regions of France being badly hit by the current trend towards increasing unemployment, but it is not at all clear that they are faring noticeably worse than some of the more prosperous regions. From this point of view, the capital, Paris, appears to be escaping the worst effects of the recession. This, at least, had been forecast by the figures quoted by Passeron, as mentioned above.

Finally, Passeron gave, *inter alia*, statistics for gross income per inhabitant and Gross Domestic Product for each region, as reproduced in Table 7.5. The gross income figures are in the form of an index with France = 100; the Gross Domestic Product figures are in the form of a share of the France total of 10,000 (i.e. essentially equal to an index of 100.00 multiplied by 100, for greater precision). In both cases the figures for 1962 and 1970 are actuals, whereas those for 1980 are projections; in view of the critical comments relating to French economic statistics appearing at various points in this volume, one should point out that the regionalisation of macro-economic statistics has been taken much further in France than in the UK, and that regional Gross Domestic Product statistics for the UK do not exist. The advantage of figures presented in index or share form is, of course, that they enable us to ignore the effects of inflation.

The gross income columns immediately make clear the enormous diversity in levels of income per head across France with, in each of the three columns, the Paris region being the only region in excess of the

Table 7.5: Regional Incomes and GDP, 1962-80

Regions	Gross Income per Inhabitant (index)			Gross Domestic Product (share)		
	1962	1970	1980	1962	1970	1980
Paris Region:						
Ile-de-France	144	137	137	2,443	2,784	3,267
Paris Basin:						
Champagne-Ardenne	100	94	98	239	273	295
Picardie	97	91	90	323	305	276
Haute-Normandie	96	98	97	366	372	413
Centre	88	93	90	333	355	356
Basse-Normandie	86	89	94	212	191	190
Burgundy	89	93	91	260	261	248
North:						
Nord-Pas-de-Calais	92	92	93	823	704	617
East:						
Lorraine	97	90	95	479	454	398
Alsace	93	96	94	282	282	272
Franche-Comté	91	87	88	184	189	179
West:						
Pays de la Loire	81	87	86	433	423	390
Brittany	80	84	84	384	323	284
Poitou-Charentes	79	88	86	241	220	210
South-West:						
Aquitaine	83	91	90	456	436	371
Midi-Pyrénées	79	87	88	340	307	246
Limousin	83	87	91	126	102	86
Centre-East:						
Rhone-Alpes	99	99	99	894	968	999
Auvergne	86	87	91	227	199	175
Mediterranean:						
Languedoc-Roussillon	99	99	88	285	239	198
Provence-Cote d'Azur-Corse	100	93	93	672	614	530
All France	100	100	100	10,000	10,000	10,000

Note: 1980 figures were projections.
Source: H. Passeron, *L'Economie Régionale en 1980* (Les Collections de l'INSEE, R31, Apr. 1978).

national average, so excessively skewed is the distribution. Average income per head in the Paris region in 1980 is shown as 37 per cent above the national average and is 63 per cent above the lowest figure, Brittany's 84. Some trend towards greater equality may be discerned from these columns, but unevenly and at a very slow pace. The Paris region is shown as losing none of its superiority over the period 1970-80, whilst the relative position of Brittany, for example, also remained static. Those for such regions as Alsace, Pays de la Loire (near Brittany) and Aquitaine declined somewhat, and that for Languedoc-Roussillon declined sharply. Regions such as Picardie, Lorraine and Provence were faring relatively less well by 1980 than they had been nearly twenty years previously. Of the 7 per cent 'outfall' from the Paris region, the main beneficiaries were those regions in the Paris *Basin* such as Haute-Normandie, Centre, Basse-Normandie and Burgundy. It is, of course, possible to dispute the significance of these gross income figures: if individuals in, for example, the Paris region are faced with substantially higher costs than elsewhere, then are their higher income figures merely statistics on paper and quite unrelated to any higher standard of living? For individuals this may well be true, but for the region as a whole it cannot, since the higher costs themselves reflect incomes of second-round multiplier effect order, for example incomes to landlords, all of which continue to increase the region's total wealth. A separate calculation, published in the CGP report cited previously and based on a survey carried out by INSEE, suggested that for 1980 the percentage of households with annual incomes in excess of 50,000 frs. (some £5,000) ranged from 60 per cent for the Paris region to only 15 per cent for the average of the regions in the 'South-West' ZEAT and 17 per cent for each of the 'East' or 'West' ZEATs. Apart from the Paris region only the 'Centre-East' (44 per cent) was above the national average of 43 per cent, the distribution being very skewed.

The corollary of the income figures are the shares in Gross Domestic Product shown in the last three columns of Table 7.5. Here the indication is clearly that the advantageous position of the Paris region *vis-à-vis* the remainder of France, although at a lower level than in the income columns, continues to improve relatively throughout the nearly twenty-year period. All the problem areas of France now contribute relatively less to GDP than they did in 1962, with the falls being very large in some cases, for example Brittany and Nord. Apart from the Paris region, the only other regions to improve their relative positions are Champagne, Haute-Normandie and Centre (all in the Paris Basin), and Rhone-Alps. Whilst it is true that some problems arise from the method of computation of these regional GDPs,[22] they are unlikely materially to affect our conclusions. From a study of Table 7.5 it is impossible to have much confidence in the view that regional inequalities are lessening over time, at least not in the direction desired by the various policy measures.

Policy Measures and Effects

One point that emerges *passim* from various of the statistics quoted
above serves to reinforce a view expressed by one of the leading observers of French regional developments, Dr Hugh Clout,[23] when discussing
the effects of jobs created in the provinces as the result of regional
measures:

> it is undeniable that the pattern of job creation is almost the inverse
> of what had been anticipated. Regions recognised as having the most
> serious employment problems, and therefore qualifying for the high-
> est rates of assistance, have received relatively few jobs. Bretagne, for
> example, received only 3.5 per cent of new factories and 5.4 per cent
> of the jobs created, and results are even less impressive in Aquitaine,
> Limousin and other western regions. By contrast, regions in the Paris
> Basin have done extraordinarily well, even though development grants
> were not generally available.

Moves of firms 'decentralising' out of Paris, i.e. either moving their
location in entirety or opening up a new factory or branch in the provinces whilst retaining those in the capital, gathered pace in the late
1950s and early 1960s and continued, albeit at a somewhat reduced
rate, thereafter and undoubtedly created many thousands of jobs in
the provinces. De Lanversin[24] cited an annual figure of 40,000 jobs
created at the peak in 1961 and a survey published by the French Embassy, London,[25] indicated that firms' moves initiated in the two years
1969 and 1970 would *eventually*, over a period of several years, lead to
the creation of some 110,000 jobs in the provinces. Clout's comment
quoted above refers to the strange paradox that *most* of such moves
over the years when effective regional policy measures were in force
went *not* to the problem regions to which the attractive investment
grants and other financial incentives applied, but to those regions not
so far from the capital, often in the Paris Basin, with no such incentives.
This would seem to establish a prima-facie case (although no more than
that) for concluding that it was the restrictions on industrial development or expansion in the Paris region (and/or the high costs of continuing to operate in the capital), and not the financial incentives applying
in certain regions, which proved crucial in connection with these moves.
In fact, many of the relocation schemes received no state aid at all. From
almost all available statistical series regions not too far away from the
capital have done very well out of these moves. Aydalot[26] gave a graphic

summary of the position in Figure 7.5: his detailed research showed that only the shaded area on the map, which extends perhaps 300 kilometres from Paris, had been significantly affected by firms relocating from the capital. The arrows on the map show the respective drifts of population towards Paris and, in smaller numbers, towards other major conurbations from the countryside, and out of city centres towards locations on or near the perimeters. It should also be pointed out that Aydalot's work was published in 1971 and that at a seminar at the London School of Economics in 1976 Monsieur Essig, the Director of DATAR, in reply to a question put to him by the writer, suggested that the above view was no longer correct and that firms were now prepared to move much further distances westwards or south-westwards. Overall the pace of such 'decentralising' moves continued to slow down throughout the 1970s and Clout points out that, in any event, such *industrial* moves must be seen as less important when set in a context in which it was the tertiary sector that was creating the majority of new jobs.

This brings us to what might be termed the second major paradox of French regional policy. Despite both the battery of regional financial incentives and the plethora of official institutions concerned with various aspects of regional development, the total funds provided by the French government each year for regional policy purposes during the 1970s were only some one-tenth of the equivalent in the UK, even though it could not seriously be doubted that regional imbalance was far more acute in France than in the UK. Perhaps this is, after all, the crucial reason why regional economic policy has been seen to work so slowly and why the general direction of change has in some respects, as indicated above, run counter to the expressed policy objectives.

The report of the regional policy committee of the Commissariat Général du Plan, issued as part of the work of preparing Plan 8, has already been cited above. It included a frank appraisal of the successes and failures of regional economic policy to date (1980), quoting as definite successes the relative shifts in the pattern of industrial job creation, the relative gains of the provinces over Paris in levels of income and standards of living, the multiplication of detailed studies of regional problems and the increased role and efficiency of the economic planning bodies in each region. It went on to admit that progress had been extremely slow and that wide disparities remained, so much so that it was still possible to refer, as a caricature, to 'three Frances' — Paris, the rich East and the poor West. It concluded by pointing to (i) the enormity of the problem and (ii) the very large number of local government organisations of one kind or another entitled to be involved and consulted – there are, for example, as many 'communes' in France as in the whole of the rest of Europe.

Figure 7.5: Industries' Geographical Mobility

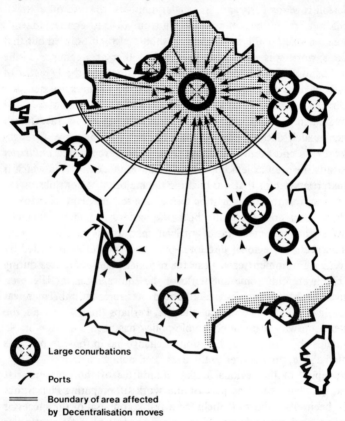

    ⊗ Large conurbations

    ↗ Ports

    ═ Boundary of area affected
       by Decentralisation moves

Source: P. Aydalot *et al.*, *La Mobilité des Activités Economiques. L'Exemple Français* (Gauthier-Villars, 1971).

An authoritative study of major trends in the French economy,[27] published in 1981, concluded that regional economic policy in France undoubtedly had achieved major successes, in three main respects. First among these would be the reversal of the trend for the Paris region to become ever more dominant in the country's economic and social life, a trend which was now 'practiquement stoppée'. This conclusion was reached via a consideration of migration flows and patterns of job creation. Second, the poorest regions of the West and South-West had seen a considerable reversal of their fortunes not only because net out-migration to other regions had greatly diminished and overall increases in population were recorded in the period to the 1975 census, but also because of the changed pattern of job creation – of the 650,000 new jobs created in manufacturing industry between the years 1962 and 1975, some 200,000 were located in the regions of the West and South-West. The former point would now need amending in view of INSEE's estimates, noted previously, that some of the poorer regions did have either declining or static populations for the years 1975-80. The latter reference to job creation appears partially valid, but does not answer the trenchant criticism put forward by Dr Clout, as noted above. The author goes on to suggest that France's system of regional incentives, although modest by international standards, is economically very efficient: thus for the period to 1975 regional incentives in France were leading on average to the creation of some 40,000-50,000 jobs per year, against some 80,000 in the UK, which had regional incentives eight times larger than those in France. Third, in the view of the same author, the effects of public expenditure in the regions had been greatly to lessen regional disparities, via improvements under such headings as transport, telecommunications, hospitals, television networks, tourism and social infrastructure. The major problem remaining to be tackled was seen as the decentralisation of tertiary-sector employment, a problem which was later to receive detailed attention in the policy pronouncements of the socialist government after May-June 1981, as discussed in Chapter 5.

Earlier Studies

A variety of earlier assessments of the effects of regional economic policy do exist, often in considerable detail, but inevitably the data on which they were based are no longer up to date. Thus Chardonnet,[28] writing of the period up to 1973, shows conclusively that the growth of industrial employment was far more rapid in the regions in the Paris Basin than anywhere else in France, that there were significant increases in the western regions but that in the Nord region the number of industrial jobs continued to decline each year. Astorg[29] also, using data up to 1971, confirmed the view that over time the problems of the western half of France, and especially the North-West quadrant, were gradually ameliorating, whereas those of the North-East were 'still giving great cause for concern, since they are still suffering from outdated facilities and strong foreign competition'.

Astorg's conclusions were, however, essentially optimistic in tone, in sharp contrast to Professor Gravier's second major study of the regions,[30] written 25 years after the first, which concluded: 'the extreme contrast between the under-populated west and Massif Central and the continued growth of Paris remains true.' Gravier admitted that the industrial growth of Paris had virtually halted, but found that the poorest regions had benefited little from such changes as had occurred. He was particularly critical of regional policy measures in the widest sense for being (i) much too fragmentary, in that various schemes, such as agricultural renovation, tourist investment, urban renewal and development of higher education seemed to be pursued without any clear links between them, and (ii) much too centralised, in that most major decisions were directed by civil servants living in Paris. Gravier concluded: 'the privileges enjoyed by Paris have been preserved and even glorified . . . and regional hopes have frequently been disappointed.'

Earlier discussions of the difficulties inherent in any attempt to assess the results of French regional economic policy were given in both Allen and McLennan[31] and Viot,[32] whilst the interrelationship between economic effectiveness and endemic political problems was emphasised by Ross and Cohen.[33] For a first-hand 'feel' of the nature of France's regional problems, one cannot do better than the many detailed studies of individual regions or departments which have appeared in various official publications in recent years.[34]

The French Regions and Europe

Finally, further mention should be made of the effects on France's troubled regions of the development of the EEC's Community-wide regional policies, to which there have been only passing references above. To ascertain whether EEC initiatives have had significant, or indeed any, effects at the level of France's regions is a far from easy matter. Late in 1981 the EEC published a series of pamphlets, one for each of most of France's economic planning regions, describing at some length the aid, of various kinds, the region had received from the EEC by mid-1981. A summary of the main sums granted is given in Table 7.6.

The amounts shown in Table 7.6 appear considerable and from those figures it would appear incontestable that the EEC's measures have had a noteworthy effect. However, a representative of DATAR, with whom the writer discussed this matter whilst in Paris in December 1981, was adamant that no EEC aid of any kind had gone direct to any of the regions. All of the sums shown, I was assured, and all other forms of assistance, are routed from the EEC to the French government in Paris and they therefore have to be seen as helping to finance the system of national regional incentives detailed earlier in this chapter. No evidence has been found in any of the sources consulted that the French government has, over the years, increased the levels of its regional incentives on account of the sums it was receiving from the EEC. Whether, therefore, the EEC's regional policies have directly been of any assistance to the French regions must remain a moot point. It should also be said, and the EEC's publications readily so admit, that it is not easy to know exactly what meaning to attach to the sums shown in Table 7.6, since they are an amalgamation of sums from different dates, all in current francs and with no attempt to translate into constant values, for example via deflation by suitable price indices.

Table 7.6: Aid from EEC to French Regions to 1981 (million frs.)

	Grants	Loans
Paris Basin:		
Champagne-Ardenne	70.1	115.2
Picardie	N/A	N/A
Haute-Normandie	46.3	40.0
Centre	101.8	936.7
Basse-Normandie	163.9	215.4
Burgundy	N/A	N/A
North:		
Nord-Pas-de-Calais	718;9	1,908.4
East:		
Lorraine	381.5	8,932.0
Alsace	59.5	433.6
Franche-Comté	N/A	N/A
West:		
Pays de la Loire	358.2	694.0
Brittany	875.6	620.3
Poitou-Charentes	344.9	168.3
South-West:		
Aquitaine	416.7	701.6
Midi-Pyrénées	558.9	461.7
Limousin	323.9	105.6
Centre-East:		
Rhone-Alpes	265.2	3,387.0
Auvergne	508.4	368.9
Mediterranean:		
Languedoc-Roussillon	702.2	101.3
Provence-Alpes-Cote d'Azur	291.1	1,186.3
Corsica	N/A	NA/
All regions for which data available	6,187.1	20,376.3

Source: Series of booklets on French regions and Europe (EEC, 1981).

Table 7.6 suggests that, in granting loans in particular, the EEC has been more minded to help regions affected by industrial decay and change (Lorraine, Nord-Pas-de-Calais) than the underdeveloped regions of the West and South-West. It is also both interesting and curious that very large loans have been given to some of the most prosperous regions of France (Rhone-Alpes, Provence-Cote d'Azur).

Some Conclusions

After such a review, using diverse data and statistical series, no neat conclusion seems possible. The difficulties involved in any such attempt at assessing the effectiveness of regional economic policy are self-evident, and must relate back to the earlier uncertainty as to the precise objectives. Undoubtedly in some sense regional inequalities are lessening and the capital's dominance over the economic life of the country is slowly, perhaps very slowly, being whittled away. The regions to the far West and South-West, for which the various policy measures were originally framed, have had some share in the increased regional prosperity, but not so much as the various regions in the Paris Basin, for which the benefits were never intended and to which indeed the major financial incentives do not apply. And finally the problems of the declining older industrial regions of the North-East, scarcely envisaged in the early years when national concern over regional inequalities was developing, have become more and more acute and to date show no signs of abating. 'Regional Policy for Ever?' was the title of a recent UK journal article: certainly in France it seems clear that regional policy will have to continue, and will have to become more refined and sensitive, for at least the foreseeable future.

Since the elections of May-June 1981 the socialist government under President Mitterrand has emphasised its commitment to the lessening of regional inequalities, as being concomitant with its policy of political decentralisation of power and decision-making. The new regional policy measures announced late in 1981 have been detailed above and by early 1982 there was every indication that regional economic policy had high priority in the eyes of the socialist government. Whether this will lead to a quickening of increasing prosperity for the poorer regions of France must, however, depend on the future path of the national (and world) recession and on how much money will be made available to finance the new system of regional incentives, both of which continued to appear problematic by early 1982. For the poorer regions of France, it may well be that things will get worse before they get better.[35]

Notes

1. J. F. Gravier, *Paris et le Désert Français* (Flammarion, Paris, 1947).
2. N.M. Hansen, *French Regional Planning* (Edinburgh University Press, 1968).
3. K. Allen and M. MacLennan, *Regional Problems and Policies in Italy and France* (Allen and Unwin, 1970).
4. Ibid.
5. Ibid.
6. Commissariat Général du Plan, *Rapport du Comité Aménagement du Territoire* (La Documentation Française, 1980).
7. Hansen, *French Regional Planning*.
8. J. Lajugié, 'Aménagement du Territoire et Développement Economique Régionale en France (1945-1964)', *Revue d'Economie Politique* (Jan.-Feb. 1964), quoted in Allen and MacLennan (p. 147), who follow the same approach.
9. Hansen, *French Regional Planning*.
10. J. Chardonnet, *La Politique Economique Intérieure Française* (Dalloz, 1976).
11. Quoted in Hansen, *French Regional Planning*.
12. Allen and MacLennan, *Regional Problems and Policies in Italy and France*.
13. This may be why Clout emphasises the latter date: see H. Clout, *The Geography of Post-War France: a Social and Economic Approach* (Pergamon, 1972).
14. For details see Allen and MacLennan, *Regional Problems and Policies in Italy and France*, p. 164.
15. As in Chardonnet, *La Politique Economique Intérieure Française*.
16. *La Lettre de DATAR* (DATAR, Dec. 1981-Jan. 1982).
17. C. Hull, *Background Notes to Regional Incentives in France* (International Institute of Management, March 1978).
18. *Statistiques et Indicateurs des Régions Françaises*, *Les Collections de l'INSEE*, Série R, nos. 45-6 (1981).
19. *Vers un Nouvel Equilibre Paris-Province* (INSEE, 1979).
20. H. Passeron, *L'Economie Régionale en 1980*, *Les Collections de l'INSEE*, Série R, no. 31 (Apr. 1978).
21. *Statistiques et Indicateurs des Régions Françaises, Les Collections de l'INSEE*, Série R, nos. 45-6 (1981).
22. Discussed in detail in Passeron's Appendix 9.
23. H. Clout (ed.), *Regional Development in Western Europe* (Wiley, 1975).
24. J. De Lanversin, *L'Aménagement du Territoire et la Régionalisation* (Libraries Techniques, 1970).
25. *French Regional Development Results 1969-70* (French Embassy, London, Ref. No. B62/4/71).
26. P. Aydalot *et al.*, *La Mobilité des Activités Economiques, l'Exemple Français* (Gauthier-Villars, 1971).
27. N. Perrin, 'L'Aménagement du territoire et le developpement régional' in J.P. Pagé (ed.), *Profil Economique de la France au Seuil des Années 80* (La Documentation Française, 1981).
28. Chardonnet, *La Politique Economique Intérieure Française*.
29. M. Astorg, 'Regional Development and Policy' in J.P. Pagé (ed.), *Profil Economique de la France* (La Documentation Française, 1977).
30. J.F. Gravier, *Paris et le Désert Français en 1972* (Flammarion, 1974).
31. Allen and MacLennan, *Regional Problems and Policies in France and Italy*.
32. P. Viot, 'Interregional Plan Formulation in France' in D. Dunham and

J. Hilhorst (eds.), *Issues in Regional Planning* (Mouton, The Hague, 1971).

33. G. Ross and S. Cohen, 'The Politics of French Regional Planning' in J. Friedmann and W. Alonso (eds.), *Regional Policy, Readings in Theory and Applications* (MIT Press, 1975).

34. Especially the series *Notes et Etudes Documentaires*, published by La Documentation Française.

35. A large collection of other statistics relating to the French regions, mostly based on census results and therefore for the period to 1975, may be found in S. Mary and E. Turpin, *Panorama Economique des Régions Françaises, Les Collections de l'INSEE*, Série R., nos. 42-3 (1981).

8 FRANCE IN THE EEC AND THE WORLD

The French economy's external relations may for convenience be divided into those with her partners in the European Community and those with the rest of the world, although a considerable degree of overlap between the two will be inevitable. In this chapter each will be considered in turn after discussion of France's balance of payments for 1980 and an overview of the economy's external constraints.

The Balance of Payments

The French balance of payments, current account, for the years 1978-80, is summarised in Table 8.1. This table immediately makes clear the very considerable deterioration of France's external position over the three years, with the overall balance on current account declining from a surplus of 16,850m frs. to a deficit of 31,113m frs. (Statistics[1] for the first half of 1981 suggested some improvement, with a further fall in energy imports in volume and agro-foods exports significantly higher. The out-turn for the year 1981 looked doubtful, however, in view of the new expansionist economic policies after the elections of May-June 1981.)

Table 8.1: Balance of Payments, Current Account, 1978-80 (million frs.)

	1978	1979	1980
Exports	336,061	400,846	454,812
Imports	−332,967	−409,179	−505,263
Balance of trade	+3,094	−8,333	−50,451
Public works and technical co-operation	+13,274	+13,390	+16,294
Dividends and interest received	+4,633	+6,771	+8,999
Tourism	+7,379	+6,969	+8,918
Non-marine transport	+3,681	+4,869	+5,418
Other items (net)	−15,211	−18,753	−20,291
Balance of invisibles	+13,756	+13,246	+19,338
Current account balance	+16,850	+4,913	−31,113

Source: Ministère du Commerce Extérieur, Communiqué, 2 March 1981.

This deterioration stemmed from the worsening of the balance of trade, almost the whole of which was caused by imports of energy,

191

especially oil and petrol. The energy deficit alone reached 132,900m frs. in 1980, an increase of over 49,000m frs. on 1979 as the 'second oil shock' hit France hard. The volume of energy imports actually fell by 15.6 per cent, but the average price expressed in francs rose by 86 per cent on the year. The net surplus from industrial exports also fell in the face of the world recession, but the net surplus from agro-foods recovered well.

The table also shows the important place of invisibles in the balance of payments, the sector consistently yielding a significant surplus to offset deficits on visible trade. It is also apparent that the invisibles balance failed to rise at all from 1978 to 1979 before recovering well in 1980. This sector will be considered in more detail below.

External Constraints: an Overview[2]

From having foreign trade that had remained small and was concentrated on France's colonial territories, France has since around 1950 seen a gradual opening up of her economy to external influences, with the pace of such change accelerating markedly from around 1960 and again from around 1970. The major trade routes have become those to other developed countries and especially France's partners within the EEC: it is easy to lose sight of the fact that the twenty years or so of the EEC's effective existence have seen a quite remarkable expansion of trade between the member states. In recent years the 'oil shocks' have required the French economy to be even more outward-looking, so that by 1980 foreign trade accounted for almost a quarter of the country's national income (against only some 15 per cent in 1970).

The prime cause for continuing concern over France's external position relates to energy: by 1981 her energy needs had reached over 5 per cent of GNP and some 88 per cent of this total had to be imported. Despite strenuous efforts to diversify, the sources of oil imports remain highly concentrated on the Middle East, with Saudi Arabia alone providing some 48 per cent of the total (in value) by 1981 and being responsible for a steadily increasing proportion of the total year by year. Small wonder then that France feels extremely vulnerable in this respect and gives the highest priority in her foreign policy to matters affecting the Middle East.

Much the largest supplier of natural gas is the Netherlands (52 per cent in 1980), followed by the USSR and Norway; the Algerian supply reached 25.6 per cent of the total in 1976 but, contrary to expectations, declined relatively thereafter. The main suppliers of coal imports were South Africa, Germany and the USA. If the country's domestic programme of nuclear power stations is allowed to continue as planned, France should be producing over 40 per cent of her energy needs by 1990: only thus can the massive external energy deficit be lessened.

During the 1970s, whilst France was achieving GDP growth averaging 3.6 per cent per year, each of her exports and imports grew on average by 8.2 per cent per year in a decade in which exports of all industrialised countries increased by an average of only 6 per cent per year. Some of France's industrial sectors have exceptionally successful export records, notably automobiles, but also shipbuilding, aircraft and arms production, each of which exports around 50 per cent or more of total output. Rather surprisingly, France has visible trade deficits in most of the modern science-based and research-intensive industries and in general imports advanced technology.

France now ranks as the world's fourth-largest trading power (imports and exports) or fifth for exports alone, a quite remarkable feat from the essentially inward-looking economy of some thirty or even twenty years ago.

This trade is concentrated within a relatively small geographical area, with almost exactly 50 per cent of exports going to five countries, Germany (much France's most important trading partner), Italy, Belgium/Luxemburg, UK and the Netherlands. France has large trading deficits, obviously with her suppliers of oil and gas but also, for industrial products, with West Germany (16.8 billion frs.) and the USA (24.6 billion frs.). Apart from the energy field, the principal deficits are concentrated in quite a narrow sectoral range, most of which may be termed investment goods, viz. industrial machinery, electronics appliances, precision instruments and appliances and machine tools. Again, rather surprisingly, France has huge deficits (totalling over 40 billion frs. in 1980) for the import from the USA of aircraft and data-processing equipment, both areas in which France is elsewhere a successful producer and exporter; both are, of course, also areas in which the products are highly specific and specialised and not easily substitutable. Imports from Germany tend to be concentrated in organic and inorganic chemicals, industrial instruments and appliances, and photographic and optical equipment, whilst those from Japan are largely in telecommunications equipment and recording apparatus (nearly 40 per cent of total), optical and photographic materials and watches, and calculators and office equipment. France's trade surpluses, on the other hand, tend to be spread more evenly over a larger number of countries, the largest being with Switzerland (9.3 billion frs.), followed by Italy, Egypt, Algeria, Greece, Tunisia and the UK (with whom she had a surplus of 2 billion frs.). Apart from the major ones already mentioned, the following French industries also have successful export records within their own spheres: perfumery and toilet articles, leather goods, clothing and medicinal and pharmaceutical products.

For agriculture and food production France has, as was shown in Chapter 3, a healthy surplus for the normal range of agricultural produce and food derived therefrom, but has an overall sectoral deficit on account of her heavy imports of such tropical or semi-tropical items as coffee, tea, cocoa and sugar. France is a very successful exporter of agro-food, especially grains, to the remainder of the EEC and particularly to Italy and Germany: the latter took 13,654m frs. and 11,745m frs. respectively of French products in 1980 and each had exports to France of only some 40 per cent thereof.

Apart from the huge deficit with the OPEC countries, France has overall large trade deficits with the remainder of the EEC and with the USA, is just in surplus with Eastern Europe, and only with the developing countries (especially her former colonial territories) has she a large and increasing trade surplus. Over one-fifth of all OECD exports to Africa came from France (1980). To both Eastern Europe and developing countries, sales of machinery and manufactures categorised as non-technology-intensive are the most important sector; in recent years the same products plus such items as arms sales have also begun to make successful inroads into the lucrative OPEC markets, thus helping to offset to some extent the huge drain of currency towards those countries.

Sectoral Changes

Sectoral changes in France's external trade over the period of 1958 to 1979 are summarised in Table 8.2, which indicates important developments under exports and imports. Thus the achievement of the agriculture and food sector in winning a slow growth in share of total exports has to be set alongside the very considerable relative decline in imports for the same sector. Over the twenty-year period, therefore, a large relative deficit was converted into a useful surplus. Similar comments are true of raw materials. It appears surprising that the figures for energy imports do not show a larger increase unless one recalls that in the earlier part of the period the prices of energy imports declined in real terms. The relative figure actually fell from 19.7 per cent in 1958 to 12.3 per cent by 1973, before rising sharply thereafter; further, the table does not include the post-1979 increases.

Table 8.2: Structural Changes in External Trade, 1958-79 (as percentage)

	Exports		Imports	
	1958	1979	1958	1979
Agricultural and food products	13.0	14.3	25.2	10.7
Raw materials	7.2	4.3	24.9	7.4
Energy	6.3	3.7	19.7	21.5
Manufactured products	70.5	77.0	30.1	60.0
Miscellaneous	4.0	0.7	0.1	0.4
Total	100.0	100.0	100.0	100.0

Source: P. Meunier, Les relations économiques et financières de la France avec l'extérieur' in J.P. Pagé (ed.), *Profil Economique de la France au Seuil des Années 80* (La Documentation Française, 1981).

Direct Foreign Investment

The post-war years have seen heavy direct investment in French industry by the USA, the UK, and to a lesser extent by other EEC states, but only in the 1970s have French firms given serious attention to making direct investments in overseas plants, raw materials suppliers or market outlets. Whilst there is still a long way to go to catch up on her competitors, the 1970s saw significant French investments in overseas energy (especially the UK) and mining sources. French industries have become involved in many joint production ventures in developing countries. At the same time direct investment in France by foreign firms continued to grow and has reached very high levels in data-processing equipment (over 70 per cent), oil/natural gas and agricultural machinery (over 50 per cent) and parachemicals and iron ore (around 45 per cent). Foreign investment flows between France and her EEC partners approximately trebled during the 1970s, perhaps the most important category relating to investment in real estate. French firms in which significant foreign investments have been made tend not to be export-orientated, i.e. they are being used to make inroads into France's domestic markets. Nowhere is this more true than in the case of electronic and data-processing equipment for which domestic demand is buoyant but production inadequate.

Finance

About one-eighth of foreign trade, especially in public works construction projects and in capital goods, is financed by export credits, often combined with aid to exporting firms in the form of loans or guarantees on preferential terms (plus a further eighth financed by the EEC agricultural policy). Assisted financing is now seen as almost a *sine qua non* for exports of capital goods and public works to the developing countries and to Eastern Europe, both categories of countries whose short-term financial resources are limited. There has been criticism from some economists that such preferential financial terms have the effect, when taken fully into account, of rendering marginally profitable business unprofitable, but it has to be remembered that they facilitate, indeed they make possible, the penetration of young expanding markets, often with excellent future prospects.

One element in the maintenance of domestic rates of interest relatively high in nominal terms (although usually low or even negative in real terms) has been the aim of attracting sufficient capital funds (both long- and short-term) from those countries which have overall surpluses on their foreign trade with France (especially OPEC), so that part of this money can be recycled towards the preferential credits and loans outlined above. Such in-flows of capital movements, especially long-term, have considerably aided the French balance of payments in recent years.[3]

In 1980 the overall deficit on current account transactions of 31,113m frs. was offset by short-term capital in-flows of 12,178m frs.; in the long-term account loan drawings brought in 20,930m frs., but commercial credits resulted in a debit figure of 17,069m frs. After all other factors had been taken into account France was able not only to maintain but even to increase her foreign exchange reserves, which leapt from 133.80 billion frs. in 1978 to 349.56 billion frs. by May 1981. As a consequence it was possible to hold the franc steady and thus avoid some of the worst effects of imported inflation (there are, of course, always two sides to any foreign currency story: whilst a falling franc would have raised the cost of imports into France, it would have lent an extra competitive edge to France's own exporters). Simultaneously some of the effects of the oil price rises were postponed by the government's policy of borrowing to cover part of the extra cost, hopefully until the time comes when France is satisfying a much higher proportion of her energy requirements from her own resources. It scarcely needs to be pointed out that both the acquisition of short-term capital funds and the incurring of debts relating to the recent oil crises cannot simply be seen as solutions to past problems: clearly the day will come when both will have to be repaid. Only latterly (in 1981) did the value of the franc, along with those of most other European currencies, fall sharply against the dollar, causing what has been termed 'the third oil shock' (since oil prices are fixed by reference to the US dollar) and occasioning new problems relating to the financial policy indicated above.

France in the EEC

Many of the most significant economic effects to result from France's membership of the EEC, and certainly those which have received the greatest publicity, have related to agriculture; these were reviewed in Chapter 3 and will not be repeated here, save to recall that the modernised part of French agriculture was extremely well placed to benefit from the new trading opportunities and did proceed to procure a substantial and growing surplus on agricultural exchanges with the rest of the EEC. The remainder of the economic effects for France related partly to how her own producers reacted to and coped with the lowering of the internal tariff barriers and partly to the consequences of European decisions and regulations, to the framing of which France had, of course, contributed. 'From an economic point of view, the Fifth Republic and French participation in the European Common Market are closely connected'[4] was how a leading French economist encapsulated the economic change that France experienced as a consequence of the Treaty of Rome. Both France's Fifth Republic (which saw the return to power of General de Gaulle) and the EEC effectively commenced in 1958, at which date the country's economy was essentially inward-looking and protected from external competition by high tariffs and quota restrictions. All this had to change. From now on, economically speaking at least, what concerned France also concerned Europe and vice versa. As one commentator wrote of France's Pinay-Rueff monetary and financial reforms of 28 December 1958 (which brought a return to internal stability after the uncertainties and devaluations of the previous era): '28 December 1958 was perhaps as important a day for the Six as that on which the Treaty of Rome was signed.'[5]

Plan 3 (1958-63) was just getting under way in the context of a considerable degree of regulation and control by the authorities, with only a low priority being assigned to external trade. Trade within the 'Franc Zone', i.e. with France's former colonial territories, was seen as largely analogous to internal trade in view of the degree of protection and preferential access which French firms enjoyed in those countries. Elsewhere external trade was seen almost as an undesirable necessity, with imports being needed to provide those goods which could not be provided, or could not be provided in sufficient quantities, by domestic suppliers and exports being required to procure the foreign exchange to pay for the imports. In the 3rd Plan both exports and imports were essentially seen as 'constraints' on the national economy.[6]

In none of the other EEC member states at that time was there such an outlook and in none of them had protective tariff barriers been maintained to the same degree as in France, with the partial exception of Italy. Foreign trade, even when trade with the 'Franc Zone' countries is included, comprised a smaller proportion of the national economy in France than in any other country in Europe. The 3rd Plan even provided that the volume of imports should be held constant in real terms and thus decline as a proportion of the economy by the close of the planning period (1961) and that exports as a proportion of the national economy should remain constant. In the eyes of the planners France was to remain largely a closed economy.[7] After all the preparatory work on Plan 3 had been completed, the Commissariat Général du Plan had to admit rather ruefully, 'the consequences of the establishment of the Common Market had not been taken into account.'[8] In reality, over the period 1956-61 imports, instead of stagnating, rose by 25 per cent whilst exports, planned to rise by one-third, actually rose by 71 per cent.

The out-turn saw serious discrepancies between the growth paths of a number of industries and the forecasts which had been enshrined in Plan 3 and there were far-reaching consequences for the planning process and for the future of economic planning in France.

At the same time the French planners were required to cease using some of the instruments on which they had hitherto relied, such as import quota restrictions and tariff barriers. Trade within the original Six gradually became tariff-free and extra-EEC trade became subject to an external tariff decided at Community level and thus outside direct French control. Any forms of subsidy to exports within the Community were also supposed to cease and the official doctrine is that all such measures have ceased. No one pretends, however, that the French government is not able to find a way to circumvent these regulations as and when they find it expedient to do so. Two separate reports, one by the Patronat Français[9] (the French employers' association) and the other by two leading American economists,[10] both concluded that these developments had played a major role in lessening the influence and importance of national economic planning in France. Economic planning was examined in detail in Chapter 5; here we may simply note that one possibility that has been mooted is that a Community-level system of indicative planning may eventually emerge at some future date.[11]

Consequent upon France's entry into the EEC a significant change took place in French economic policy which post-1958 became of a more general and non-discriminatory nature, rather than one favouring particular industries or firms.[12] Thus fiscal and monetary measures encouraged investment, particularly relating to new industrial products, and aided, *inter alia*, regional relocation and industrial concentration (for the latter, special tax exemptions and low-interest loans became available). The results of these measures in turn contributed to the significant growth in French exports.

Competition

At the time of the signing of the Treaty of Rome, the attitude towards more open competition, on the part of both business circles and governmental bodies in France, can only be described as one of suspicion. From being initially seen as a regrettable necessity if the political and strategic objectives of the Community were to be achieved, external competition had by 1958 come to be seen as an instrument for the achievement of greater productivity and efficiency on the part of French industries. Suspicions remained, however, especially on the part of the employers' associations in France, which sought to have included in the Treaty of Rome (i) measures tending to equalise employers' 'social costs', especially what they referred to as the 'trois vaches sacrées' (three sacred cows), viz. length of paid holidays, length of the working week and female/male wage equality, (ii) longer transition periods, and (iii) rights to re-introduce protective measures in the event of balance of payments difficulties. Although some additional clauses were inserted in the Rome Treaty, the Patronat were far from satisfied with the outcome.[13]

Economic Development Post-1958

If certain French organisations were anxious regarding France's membership of the Community, the record of the post-1958 period suggests that their fears were groundless. For the ensuing fifteen years economic growth averaged 5.5 per cent (against 4.8 per cent for the five years to 1958), a record considerably better than that of any other country in Europe. Even West Germany, with a growth rate averaging 5 per cent after 1958, was consistently less successful than France, whereas pre-1958 the reverse was true. It was these same years that saw what has been described as the change from an essentially closed to an essentially open economy. As Table 8.3 shows, France's exports as a percentage of Gross National Product mushroomed from 8.9 per cent in 1958 to 14.7 per cent fifteen years later and continued to rise thereafter. Provisional statistics for 1980 give a figure of 18.2 per cent.[14] The figure for France is still smaller than that for either West Germany or the UK, but the gap has been appreciably narrowed over the period of some twenty years. France's manufacturing industries acquired a much-increased export orientation. As a result, exports (in volume) grew at rates usually between 10 and 17 per cent during years when household consumption was rising at only some 4.0-6.5 per cent. From 1978 to 1979 exports in value rose by 19.2 per cent, in a year in which inflation finalised at just over 10 per cent: the rate of growth in real terms was therefore less than in the pre-crisis years, but must be considered a remarkable achievement in the prevailing world circumstances. From 1979 to 1980 exports in value rose by 13.4 per cent, a rate just about equal to the rate of inflation, and therefore failed to rise in real terms.

Table 8.3: Exports/Gross National Product, 1958-79 (per cent)

	1958	1969	1973	1979
France	8.9	10.6	14.7	17.3
West Germany	16.0	18.9	19.7	22.7
UK	14.3	16.8	18.8	23.2

Source: 'Statistiques du Commerce Extérieur' quoted in Pagé, *Profil Economique de la France au Seuil des Années 80*.

Far from certain industries disappearing as the result of France's membership of the EEC, as had been feared, the effects of membership included greatly increased industrial specialisation and intra-industry trade, both within France and throughout Europe. France's competitive position improved rapidly, with the result that its trade outside Europe also grew more rapidly than had been anticipated. Only in the case of consumer durables did the position of the French economy clearly deteriorate, with large quantities of cheap products such as refrigerators being imported, especially from Italy.

According to one respected survey, 'industrial structures changed more in ten years than in the previous fifty.'[15] It is, of course, impossible to prove that changes in France's internal industrial structures (especially increased concentration and investment, mergers of smaller units into larger ones, rationalisation and increased specialisation) were caused by the country's membership of the EEC, but it does appear undeniable that the latter provided a direct stimulus for such change. The scene had also been set by the Pinay-Rueff financial and monetary reforms which greatly increased business confidence as to future stability (even though after 1958 the rate of inflation in France in fact remained higher than that in other EEC countries). It is not without interest, particularly in view of recent developments in the UK, to note that when in the later 1960s General de Gaulle had become so disenchanted with European developments that he considered withdrawing France from the EEC, French business circles made clear how strongly they would oppose such a move.[16]

Industrial Success

A survey by Régis Paranque[17] showed how French industry, from a precarious and vulnerable initial position in 1958, had reaped undeniable success from France's membership of the EEC, increases in external sales of industrial products becoming one of the prime motors of sustained economic growth. Within a steadily rising total volume of French exports, the percentage going to other EEC member states leapt from 27 per cent in 1958 to some 50 per cent by 1975. Within two years from the signing of the Treaty of Rome French exports to Italy alone had grown by 133 per cent.

In the new export drive the industries which led the way were chemicals, electrical equipment, mechanical engineering (especially cars), paper and cardboard and, to a lesser extent, textiles and clothing. French industrialists discovered, often for the first time, that export sales gave them new and secure bases, widened market power and all the advantages of significant economies of scale.

France had always been confident that her agriculture would fare well in Europe, as was indeed to be the case, but one of the main elements in both Plan 5 and Plan 6 was to aid the development of those industries producing investment goods and semi-manufactured products. Increased size and specialisation were essential components of this development. In general, the outcome was successful but still Plan 7 (1975-80) had to refer to insufficient competitiveness in the investment goods sector. This may be contrasted with the outstandingly successful export record of the French automobile industry.

A major worry has been that, whilst French exports to the rest of Europe have done very well, imports into France from other EEC states have risen at just about the same rate, in fact slightly more rapidly, so that the balance from such trade has not improved. At the same time it has become clear that industrial concentration and specialisation have been pursued even more rapidly in other European countries than in France and that some individual industries in other European countries have rather better records than their French counterparts. Thus the German chemical industry exports over 34 per cent of its products against the French industry's 23 per cent; total production from the German steel industry is double that from the French, and Germany produces far more of her own energy requirements. Paranque's conclusion was that French industry, confronted with a new era of 'savage international competition', was 'well-placed but vulnerable'.

De-industrialisation

After such emphasis on developments within French industry, it may be a matter of some surprise to find that economists are now concerned over the phenomenon of 'de-industrialisation', defined as a situation in which there is a contraction in industrial production and employment and a persistent deficit on the balance of trade so that exports are unable to cover imports.[18] This phenomenon is seen as international and as characteristic of the major developed countries in recent years. For France it is certainly true that industrial employment has been in relative decline for some years: as a percentage of total employment it fell steadily from 40.4 per cent in 1968 to 37.7 per cent in 1977, in common with most other European countries. Similarly, the share of industrial value added in GDP at market prices in constant francs fell slowly but steadily throughout the 1970s, again a common feature throughout much of Europe. Perhaps none of this need detain us unduly here except to note that the trend towards a greater proportion of the economy being devoted to the services sector is not unexpected and is found in all comparable countries. What may be considered more surprising is a table of developed countries' shares in total exports of manufacturing industries by all such countries, over the long period 1950 to 1977: years which saw the UK's share fall from 25.5 per cent to 9.3 per cent and Japan's share rise from 3.4 per cent to 15.4 per cent saw France's share remain constant at 9.9 per cent.[19] This finding adds a considerable qualification to the comments above regarding France's successfully increased export performance: she did not in fact do any more than hold constant her relative export performance *vis-à-vis* all other developed countries. Subsequent statistics suggested that the same trend continued until at least the end of 1979.[20]

Franco-German Trade

Much attention has naturally focused on France's trade with her largest and most serious competitor, West Germany, trade which has mushroomed in the years since the signing of the Treaty of Rome. The net balance of all such trade each year shows a large and growing surplus in West Germany's favour (= a deficit for France), which in 1979 amounted to DM 6,798m (= approx. 16,355m frs. or £1,524 m). Much the most important category of trade was capital goods (including mechanical and electrical engineering, automobiles and aeroplanes) with a net surplus to West Germany of DM 5,923m (14,249m frs. or £1,328m). Only agriculture recorded a significant surplus to France of DM 1,688m (4,061m frs. or £378m), but this surplus had tended to fall throughout the 1970s as West Germany sought to build up her agricultural self-sufficiency. Clothing and textiles between them had a surplus for France of DM 542m. For most categories of product, both industrial and agricultural, the share of Germany's imports coming from France has tended to decline over the last decade as Germany has sought alternative, and cheaper, sources of supply.[21]

France as a Community Member

Just as the Treaty of Rome may be said to have evolved from earlier European initiatives, such as the inauguration of the European Coal and Steel Community in 1951, so too the EEC itself has continued to evolve since 1958. The single most significant development was, of course, the admission to membership of the UK, the Republic of Ireland and Denmark by the Treaty of Brussels in 1972 followed by the admission of Greece in 1981 and possibly those of Portugal, Spain and eventually Turkey, from dates not yet known. Apart, however, from such major turning-points, inter-state negotiations take place more or less continuously in Brussels, Luxemburg or Strasburg, and France is never slow to put forward her own point of view in such negotiations. The successive crises over the development of the Common Agricultural Policy, notably the French decision to boycott the Community in 1965, the precipitate decision to devalue the franc in 1969 and the illegal imposition of a levy on wine imports in 1976 were dealt with in Chapter 3.

Problems have also arisen in a number of other fields. The development of a common transport policy went through a long period of stalemate before agreement was finally reached in 1965. France had only been prepared to accept a settlement of the problem of the size of the quotas to be issued to member states for the granting of road transport licences (France would initially get 210, the same as West Germany) on condition that agreement was also reached on the rate-bracket issue (most member states operated controls over transport rates in some form or another: France had wanted tariff brackets to be applied to all forms of transport, but in 1965 gave way and agreed that these be limited to international transport only). Since, however, the French boycott of the Community followed almost immediately and since discussion of the finer points of the agreement ran into a series of snags, the agreement was not implemented until 1968, with France receiving 286 licences. In view of her own regional problems, which were discussed in Chapter 7, France actively urged the implementation of a Community regional policy, from which her poorer areas stood to benefit. France vigorously proposed close links between the Community and developing countries, on account of her close links with her former colonial territories, and this led to the 'association' of such countries with the Community. Problems arose over the varying taxation systems in operation in the member states, but although negotiations continued fitfully over many years the path towards harmonisation of taxation systems was extremely slow. The French system of corporation tax already included some compensation for the double taxation effect arising from international transactions but, by allowing tax credits only for residents and for companies registered in France effectively induced French investors to invest in French companies and discriminated against investors from other EEC countries. A major victory for France was in converting the rest of the Community to Value Added Tax, from their previous cascade-type systems.

France initially favoured a supra-national element in the Community organisation with a Secretary-General empowered to act independently on major problems but subsequently, as we saw in Chapter 3, shied away from the Community having its own source of income and thus a degree of immunity from the wishes of the member states. A problem within the Council of Ministers was as to whether their decisions had to be reached by majority vote or unanimously, with France favouring the latter, at least on major issues. A compromise agreement was signed in 1966, but with such a tortuous wording that it did little to make matters any clearer. General de Gaulle's opposition to UK membership of the Community in 1962/3 and again in 1966/7 is well known. After his resignation in 1969 and the re-opening of negotiations in 1970, the French attitude was again crucial: initially she proved obdurate, particularly over the role of sterling and the monetary implications of UK membership, but at the Heath-Pompidou 'summit' at The Hague in May 1971 she gave way on this issue. The difficult question of the role of sterling was to be discussed after British entry in exchange for the UK's agreeing to stabilise, and eventually to run down, the size of her sterling balances. Finally, when the oil crises arose, France urged that the Community's best interests lay in adopting a low-profile policy.[22]

Conclusion

If a conclusion is needed regarding the overall effects of France's membership of the EEC, it may be taken from Tardy:

The building of Europe . . . has had an overwhelming influence on
the economic development of France. It has directly contributed to
the opening of its external frontiers. It has accelerated the modernisation of its agricultural and industrial structures by favouring economic growth over the last twenty years (writer's translation).[23]

France and the Rest of the World

If a gradually increasing share of French external trade takes place
within the (now enlarged) European Community, a purely statistical
consequence is that the share with the rest of the world must be declining. By 1979 over 50 per cent of French exports went to other EEC
member states, a further 12 per cent to other European countries, 6 per
cent to OECD countries outside Europe (i.e. USA, Australia, Canada,
Japan) and some 31 per cent to the rest of the world.

The overwhelming problem for the French economy from an external point of view is its huge energy deficit: in 1980 the deficit for
'energy and raw mineral materials' amounted to 139,000m frs., of which
energy alone accounted for 133,000m frs. It therefore urgently needs a
much-expanded export performance just at the time when this is most
difficult to achieve. All other developed countries are in essentially the
same position as France and have naturally taken steps to protect their
own interests whilst the developing countries, until recently seen as
relatively easy markets for French exporters, are now making strenuous
efforts to develop their own industrial capacity. For the years 1971-3
France had relatively modest balance of trade deficits of between
4,000m frs. and 6,500m frs. each year; by 1976 the figure had leapt
to 41,600m frs. As early as 1973 the Marjolin Commission warned
against excessive reliance on external trade within the EEC and urged
the need to maintain and develop markets elsewhere.[24] Now that the
annual trade deficit to the USA alone reaches nearly 24,600m frs.
(1980) their words seem prophetic. The traditional rectifying instrument of devaluing the franc should be avoided, since this would merely
accelerate once again the increase in the bill for imported energy,[25] but
a further devaluation of the franc became unavoidable in October 1981.

In the general decline in world trade in the latter half of the 1970s
French finished products fared particularly badly, and nowhere was this
more true than in the case of exports to the USA. French exporters
have effectively failed to penetrate USA markets to significant levels
and less than 5 per cent of all French exports go to the USA. French

exports to the USA consist largely of agro-foods and semi-manufactured goods and rather little in the way of finished products (with the notable exception of cars). Rather similar remarks apply in the case of Japan where the only consistently successful French exports are textiles and clothing. Overall some 15 per cent of French exports relate to agro-foods and other raw materials, a higher percentage than for most other European countries. Over 70 per cent of her exports are industrial products, a figure that is considerably below those for most of her competitor countries, and has only increased very slowly over the last twenty years.

On the other side of the balance of trade coin, nearly a quarter of the cars sold in France now come from overseas, as do 98 per cent of tape-recorders, 86 per cent of hi-fi sets, 75 per cent of domestic freezers, 66 per cent of refrigerators, 58 per cent of machine-tools and 50 per cent of textiles: French industry needs to make, and is now making, serious efforts to re-conquer these domestic markets. The dominant position of French exports to Africa has been maintained, but French firms have had rather little success in penetrating markets in Central or South America, or in Asia. In the list of countries supplying Japan's imports, France ranks twenty-third! In terms of trends over time, only with African countries and with the countries of Eastern Europe has France been steadily improving her net trading position, via increasing surpluses.[26] Both the Lomé Convention of 1975 (between the EEC and 52 states in Africa, the Caribbean and the Pacific) and the Maghreb Agreement of 1976 (between the EEC and Tunisia, Morocco and Algeria) should help to maintain the dominant positions already enjoyed by France in those areas. It has to be said, however, that from a strictly economic point of view, France's continued stress on trade with her former colonial territories includes an element of the sentimental or nostalgic: whereas those countries took over 20 per cent of all France's exports in 1960, by the end of the 1970s this figure had shrunk to some 5 per cent.[27] Nevertheless, by 1979 France had healthy surpluses from inter-Mediterranean trade, including with each of Egypt, Greece, Algeria, Morocco, Yugoslavia, Tunisia and Italy, these surpluses totalling some 17,000m frs.

When, at the request of the Prime Minister, an official committee of enquiry published in 1978 a detailed study of France's external trade to 1985 they concluded that one of the most serious causes of concern was France's relatively weak export performance in the fields of capital goods and consumer durables (other than automobiles) and the invasion of French domestic markets in those same sectors by imported products from both within and outside Europe.[28] There appears to be no good reason why France should not do well in these sectors, and it seems probable that they will be given increased attention by both government and industrialists in future.

Financial and Monetary Aspects

Over the period 1958-66, i.e. for the first eight years of France's membership of the EEC, the country had surpluses on the balance of payments current account, which led to a strong and stable franc and the attraction into the country of longer-term capital funds. Even though the relative weakness of the French financial sector meant that the country derived rather little benefit from the rapidly growing Euro-dollar market, the government was able in these years to more than treble its reserves of gold and foreign exchange (especially the former) and repay over $1,700m of external debts.

The year 1967 saw the return to a quasi-totally free foreign exchange system after some 25 years of close control; it also saw a marked deterioration in the French balance of payments, a period of instability in the international monetary system and a flight to gold in which French citizens were prominent participants. The ensuing weakness of the franc continued until late 1969, when the continuing balance of payments deficit required, in the eyes of the French government, a devaluation of the franc by 12.5 per cent on 12 August, to the consternation of her EEC partners. Soon afterwards there began the long series of negotiations leading eventually to 'the snake in the tunnel': some (but not all) European currencies would be linked together but liable to fluctuate ('the snake') within the context of a link with the dollar ('the tunnel') which could fluctuate by a rather wider margin. After renewed instability in the international financial system in 1972 and early 1973 there followed only a short peaceful interlude before the oil crisis erupted in December of that year.[29] The story of the ensuing years is well known with successively mounting balance of payments deficits by most European countries, the accumulation of huge surpluses within OPEC countries and the eventual 'recycling' of these, and the era, consequent upon the escalating inflation, of rates of interest which nominally seemed very high but were frequently negative in real terms. France herself actually managed to convert the deficits of the years 1974-7 into the current account surpluses of 16,850m frs. in 1978 and 4,913m frs. in 1979, shown in Table 8.1, a remarkable achievement matched by no other country in Europe, before slipping back into a large deficit of 31,113m frs. in 1980.

After the initial upsets (which saw France withdrawing from the snake in January 1974 and rejoining in July 1975 only to withdraw again in March 1976), 'recycling' of OPEC funds enabled France to finance her oil bill without immediately drawing on her national income and whilst maintaining the value of the franc, but at the expense of mounting long-term debts, a policy with obvious attractions but not without its dangers. (Potential UK critics of French action should note that the UK joined the snake in May 1972 but left it only one month later.)

From March 1976 the Banque de France no longer had to maintain the external value of the franc within fixed limits and its value was allowed to float gradually downwards. This period lasted for three years. It was followed by the creation of the European Monetary System, which was agreed by the EEC heads of government in December 1978 and came into force in March 1979. In the words of one respected commentator, 'A year later it had fulfilled neither the fears nor the hopes to which its creation had given rise.'[30] In fact on the EEC foreign exchange markets rather little happened of any interest: the mark was revalued by 2 per cent in the autumn of 1979 to take account of the prevailing economic conditions. There was no sign of a gradual convergence of the various rates of inflation in the eight EEC countries which had joined the EMS (excluding solely the UK) which was contrary to the hopes of the EEC Commission and to the theory on which the scheme was based. The only major noticeable change was that adjustments of exchange rate parities could no longer be decided on unilaterally by individual member governments but had to be agreed at Strasburg, as was to happen in October 1981 when, *inter alia*, the franc was devalued by 3.0 per cent.

The European Monetary System (EMS) is based on the European Currency Unit, which is the reference basis for all the national currencies, a grill of bilateral rates of exchange between all the national currencies and a 'divergence indicator' governing the extent to which individual rates of exchange shall be permitted to vary. All being well, the system is due to lead to the creation of the European Monetary Fund in 1982. By early 1982 the EMS appeared to be working well: even the exchange rate adjustments of October 1981 were achieved with, for the EEC, rather little in the way of disagreements and late-night sittings. Whether, however, the EEC states will feel able to proceed in the near future to the original aim of full monetary union must at present seem rather doubtful.[31]

Invisibles

If France's balance of payments has been dominated in recent years by the costs of her imported energy, there are also major items of invisibles which are worthy of note. The invisibles sector yielded a total surplus of 36,216m frs. in 1980, which greatly helped to mitigate the effects of the visible trade deficit of 50,451m frs. Within the invisibles sector the most important contributors to the surplus were 'Public Works and Technical Co-operation' (16,294m frs.), Dividends and Interest Received (8,999m frs.), Tourism (8,918m frs.) and non-marine transport (5,418m frs.). One of the causes of concern relating to France's greatly increased export performance has been over the inadequacy of her merchant fleet to carry the goods in question, thus forcing her to rely on foreign shipping. Other European countries, led by the UK, look to their banking and insurance sectors for significant positive contributions to their balance of payments under 'Services', but with France this is not the case. Neither of these sectors has reached full development within the domestic economy and foreign banks and insurers have for many years made profitable inroads into French domestic markets. Equally French banks and insurance companies until the early 1970s made rather little attempt to develop foreign business, despite being urged to do so.[32] In the later 1970s, however, there were at last signs that such development was being taken seriously, partly at least on account of the intense competition now being met within the domestic market.[33]

Under 'Transfers', interest and dividend payments from overseas yielded a surplus of around 1,000m frs. annually until 1970 but thereafter the net annual balance has shrunk and even became a deficit in 1972 before reverting to a relatively small surplus and only thereafter recovering well. The exceptional circumstances relating to the year 1972 have already been referred to above; the longer-term effect includes the substantial foreign investments in French domestic companies. Quantitatively far more important than these, however, are the escalating but little-noticed remittances home of part of their wages by immigrant workers temporarily in France, especially from the poorer countries of southern Europe. Such payments now exceed some 5,000m frs. annually and continue to rise steadily each year.

With regard to capital account movements, until 1967 French residents were net disinvestors in foreign stocks and shares, but since that year have been net investors overseas: annual totals have varied but have often exceeded 2,000m frs. In addition, direct investment in and loans to foreign companies by French resident companies have usually exceeded 3,000m frs. in recent years. The French authorities have not been entirely sorry to see these outward currency movements but they have been offset, and often exceeded, by investments in French companies from external sources.

Overall, the surplus on the invisibles sector is now an important aspect of France's balance of payments situation, but it is a phenomenon of quite recent origin: invisibles recorded a net deficit every year until 1977. These declined year by year, that for 1977 being only 600m frs., and thereafter each year has shown significant, and growing, surpluses.

Foreign Exchange

The general tendency since the 1972/3 crises has been for exchange rates to float, but with continued intervention from the respective monetary authorities from time to time. Such a solution may be theoretically unsatisfactory, but in practice works well and enables foreign trade to continue and develop without undue worry as to the foreign currency or exchange rate implications. The French foreign exchange market has had no difficulty in developing throughout the 1970s to keep pace with (i) the greatly increased volume of France's external trade, (ii) the escalation of the Eurodollar market and (iii) greatly increased foreign currency speculation.[34] The Exchange Stabilisation Fund is used by the Banque de France no longer (since 1973) to keep the value of the franc within fixed predetermined limits, but rather to 'smooth out the foreign exchange markets whenever any abnormal distortions appear.'[35] Thus the external value of the franc is maintained at a relatively stable level, with consequent benefits for French exporters and importers. Devaluations of the franc from time to time, such as that announced in October 1981 after EEC agreement, are discussed elsewhere, including in Chapter 9.

External Debt

The available statistics relating to France's external debt are quite inadequate[36] and a margin of error must be allowed for in any figures quoted. By the end of 1981, however, France's total gross external debt (public and private sectors combined) totalled some 125,000m frs., or just over $22,000m, well below the UK's $31,000m. Medium- and long-term debt comprised over three-quarters of the French total, which has been calculated as equal to around 8 per cent of GDP or about four months' exports and which is growing much more slowly over time than the growth rate of the national economy. On the other side of the balance-sheet France's external credits are even more difficult to assess reliably, but they have been estimated approximately to equal the total debts indicated above, although the last three years or so have seen a gradual deterioration in this position. The two are not, however, comparable, in two respects: first, whereas France tends to borrow on the Eurodollar market and from sources in the USA, she tends to lend principally to developing countries; second, whereas she generally borrows in external (and hard) currencies, she generally lends in francs.[37] Perhaps the most disconcerting aspect of the external borrowing, from the point of view of the French authorities, has been the tendency for this artificially to swell the growth of the money supply — as much as one-fifth of the increase in the latter may have come from the former — but overall the authorities seem to have accepted the growth of such indebtedness as inevitable and possibly even as desirable in some respects.

Franc Zone

The historical links between the currencies of Metropolitan France and those of her former colonial territories naturally changed somewhat after the majority of the latter states achieved independence. During the 1960s a total of 14 African and Malgasy (Madagascar) states left the Franc Zone and their currencies became recognised as quite separate and distinct from the French franc, but tied to the latter at fixed rates of exchange. Their currency reserves continued to be held in francs in Paris. Those territories continuing to have the status of colonies were regarded, by what might be called a legal fiction, as an integral part of Metropolitan France, and French francs circulated freely there. In general these links have never reached the status or importance of, for example, the UK's overseas balances held in sterling; nor can they be said to have acted as a serious constraint on France's domestic policies. France has, however, provided a considerable volume of aid, in the form of grants and loans, to such countries, reaching over 12,000m frs. per year by the late 1970s. Almost the whole of French aid to developing countries goes to those states.

Recent Trends[38]

During the later 1970s there occurred a significant geographical reorientation of French trade towards countries outside OECD, i.e. towards the developing countries, particularly of investment (capital) goods. The increased surplus from this trade, in which electric and electronic equipment and apparatus were especially important, helped to offset both the growing deficit for industrial exchanges with other OECD countries and also the growing oil bill. In the case of the inter-OECD trade the place of household consumer durables was continuing to become more important by the end of the decade and there seemed to be an urgent need for French industry to take steps to endeavour to recover this market. In the case of cars, on the other hand, exports of French products remained more than double those of imports, with a healthy surplus, which reached by 1979 over 19,000m frs. for vehicles and 8,800m frs. for parts, largely for assembly plants located abroad.

The agro-foods sector's external balance has developed well, as noted above, but remains subject to wide fluctuations from year to year, from natural causes. In view of the (still) relatively large share of agriculture in the French economy, this gives rise to larger balance of payments fluctuations from this cause than is the case for almost all other developed countries. As one example, by the beginning of the 1980s French meat production had still not fully recovered from the wholesale slaughterings of livestock that were necessary during the drought of 1976.

Within the invisibles sector the category 'Public Works and Technical Co-operation' was continuing to develop, to the extent of dominating the invisibles account, and was particularly important in that the work involved frequently gave rise to large and valuable sales of investment (capital) goods or other equipment, the results of which would eventually show up in the trade balance.

Finally, if one may judge from various Ministerial pronouncements since the elections of May-June 1981 and from a reading of the Plan Intérimaire, the socialist government under President Mitterrand may give less priority to matters relating to international trade than did their predecessors. The Plan Intérimaire contains surprisingly few references to any aspects of international trade.[39]

Notes

1. Source: *Les Notes Bleues*, no. 34, 6 Sept. 1981.

2. This section draws heavily on 'The External Constraint on the French Economy' in *Conjoncture*, Monthly Economic Bulletin of Banque de Paris et des Pays-Bas (Jun. 1981).

3. This point was made to the writer when he visited the Ministère du Commerce Extérieur in Paris in December 1981. The Ministry disagreed with the emphasis on short-term capital funds in the *Conjoncture* cited above, and supplied me with some of the further statistics which follow.

4. B. Balassa, 'L'Economie Française sous la Cinquième République', *Revue Economique*, no. 6 (Nov. 1979).

5. P. Drouin, *L'Europe du Marché Commun* (Julliard, 1968).

6. J. Benard, C. Roux and C. Girardeau, 'L'Exécution du IIIe Plan Français', *Bulletin du CEPREL* (Jul. 1964).

7. Balassa, 'L'Economie Française sous la Cinquième République'.

8. *L'Equilibre économique en 1961* (Commissariat Général du Plan, 1957).

9. *De la forme et des méthodes d'un plan national dans un système d'économie de marché* (Conseil National du Patronat Français, 1965).

10. J.H. McArthur and B.R. Scott, *Industrial Planning in France* (Harvard, University Press, 1968).

11. Balassa, 'L'Economie Française sous la Cinquième République'.

12. A. Cotta, 'Réflexion sur la politique industrielle de la France', *Etudes de politique industrielle*, no. 17 (Ministère de l'Industrie, 1977).

13. Balassa, 'L'Economie Française sous la Cinquième République'.

14. Source: Ministère du Commerce Extérieur.

15. B. Guibert *et al.*, *La Mutation Industrielle de la France* (Les Collections de l'INSEE, Série E, nos. 31-2, Nov. 1975).

16. Balassa, 'L'Economie Française sous la Cinquième République'.

17. Régis Paranque, 'L'Industrie Française dans le Marché Commun', *30 Jours d'Europe* (Dec. 1976).

18. A. Jacquemin, 'Le Phénomène de Désindustrialisation et la Communauté Européenne', *Revue Economique*, vol. 30, no. 6 (Nov. 1979).

19. F. Blackaby (ed.), *De-Industrialisation* (Heinemann, 1979).

20. P. Meunier, 'Les relations économiques et financières de la France avec l'extérieur' in J.P. Pagé (ed.), *Profil Economique de la France au Seuil des Années 80* (La Documentation Française, 1981).

21. 'L'Evolution des Echanges Franco-Allemands au Cours des Années 70', *Problèmes Economiques*, no. 1693 (15 Oct. 1980).

22. D. Swann, *The Economics of the Common Market* (Penguin, 1978).

23. G. Tardy, 'La France dans l'Europe' in Pagé, *Profil Economique de la France au Seuil des Années 80*.

24. 'Relations économiques et financières avec l'extérieur', *Preparatory Document for the Seventh Plan* (Commissariat Général du Plan, 1973).

25. 'Le Commerce Extérieur Français', *Problèmes Economiques*, no. 1563, 8 Mar. 1978.

26. 'Le Poids de la contrainte extérieure', *Economie et Industrie* (Sept. 1977).

27. Meunier, 'Les relations économiques et financières de la France avec l'extérieure'.

28. 'Les Perspectives du Commerce Extérieur Français', *Economie et Statistique* (Dec. 1978).

29. H. Baronne, 'Les Relations Monétaires et Financières de la France avec l'Extérieur' in Pagé, *Profil Economique de la France* (La Documentation Française, 1975).

30. Meunier, 'Les relations économiques de la France avec l'extérieur'.

31. For an excellent review of this topic, see D.C. Kruse, *Monetary Integration in Western Europe* (Butterworths, 1981).

32. A. Cotta, 'La Banque Française et l'Impératif International', *Bulletin d'information économique de la Caisse Nationale des Marchés de l'Etat* (3rd quarter, 1978).

33. P. Coupaye, 'L'Internationalisation des Banques Françaises', *Eurépargne* (June 1979).

34. J. Blanc, 'Le Marché des Changes', *Notes et Etudes Documentaires*, 17 Mar. 1978.

35. *Le Fonds de Stabilisation des Changes en France* (Banque de France, Dec. 1978).

36. A. Costabel, 'L'Endettement Extérieur de la France', *Problèmes Economiques*, no. 1676 (4 Jun. 1980).

37. Costabel, 'L'Endettement Extérieur de la France'.

38. This section draws on Meunier, 'Les relations économiques de la France avec l'extérieur'.

39. The whole of this chapter has greatly benefited from an extended discussion the writer had in Paris in December 1981 with Monsieur Remond of the Ministère du Commerce Extérieur, to whom my grateful thanks are due.

9 CONCLUSIONS AND PROSPECTS

Recent Economic Trends

The Energy Crisis

Any examination of current economic developments affecting the French economy and any attempt at a prognosis for the future must begin with the dominating question of energy. As Table 9.1 shows, the 'first oil shock' of 1973-4 was succeeded by further price increases each year until the 'second oil shock' of 1979-80.[1] Thereafter the further, if less dramatic, price rises and exchange rate adjustments combined to produce in 1981 what came to be known as the 'third oil shock'. By early 1982 the price appeared to have settled, temporarily at least, at a level just 29 times greater than that of 1970, as Table 9.1 makes clear. The revenues produced to the OPEC countries, at the rate of around US $400 billion per annum by early 1982, are quite staggering.

Table 9.1: Arabian Light Oil — Average Posted Price per Barrel, 1970-81 (Ex Gulf)

	Price[c] ($)	Index, Current $ 1974 = 100	Index, Constant $ 1974 = 100
1970	1.20		
1971	1.48		
1972	1.65		
1973	2.20		
1974 c	9.38	100.0	100.0
1975	9.82	104.7	95.5
1976	11.51	122.7	106.3
1977	12.33	131.4	107.6
1978	12.70	135.4	103.4
1979	18.65	198.8	139.4
1980[a]	31.50	330.3	210.5
1981[b]	35.37	370.8	216.8

Notes: a. After the May 1980 increases, and taking account of the Algiers conference (deflator: 10%).
b. Taking account of the indexation principles agreed at Taif (deflator: 9%).
c. Previously to 1976, the series of values — which matches with the prices fixed subsequently — must be established, taking into account the price distinctions made at the time between concession and participation crude.

For France the effects of the successive waves of oil price increases have been particularly acute because, with only limited natural sources of energy of her own, she is heavily dependent on imported energy. During the 1970s the country's net oil bill as a percentage of Gross National Product rose from just over 1 per cent to 4 per cent and oil imports as a percentage of all imports rose from under 10 per cent to close on 20 per cent. Around 80 per cent of all energy consumed in France is imported, against about 70 per cent for West Germany, just over 20 per cent for the USA and, now, nil for the UK. When the oil price is expressed in national currencies to give the Imported Oil Price Index, over the period 1974-80 the increase, in current values, was steeper for France than for any other comparable country.[2]

References to France's continuing energy problems have appeared throughout this book. In the Plan Intérimaire, published in late November 1981, a whole chapter was devoted to 'A new energy policy' and contained a series of new measures relating to the generation and conservation of energy. The Plan forecast that France's total energy needs would rise from 189.0 Mtep units in 1981 to 232.0 Mtep units in 1990, or an increase of some 23 per cent on the decade, with the more rapid increase coming from industrial uses. The Plan hoped that the contribution of petrol to the country's total energy requirements would fall from 93 Mtep units in 1981 to 70-75 in 1990, with the shortfall being made good by increased output of gas, coal and, especially, nuclear energy. The latter produced 19.5 Mtep units in 1981 and was forecast to achieve 60-66 units in 1990, i.e. more than trebling of output. Finally, it was stated that the next five-year Plan, covering the years 1984-8, would have as one of its major points of focus the development of a flexible long-term energy policy.

Overall France continues to feel extremely vulnerable on the energy front and in particular to be conscious that it is the rapid rise in oil imports that has been primarily responsible for the growing deficit on the balance of payments current account which in turn has tended to act as a brake on economic and social policies. The energy problem is not, however, going to go away and there seems to be no way in which France can free herself from this constraint over at least the next decade.

The Economy at the Start of 1982

If the present book had been written at any time up to about 1975 it would have been *de rigueur* for the concluding chapter to refer admiringly to 'le miracle français', as did a number of other works of economic analysis at that time. By the commencement of 1982, however, the economic 'miracle' was looking decidedly precarious.

Unemployment rose to the unprecedented level of 2.1m by the end of 1981; inflation for the year averaged out at 15 per cent, but the annual rate was still rising and was forecast to reach 20 per cent. Raw material prices were rising by some 22 per cent, bank base rate had at one point reached 18.5 per cent and the balance of payments deficit for the year was expected to end up at around £10,000m. Results of an INSEE Survey of expected industrial investment for 1982 suggested that this would fall by some 4-5 per cent in volume.[3]

The exchange rate adjustments agreed by the EEC Finance Ministers in October 1981, i.e. the devaluation of the French franc and the Italian lira by 3 per cent and the revaluation of the West German mark and the Dutch guilder by 5.5 per cent came in the wake of the fall in the value of the US dollar which threatened to disrupt the fixed currency rates in the European Monetary System: the flood of international money being switched into marks threatened to break its link with the franc and the French Finance Minister, Monsieur Jacques Delors, was particularly vociferous in urging that agreement should be reached. The French threat to introduce a system of foreign currency import deposits caused the West Germans to remark that this could 'mark the beginning of the end of the European Monetary System'. In the event France modified her insistence on a franc-mark adjustment of 9 per cent and accepted the outcome of, effectively, 8.5 per cent. The other EEC Ministers apparently believed that the problem was largely one of France's own making, the flight from the franc being precipitated by the reformist measures being promulgated by President Mitterrand's government.[4]

After the exchange rate adjustments the downward slide of the franc was arrested and it maintained its exchange value at just under 6 frs. = US $1. This new stability enabled the government both to reconstitute some of its lost foreign currency reserves and to lower short-term interest rates from 18.5 per cent to 15.86 per cent at the end of October 1981. Unfortunately just at that time revised statistics were issued, showing that the central government's budget deficit had reached a huge 106,940m frs. (some £10,000m) by the end of September, well over double the equivalent figure for 1980, and that the annualised growth rate of the money supply (M2) had reached 17.6 per cent, against lower rates in all other comparable countries and against France's out-turn of 9.6 per cent for 1980.

Nevertheless by late 1981/early 1982 a number of hopeful signs had appeared. Household demand was holding up well and the tendency for industries to run down stocks of finished products had nearly ceased:

there were therefore forecasts of a considerable up-turn in economic activity as 1982 progressed although, as a leading bank commented, 'Unfortunately, at the moment it is not being accompanied by the slightest flutter on the productive investment front.' The commentary continued, with regret, that government action to check this economic upswing would become inevitable during 1982 on account of the excessive increases in monetary aggregates, budgetary deficit and balance of payments deficit. The general government borrowing requirement was forecast to reach some 2.5 per cent of Gross Domestic Product during 1982, whereas the government had undertaken to hold this to 2 per cent.[5]

The Mitterrand Government and the Economy

In the wake of the exchange-rate adjustment, the government introduced a freeze of prices of essential goods and services, including such basic items as bread, milk, butter, margarine, sugar and coffee, and a curb on wage demands, in an effort to control the higher inflation that might result. Profit and wholesale margins and public service charges would be kept down to increases of 8 per cent. The government found itself under attack from the Gaullist opposition on account of the devaluation and from the trade unions on account of the curb on wages; the effect of the new measures was summarised as 'likely to bring an end to the political honeymoon the French call the "state of grace"'.[6] Certainly the economic climate now confronting the socialist government appeared far removed from the optimistic pronouncements and expansionist policy measures of their first few months in office as referred to in Chapter 1 and *passim* throughout this book. Nor were the difficulties of President Mitterrand and his Ministers in late 1981 confined to economics alone as they sought to hold together the range of opinion in the government ranging from the Social Democratic wing of the Socialist Party to the Communists.

One policy measure, the announcement of the shelving of some £1.5 billion of public spending which had been announced only the previous week, threw into relief not only the economic policy difficulties but also the problem of communication within the Cabinet: they led to a public squabble between the Minister for the Economy, Monsieur Delors, and the Minister for the Budget, Monsieur Fabius, who reportedly 'work in the same building but rarely meet'.[7] The latter had for some time been in sympathy with the optimism exuded by President Mitterrand, who believed that France must buy its way out of the recession, whereas Monsieur Delors succeeded in persuading the Cabinet to accept his anti-inflationary measures because of his conviction that without them further devaluations would be inevitable during the course of 1982.

These difficulties did not stop the government from proceeding with the nationalisations of the remaining private banks or of steel in the wake of the industry's massive deficits,[8] or proposing to other EEC countries a 'European recovery' strategy based on an EEC-wide dose of mild reflation, although the motives for the latter were suspect. According to one comment, 'the suspicion must be that the EEC, and its inability to agree on any coherent "wet" strategy, will provide the Government with an alibi when faced — as it already is — with a growing chorus of criticism at home.'[9]

The onset of a new wave of strikes,[10] the publication of figures showing that unemployment had exceeded 2 million[11] and the onset of a new concerted opposition campaign led by the Gaullist ex-Prime Minister Jacques Chirac[12] all failed to deter the government who were doubtless encouraged by the results of three separate public opinion polls which showed, perhaps rather surprisingly, that the President's standing remained very high, perhaps even higher than at the time of the 10 May election.[13] The government increased the social security contributions of both employers and employees, despite the opposition of the Communist Minister of Health Monsieur Ralite, in an endeavour to curb the expected social security system deficit of 30,000m frs. (some £3,000m) for 1982.

By the close of 1981 the government had infuriated the opposition by announcing that major social reforms, including shorter working hours and earlier retirement, would, to save time, be introduced by ordinance, thus bypassing parliament,[14] provoked a strike by Paris hospital doctors over the introduction of '"socialized medicine" after the British pattern',[15] aroused demonstrations by French farmers over what they saw as inadequate agricultural subsidies for 1982,[16] and had its nationalisation measures referred to the national Constitutional Council, thus arousing the spectre of a major constitutional crisis[17] (which threatened more acutely when the Council rejected the nationalisation programme in January 1982).

Nevertheless most end-of-year assessments remained cautiously optimistic and praised the pattern of leadership of President Mitterrand to date.[18] Production had increased by 4 per cent with no discernible rise in inflation, although the hoped-for increase in productive investment had still not taken place. The flow of foreign funds into France for direct investment purposes had increased significantly since the socialist government came to power, above the level of $2 billion per annum at

which it had stagnated since 1976, as international businessmen anticipated that the regime would be less protective of domestic companies
than were their predecessors.[19]

In the early days of January 1982, the food prices frozen in October
were decontrolled and rules on prices and consumer services were
eased,[20] whilst the Minister of Finance announced that he hoped to
bring inflation down to 10 per cent for the year 1982.[21] By the middle
of the month the government announced twelve decrees intended, in
various ways, to alleviate the problem of unemployment – including
much more on-the-job training for young people. Critics were not slow
to point out that the postponement of the stated intention to reduce
the period of military service from twelve months to six might well be
related to the same aim.[22]

France could be pleased with having at least some success in persuading the EEC to embark on a limited programme of supplementary loans
and economic recovery,[23] although in other respects the various socialist
Ministers showed no signs of being any less intransigent at the European
level than were their Gaullist predecessors. 'Mitterrand seems destined
to effect more economic, political and social reforms than any of his
Fifth Republic predecessors'[24] was how one commentator summarised
the new regime after its first few months in office.

Assessment and Prognosis

Clearly the French economy today is in a radically different position
compared with that it enjoyed until the mid-1970s. The experience of
the first thirty years after Liberation was continuous economic growth
and increasing prosperity on a scale and to an extent without parallel
in the country's history.

The period since around 1975 is, however, as has been seen in each
chapter of this book, much more difficult to assess. The large-scale unemployment and balance-of-payments deficits would each on their own
constitute a major problem for the national economy; when these are
combined with inflation which obstinately refuses to fall into single
figures, lowered industrial investment and productivity, renewed tensions in the agricultural sector as farm incomes fall in real terms, mounting labour unrest at the combination of national economic difficulties
and disappointment with the socialist reforms, and a problem of regional imbalance which is at best stagnating, the picture may appear
quite bleak. Each of these aspects of the economy has been considered

in detail in this book and in each case the aim has been to show that the problem in question is remarkably complex and offers no easy solution.

That would, however, be to give a distorted impression of the situation in which the French economy finds itself in the early 1980s. Economic growth in France post 1975, although much more disappointing than that of the previous period, has in fact been more buoyant than the average for all developed countries and much more so than the record for some of France's major competitors, including the UK. Some aspects of the economy, especially the tertiary sector but also some major industrial sectors, have withstood the world recession well.

The previous 'opening up of the French economy to foreign trade' remains true and there is every prospect that France will emerge as an even stronger competitor on the international trade scene once the energy problem can be mastered or at least reduced in its impact. Active steps to hasten the latter objective have already been taken, as noted above, although it will certainly remain a major, perhaps the major, economic problem for at least the next decade. The contrast between the French economy, struggling to overcome the handicap of having only very limited domestic energy sources, and that of the UK, faring so badly in almost every respect despite the remarkable 'gift' (as it appears from France) of North Sea oil, could not be more acute.

Although the very eulogistic tone of earlier assessments of the French economy might not now be appropriate, there remains much to admire in an economic performance which by early 1982 had settled at a steady level of economic growth of around 3 per cent per annum, a level achieved by the UK only in quite exceptional years.

For the writer at least, therefore, whilst the nature and gravity of the nation's present economic difficulties should not be minimised, there are grounds for definite, if cautious, optimism regarding continued prosperity for France in future years. Perhaps the most difficult aspect to assess – it might almost be called the joker in the pack – must be the impact of the new economic and social policies being pursued by the Mitterrand government. If President Mitterrand is right, these could lead to increased economic growth and national prosperity; if not, there is every prospect of them leading to economic crises involving massive deficits on the current accounts of both the balance of payments and the central government, and possible further devaluations. France's friends must hope that this will not prove to be the case.

Notes

1. 'The second oil shock', *Conjoncture* (Paribas, Jul. 1980).

2. Ibid.

3. *Le Nouvel Economiste*, no. 315, 14 Dec. 1981.

4. J. Palmer, 'Ministers juggle mark and franc', *Guardian*, 5 Oct. 1981.

5. 'France after the exchange rate adjustment', *Conjoncture* (Paribas, Nov. 1981).

6. W. Schwarz, 'Price freeze follows on devaluation of Franc', *Guardian*, 6 Oct. 1981.

7. P. Webster, 'French cut £1.5 bn. in public spending', *Guardian*, 8 Oct. 1981.

8. P. Webster, 'France nationalises steel in good mettle', *Guardian*, 10 Oct. 1981.

9. J. Palmer, 'French may have to back-track on reflation', *Guardian*, 19 Oct. 1981.

10. A. Moutet, 'Strike wave muffles the Mitterrand magic', *Sunday Times*, 25 Oct. 1981.

11. 'French jobless figure passes the two million mark', *The Times*, 6 Nov. 1981.

12. W. Schwarz, 'Optimist Chirac already sees a Right comeback', *Guardian*, 9 Nov. 1981.

13. J. Fenby, 'Mitterrand's poll rating rises despite problems', *The Times*, 11 Nov. 1981; and 'Mitterrand remains popular', *The Times*, 24 Nov. 1981.

14. W. Schwarz, 'Mitterrand curtails debate on jobs law', *Guardian*, 20 Nov. 1981.

15. C. Hargrove, 'Paris doctors strike to defend pay beds', *The Times*, 11 Dec. 1981.

16. C. Hargrove, 'Anger of French farmers erupts', *The Times*, 12 Dec. 1981.

17. C. Hargrove, '"Nine sages" to decide on nationalization bill', *The Times*, 22 Dec. 1981.

18. W. Schwarz, 'Mitterrand's Socialists seize De Gaulle's Fifth Republic', *Guardian*, 31 Dec. 1981.

19. D. Bodanis, 'Election of French Socialists has not slowed foreign funds', *Guardian*, 5 Jan. 1982.

20. P. Webster, 'Paris starts anti-inflation campaign', *Guardian*, 7 Jan. 1982.

21. C. Hargrove, 'Unemployment at record level in France', *The Times*, 6 Jan. 1982.

22. B. Brune, 'Twelve decrees to tackle France's unemployment', *Guardian*, 8 Jan. 1982.

23. W. Schwarz, 'French dream of more prosperous, caring society in Europe', *Guardian*, 11 Jan. 1982.

24. J. Swain, 'The 100-day gallop in Paris', *Sunday Times*, 19 Aug. 1981.

INDEX